A JOURNAL OF
CONSCIOUSNESS AND TRANSFORMATION

ReVision

CONTENTS

I0118711

Ecopsychology

Douglas A. Vakoch & Fernando Castrillon, Editors

Cover photo by Glenn McCrae

Spring 2010 • Volume 31 • Numbers 3 & 4

Artwork: Mariana Castro de A

Volume 31, Nos. 3&4 (ISBN 978-0-9819706-5-3)

ReVision (ISSN 0275-6935) is published as part of the *Society for the Study of Shamanism, Healing, and Transformation*.

Manuscript Submissions
We welcome manuscript submissions. Manuscript guidelines can be found on our webpage http://revisionpublishing.org.

POSTMASTER: Send address changes to
ReVision Publishing, P.O. Box 1855, Sebastopol, CA 95473.

Subscriptions
For subscriptions mail a check to above address or go to
www.revisionpublishing.org.

Individual Subscriptions
Subscription for one year: $36 online only,
$36 print only (international $72),
$48 print and on-line (international $84).

Subscription for two years: $60 online only,
$60 print only (international $96),
$79 print and online (international $115).

Subscription for three years: $72 online only,
$72 print only (international $108),
$96 print and online (international $132).

Institutional Subscriptions
$98 online only (international $134),
$134 print and online (international $191).

Please allow six weeks for delivery of first issue.

Adams, W. W. (2010). Intimate Participation As Our Essence, Calling, and Path: Nonduality, Buddhist Psychology, and Our Ecological Imperative. ReVision, *31*(3&4), 48-53. doi:10.4298/REVN.31.3.4.48-53.

This article offers a perspective for collaborative consideration and an invitation for further experiential inquiry. This perspective (or, better, experience) may help us subvert humankind's perilous dissociation from the rest of nature and cultivate mutual well-being in our relationships within the shared earth community. Specifically, the present study proposes that intimate participatory interrelating is our essence, our calling, and our path. This nondual yet interresponsive perspective is so obvious that we tend to miss its significance. Yet what if we experienced it vividly (again and again), not just conceptually but in a deeply heart-felt, fully thought, and thoroughly lived way? This possibility is explored and enacted here via phenomenological evidence from everyday life and revelatory insights from Buddhist psychology.

Beyer, B. (2010). A Phenomenology of Intimacy: Depthful Experience vs. Barnacle Mimicry (and The Tale of the Woefully Misguided Aspirations of the Common Land Barnacle). *ReVision*, *31*(3&4), 1-6. doi:10.4298/REVN.31.3.4.1-6

Modern, anthropocentric culture coaxes us into a survival strategy which involves constructing, identifying with, and inhabiting the constricted and impermeable boundaries of a supposedly separate and detached self. Habitually experiencing ourselves as separate from nature, we become alienated from the breadth and fullness of the experience of our whole selves, and we impart devastating effects on the rest of nature. As a remedy, the appeal is made to the direct experience of "self as part of nature" to experience the transcendence, connectedness, and identification of a more ecocentric sense of self. A brief description of this kind of experience is elaborated using results from phenomenological research on the structure of the experience.

Beyer, B. (2010). Global Warming, Ecological Psychology, and the Call to Higher Maturity. *ReVision*, *31*(3&4), 109-114. doi:10.4298/REVN.31.3.4.109-114

Our relationship with the rest of nature is being called into question urgently, ominously, by people from every corner of the earth. Short term, ill-advised solutions to environmental problems have long been the norm. The predictable result is that we are now faced with the real possibility of unprecedented natural catastrophe. The way we live our lives has put us in danger of rendering the planet uninhabitable. The maturity and wisdom necessary to meet this challenge can only arise from the ground of genuine intimate relating with nature. Will this terrifying predicament hasten the demise of the prevailing anthropocentric posture which gave rise to sustainability problems in the first place, ushering in a new era of mature human-nature intimacy?

Castrillon, F. (2010). Digitizing the Psyche: Human/Nature in the Age of Intelligent Machines. *ReVision*, *31*(3&4), 96-102. doi:10.4298/REVN.31.3.4.96-102

This article systematically explicates and examines a deep psychological and cultural process I have come to term the digitization of the psyche, also referred to as the production of digitized subjectivities. The digitization of the psyche refers to an internal and relational mirroring of our larger discursive interaction with progressively digitized culture. I regard the digitization of the psyche as a subset of a larger cultural process of digitization that is currently in ascendancy within Western culture and in many respects globally. I define this larger process of digitization as the privileging of instrumental rationality, computational logic and symbolic manipulation over intuition, emotion, nonlinear logic and the ebb and flow of the natural, undomesticated world. The article examines various ecopsychological responses to this process of digitization.

Chalquist, C. (2010). Earth is Not My Mother: Towar Contemporary Styles of Earthly Discourse. *ReVisio 31*(3&4), 7-12. doi:10.4298/REVN.31.3.4.7-12

As a cross-disciplinary approach to understanding the health and pathology of our psychological relationship to the natural world, ecopsychology challenges conventional thinking about mental healt high finance, government, and the environment. Yet its "back-to-nature" emphasis can express an unconscious conservatism that requir diagnosis before this fruitful field can turn to the task of fashioning more contemporary forms of discourse for healing our troubled relationship to our home planet.

Cochran, M. (2010). The Eros of Erosion: Revealing Archetyp Geology. ReVision, *31*(3&4), 36-41. doi:10.4298 REVN.31.3.4.36-41

This essay wanders resolutely into the deepening process of erosion as a personal, cultural and psychological phenomenon. Erosion unmasks denial, cracks our petrification, and thaws our psychic numbing, shaping and sculpting us into the essence of being. Throug erosion's relentless love, its elemental symptoms reveal our pathologies by shaking our foundations, washing us down, burning us out, blowing us away, or stunning us with vast silences. This essay scout ways to seep back into nature's sources bringing about the ecologica restoration of disconnection. It introduces an archetype of geology, a geo-logic catalyzed by the process of erosion itself. By sustaining a glimpse of ourselves as deeply earthed creatures we can feel our way back into lost natures.

Conesa-Sevilla, J. (2010). Intimations About a "Sense of Place *ReVision*, *31*(3&4), 42-47. doi:10.4298/REVN.31.3.4.42-4

This essay explores the elusive state-nature of what we try to mean when we say "a sense of place" and we think a clear answer has been given. Typically, a sense of place is experienced, transferred, communicated, interpreted, and internalized into a definite feeling, and certainty that our body-psyche has taken deep root somewhere in nature. At the heart of all our discussions about what a particular environment may mean for or elicit in each and every one of us (specifically, an authentic sense of place) is the psyche representing any reality anywhere and, in principle, occupying any "place," surel any space.

Davis, J. (2010). Diamond in the Rough: Primitiv Ecopsychology, the Diamond Approach, and Transperson Ecopsychology. *ReVision*, *31*(3&4), 13-18. doi:10.4298 REVN.31.3.4.13-18

The Diamond Approach of A. H. Almaas and the "primitive ecopsychology" of Steven Foster and Meredith Little are integrated into thi wilderness retreat. Primitive ecopsychology is based on direct contac with the natural world, ceremonies of threshold-crossing (such as vision fasts), and a four-fold model of nature, including human nature. The Diamond Approach brings an orientation to inquiry, the engaged open, and open-ended exploration of experience, and an understanding of the soul and its qualities of dynamism, sensitivity, maturation, and potentiality. This integration leads to a call for a transpersonal ecopsychology.

Dunn, S. (2010). Cosmic-Symbolic Transformations: Religiou Architecture and the Epic of Evolution. *ReVision*, *31*(3&4 72-77. doi:10.4298/REVN.31.3.4.72-77

Thomas Berry dedicated Evening Thoughts to his "monastery community". In Toronto, Canada, that Communty was able to build Nort America's first "gold" ecological church. It architecturally wed religious symbolism and the Epic of Evolution described in the Univers Story by Brian Swimme and Berry. To do it, architects, artists and th onastery community joined forces to confront what Thomas Berry s called being "between stories." This article details how areas of church setting transform familiar religious symbols. Garden be- mes sacred space. A curtain wall of clear glass facing south tracks sun's arc through the seasons. Skylights along the other walls splay constantly varying brilliant colors on the exposed concrete rfaces. The Sun fashions the constant context of liturgy.

re, M. (2010). The Nature of Transformation: Ecopsychology in Practice. ReVision, 31(3&4), 54-59. doi:10.4298/ REVN.31.3.4.54-59

opsychology asserts that contact and connection with one's natural vironment is not only vital for the preservation of that environment, t also for one's psyche. And, that reconnecting with and experienc- g this connection holds great transformative potential. This article plores the foundations of this still emerging field, elucidating the riety of theories for why contact with the wilderness may be a werful ingredient for psychological health. Whether it is an innate pacity of the natural world, a confrontation with dormant aspects of e unconscious, the experience of nondual reality, or any number of her experiences, facilitating transformation, via an ecotherapeutic odel, is possible. Drawing from the many authors and researchers o have explored these questions, as well as the author's own work a professional outdoor guide and educator, this article offers a per- ective on the history and importance of ecopsychology in facilitat- g health and transformation.

hnson-Pynn, J. S., Johnson, L. R., & Pynn, T. M. (2010). Connecting with Nature, Caring for Others: An Ecopsychological Perspective on Positive Youth Development. ReVision, 31(3&4), 78-84. doi:10.4298/ REVN.31.3.4.78-84

this article, we describe a positive youth development program that eks to optimize youth's capacity to create sustainable solutions to cial and environmental challenges. Results on measures of self ef- acy, civic attitudes and skills, and connection to nature from youth different cultural and program contexts are reported. Similarities survey measures included, feelings of connectivity to others and ture, commitment to civic action, and lack of political awareness d leadership skills. There were differences between genders, coun- es, and urban and rural locations on some measures. Collectively, r research indicates that an ecopsychological approach to youth velopment has broad multicultural applications, especially for psy- ologists interested in youth programs and the relationship of human ctors to environmental sustainability and conservation.

cKinley, M. The Western Mind, Terror of Death, and Environmental Degradation. ReVision, 31(3&4), 103-108. doi:10.4298/REVN.31.3.4.103-108

iis article explores the psychological underpinnings that inhibit anges in social attitudes and behaviors that are required to mitigate e environmental crisis. The author uses the theoretical framework terror management theory to examine the psychological founda- on of the Western mind and traces the historical development of the minant Western worldview. From this vantage point, the author monstrates how terror management theory elucidates the psycho- gical mechanisms behind environmental degradation and offers sights into the challenges in developing an alternative worldview at values ecological sustainability.

lerritt, D. L. (2010). A Jungian Perspective on Ecopsychology. ReVision, 31(3&4), 65-70. doi:10.4298/REVN.31.3.4.65-70

ng, the prototypical ecopsychologist, represented his deep connec- on with nature in his psychological theories. Jung described how r split God image affects our relationship with our bodies, the minine, sexuality and nature. His concept of the Self is best framed complexity theory and represented by the archetypal concept of e organism. Hermes, god of complexity theory and dreams, can be en as the god of ecopsychology. Dreams can be used to connect us the land and develop a sense of place. Hermes represents a rela- onship with the animal soul level of the psyche, the psyche's myth d symbol generating capacity, and the diplomacy needed to make

the major changes that will enable us to live sustainably.

Mickey, S. (2010). Imagination: Showing the Sense of Environmental Ethics. ReVision, 31(3&4), 90-95. doi:10.4298/REVN.31.3.4.90-95

The author describes how participation in the elemental force of imagination enacts a sense of environmental ethics that overcomes the dichotomy between anthropocentric (i.e., human-centered) and non-anthropocentric orientations to the natural world. A phenom- enological description indicates how imagination shows the human and the world as mutually constitutive vectors of sense, such that, in adhering to what shows itself through imagination, ethical action is not anthropocentric or non-anthropocentric, but anthropocosmic. With this elemental sense of environmental ethics, deliberative ac- tions are determined not by referring to a human or non-human center of value, but by attending to the exorbitant sense of what shows itself in the intimate intertwining of the human and the world.

Mitchell, L. H. (2010). Earthmind: Deschooling Education The Imagination of the Earth for Us. ReVision, 31(3&4), 30-35. doi:10.4298/REVN.31.3.4.30-35

The view that our place-worlds and our experiencing bodies are mutually mapped within each other and that they together form an in- separable unity has significant liberatory implications for education. I explore this core understanding of our primal locatedness in the earth as a transformational philosophical vision for realigning education with earth systems from a phenomenological perspective. I also look at actual "deschooled" grassroots organizations as a nomadic force breaking down cemented and destructive structures in the status quo and configuring and experimenting with new paradigms for creative thinking and action conducive to dealing with the escalating ecologi- cal crisis

Oei, C. (2010). On Building a Personal Relationship with Nature. ReVision, 31(3&4), 19-23. doi:10.4298/REVN.31.3.4. 19-23

This article describes the author's experiences of connecting with nature and describes how this connection proved to be a healing factor in her life. Aspects of ecopsychology that illustrate the basis for the human-nature relationship are discussed, along with sugges- tions of how one might employ the practice of sensory awareness and nature observation to connect with the natural world in everyday life. In addition to building this relationship with nature, the importance of nurturing and maintaining such a relationship is also highlighted.

Sharps, M. J., & Hess, A. B. (2010). Ecocognition: Decision and Understanding in Environmental Context. ReVision, 31(3&4), 85-89. doi:10.4298/REVN.31.3.4. 85-89

"Ecocognition," the application of cognitive science to environmental issues, is an important but relatively neglected area within environ- mental psychology. Decisions involving environmental concerns and policy are often made without reference to vital relevant informa- tion, even when such information is readily available. Our previous research explained these effects within the Gestalt/Feature-Intensive (G/FI) Processing theory of cognition (Sharps 2003); in the absence of relevant information in the immediate decision context, respon- dents tend to rely on gestalt processing, which is relatively likely to result in premature or inaccurate decision making (Sharps 2003; Sharps & Nunes 2002). Feature-intensive information, presented in the immediate context of a decision to be considered, can compensate for this effect and improve decision understanding in the environmen- tal realm.

Tucker, T. (2010). Natural Presence: Teaching to Recover Our Love of Nature. ReVision, 31(3&4), 24-29. doi:10.4298/ REVN.31.3.4. 24-29

Natural Presence re-envisions college science education to deepen and enhance the love of nature with which we began our lives. The Natural Presence approach integrates two powerful traditions that bring us as whole humans into authentic relationship with the natural world: natural history and contemplative practice. Natural history evokes our full humanness by engaging not only the cognitive, but also an array of other dimensions of intimate human relationships with the nonhuman: sensory, aesthetic, creative, affective. Contemplative practice honors our human need for reflective space as we build new information, ideas, intuitions into a framework of meaning. Natural Presence students develop attentive minds, hearts, and spirits as they embrace a renewed, vibrant, authentic relationship with nature.

West, R. (2010). Eating the Shadow: Polluted Nature in *A Thousand Acres*. *ReVision*, *31*(3&4), 60-64. doi:10.4298/ REVN.31.3.4.60-64
Jane Smiley's *A Thousand Acres* retells the story of *King Lear* from the point of view of Ginny Goneril. This paper explores how, like Shakespeare, Smiley understands consciousness and the problem of shadow in terms of the human relation to nature. The abuse of power over nature is reflected in two farm families whose bulging barns and tidy houses hide toxins and whose soil itself rests on tiles that tried to control an underground sea. Larry (Lear) has used his daughters as he used the land. His decision to divide the farm among his daughters frees both Shadow and Self and plunges Ginny into a process of growth. She retrieves painful memories of incest and confronts her own complicity in the family- and farm- systems, bringing evils that had been hidden, private, and plowed under into consciousness and into the political realm.

28th INTERNATIONAL CONFERENCE

OF THE SOCIETY FOR THE STUDY OF SHAMANISM,

HEALING, AND TRANSFORMATION

LABOR DAY WEEKEND - September 3 - 5, 2011

SANTA SABINA RETREAT CENTER, SAN RAFAEL, CA

An opportunity to engage with shamans, healers, scientists, anthropologists, medical doctors,

psychologists, and artists and to explore new directions of cross-cultural healing in the 21st century

For more information and to register, visit our webpage:

www.shamanismconference.org

A Phenomenology of Intimacy

Depthful Experience vs. Barnacle Mimicry

(and The Tale of the Woefully Misguided Aspirations of the Common Land Barnacle)

Jeff Beyer

First, a tale about barnacles. There are two kinds of barnacle: the marine barnacle and the land barnacle. The marine barnacle belongs to the class *Crustacea,* Latin for "the shelled ones." Interestingly, the developmental journey for a marine barnacle involves a dramatic shrinkage of the body area and a corresponding expansion in the relative size of the head. Infancy involves several jellyfish-like stages during which it swims freely in the open sea, carrying with it in its shrinking gut an ample endowment of nurturing nutrients, everything it needs for a good start in life. But it is soft and vulnerable, so as it approaches adulthood it searches for other barnacles, others who have presumably found a safe and prosperous place to be. When it finds that place in the security and comfort of others, its head grows more prominent and secretes

Jeff Beyer received his Ph.D. in Clinical Psychology from Duquesne University. His professional interests concern psychological maturity and intimate relating in all spheres, including with the rest of nature. He has worked as a psychotherapist for more than 25 years, currently in private practice in Pittsburgh, Pennsylvania, and also at Carnegie Mellon University, Counseling and Psychological Services. Contact Information: Counseling and Psychological Services, Morewood Gardens – E Tower, 1060 Morewood Avenue, Carnegie Mellon University, Pittsburgh, PA 15213-3890, 412-268-8072, jbeyer@andrew.cmu.edu

a metaphorically evocative substance. This substance does two things: first, it firmly secures the barnacle to something, maybe a rock, a boat, another barnacle. It attaches itself there and remains safely in that place—permanently. It has found what appears to be the best available place to be and it intends to stay there. Second, this cerebral secretion hardens into a thick protective shell within which the barnacle remains, never to emerge. Through a trap-door-like opening for its appendages, which itself slams shut in the presence of perceived danger, its limbs reach out to gather in sustenance from whatever by chance may pass by. It's a wonderful survival strategy and it usually works — it works, at least, for the marine barnacle: the creature builds a protective and mostly impermeable barrier around its vulnerable self, effectively separates itself from danger and all else by escaping to the inside, taking refuge in the hardened secretions of its head, holds on to something it deems safe, and never lets go.

That's the marine barnacle. The "land barnacle" belongs to the class *Homo*

> **Land barnacles do not intend to lose the little battles, even if it means losing the war.**

*Sapiens Pseudo Crustacean.*Human beings are the only species of land barnacle. We find ourselves in the same class with marine barnacles for our similar survival strategies. We, like the marine barnacle, attempt to protect our vulnerable selves from harm by abandoning our bodies (and with it the experience of any larger sense of self) and fleeing into our cerebrally enhanced heads. We, too, attempt to separate ourselves from danger by building impermeable psychological walls and escaping to the inside.

And we, too, attempt to attach ourselves to something — our egoic identity — and we commit ourselves to it and hold on as if our lives depended on it. Of course, one difference between us and the marine barnacle is that we humans, ever the clever ones, do all of this psychologically. Though the building of walls, the escaping within, the holding on to something is the very stuff of our experience, it is all invisible except for its effects, which are profound and often very visible; it is the development of the habitual egoic self and its way of functioning and defending itself; it is the living out of the unfolding strategy for surviving and sustaining ourselves through our vulnerable youth and throughout our development towards greater levels of maturity. Across the entire span of our lives we find ourselves already and always caught up in what we take to be a serious game of psychological survival. In our attempts to insulate ourselves from harm and pain, as a pre-emptive inoculation against danger, we reflexively and habitually endeavor to psychologically "take up residence" (Maslow, 1971, p. 336) within — not a hard shell made of calcium carbonate, like a true barnacle — but rather within the constricted and impermeable boundaries of a supposedly separate and detached self. This is the sense of self with which we eventually come to identify, yearning to once and for all have a safely fixed identity — not safely fixed by attaching to a rock or a boat or others of our kind — but by attaching to something at least, something we can at least then pretend is safe. We spend the days of our lives being doggedly committed to sustaining and enhancing this supposedly secure fortress, and experiencing ourselves as somehow separate from the rest of nature.

Our modern, barnacle-incubator culture coaxes us along this anthropocentric path. It's a path from which it is hard to veer, if we even know to do so, though a different path is never too far out of our reach, as we shall see later. From the beginning we are instructed that the boundary region of the self is found somewhere deep within the skin: "You are a separate individual." Further, the instruction goes, you are in reality separate from your body, separate from each other, and separate from nature. Moreover, any experience to the contrary is not to be admitted to or taken seriously — it is taboo: experience to the contrary would, after all, undermine

the illusion of safety. In fact the best one should hope for from behind these walls is to send and receive "communications" across the self's impenetrable bureaucracy of otherwise impermeable defenses. And for all your intimacy needs, if you must, simply "attach" yourself to another, shell to shell, and then work to maintain the attachment by engaging in regular volleys of reassuring communication. As part of the compensation for this self-seclusion, we are convincingly advised: "You are not just separate from the rest of nature, you are above nature, indeed, the pinnacle of evolution;" and "Nature is simply the background, the stage on which your singularly important human drama is played." Nature out there, which includes your fleshy body, is intrinsically other than you, an object for you as subject, and it is there for you to dominate, control, use or abuse as you see fit. In exchange for the reciprocal posture characteristic of mature intimate relating, we default to the "one-up, one-down" game, and we do not like to be the one down, submissive, and vulnerable. So on we strive, guided by our firmly held aspirations for the kind of safety and security enjoyed by the marvelous marine barnacle, with little else now to strive for except the further fortification and resulting comforts promised by the ideal of a separate self, shaping the world according to our land barnacle demands.

We may thus come to admire the marine barnacle and aspire to be like it, but we should be careful what we aspire to because we might succeed in

achieving it, and that may not be good. To the extent that we succeed in habitually experiencing ourselves as removed from the rest of nature, we are effectively alienated also from the true breadth and fullness of the experience of our whole selves. We come to experience ourselves as "next to" others and the rest of nature but not really intimately "with" them; we experience ourselves as alone. We wall ourselves off from the source of our sense of wholeness, we feel empty, needy, lacking, never really fulfilled or content. We are psychologically underfed because we nourish ourselves through clogged filters. Ever committed to our barnacle aspirations, we nevertheless try in vain to fill ourselves up and comfort ourselves in any of a variety of compensatory ways: we consume addictively — food, drink, drugs, things, fame, status, power, seeking comfort from the well that can never really satisfy us (Glendinning, 1994).

And since this becomes a habitual way of relating, rarely if ever questioned and not often shaken, we forget about the fact that it is, after all, barnacle mimicry, an attempt to feel safe. We forget, and then forget that we forget, perhaps becoming only vaguely aware of it in one of those rare, flashing moments of clarity. We come to believe our own mimicry, and so we are at a loss for understanding why we feel less than whole and less than fully content. Our very experience itself is now more or less muted by the thick and heavily fortified maze of relatively impermeable psychological walls. We are now condemned to experience the precious moments of everyday life with a relative shallowness, with an unnecessary impoverishment, like experiencing life with all the clarity of listening to a Beethoven symphony through a cheap transistor radio and with cotton in our ears. We thus come to surf experience

So on we strive, guided by our firmly held aspirations for the kind of safety and security enjoyed by the marvelous marine barnacle, with little else now to strive for except the further fortification and resulting comforts promised by the ideal of a separate self, shaping the world according to our land barnacle demands.

itself like we surf the television channels or the internet, missing most of the saturated richness and depth which is always available and which would otherwise be experienced. The mostly lost experience of genuine intimate intermingling is replaced by a relating from a distance, relating at arms length, surplus mediation relating. Still, we push on the best we can, habitually constricted and impermeable, repeatedly playing what we consider to be our trump card, our supposed separateness, heavily armed with the will, the need, and the belief in the right to dominate and control, to shape the world to fit and support our now alienated existence.

The psychological effects of the alienation accompanying our barnacle aspirations are problematic enough, but there is yet another consequence. In spite of the magnitude of its implications, it can be mentioned only briefly here: the effects of such alienated relating on the rest of the natural world. I suggest, along with many from deep ecology and ecopsychology, that this habitual alienation from the rest of nature provides the experiential basis for the possibility of carelessness toward and destruction of the natural world, those dynamic and living systems upon which our survival depends. Since we so rarely relate intimately with the rest of the natural world, we are deprived of the experience necessary for an intimate identification with all of nature, we are deprived of the requisite ecocentric (as opposed to the prevailing mainstream anthropocentric) basis for identification (Fox, 1995). Ecocentric awareness is borne through experiences of intimate relating with the rest of nature. It is an experienced identification which necessarily involves deep compassion and care for all of nature (including humans), it involves those same kinds of feelings and inclinations we hope to have for our loved ones.

Lacking these experiences, we fall into identifying instead with modern culture's anthropocentrism, the institutionalized barnacle incubator which promotes wall building and pathogenic alienation. Our predominantly anthropocentric identity instead promotes an antagonism with the rest of nature and engenders paranoid fearfulness, and it inclines us toward an often misguided posture of domination and control. From an anthropocentric posture, environmental issues become "us vs. them" issues, loggers vs. the spotted owl, or human progress vs. the snail darter, etc. At best, nature "out there" becomes only the means to an end, objects to be used and exploited — "natural resources" the raw material for our barnacle aspirations, and we are benevolent stewards. At worst, nature becomes an impediment, and it and those who want to protect it become the enemy to humankind and its purposes. Land barnacles do not intend to lose the little battles, even if it means losing the war.

Perhaps we might remind ourselves that we are not true barnacles, that our separateness and impermeable walls represent only one way of being human. What if these barnacle aspirations and mimicry are well intentioned but misguided and there is another way, a more properly human way? What if the entire premise which defines barnacle mimicry — our separateness — is illusory (Adams, 1996)? What if the whole self does not in fact exist entirely within the constricted and impermeable boundaries of a supposedly fixed and safely separated self? Where could we find the evidence to support this?

Luckily, we need not appeal only to tongue-in-cheek metaphors and clever arguments to make this case. The most powerful case may be made through a simple appeal to your own direct experience. There is a kind of experience which could be called the "self as part of nature" experience. Most of us have had this experience at some time or other in our lives, and some experience it regularly. It's an experience which reveals the folly of self protection through alienation, and it suggests an alternative. It's the experience of intimacy with the rest of nature, a kind of intimate relating which is not altogether different from our experience of intimacy with others. It is sometimes an elusive experience, often slipping away from reflective awareness only moments after it occurs, perhaps for reasons mentioned above. Even if it does stay with us, it seems that usually we do not talk about it — many people have suggested to me that the experience can be so powerful, personally valuable, meaningful, and unusual, that they are afraid to bring it up for fear that it will not be well received by others. Some have said that the experience was so powerful that they believe it transformed their life, yet they have not talked about it to anyone; it becomes another intimate experience kept secret (Beyer, 1999). Talk about this kind of experience apparently does not often fit in that well in an anthropocentric culture which highly values analytic and reductionistic rationality, and productivity and purposefulness, and individuality and competitiveness, and domination and control. Ours is a culture in which people talk very little about relating at all, much less about intimate relating.

Few are able or inclined to articulate what an intimate relationship is, or how to do it — even human to human, much less in our relationship with nature. Left

Ever committed to our barnacle aspirations, we nevertheless try in vain to fill ourselves up and comfort ourselves in any of a variety of compensatory ways: we consume addictively — food, drink, drugs, things, fame, status, power, seeking comfort from the well that can never really satisfy us.

to existing forces and chance, it is easy and all too common for people to fall into barnacle-like aspirations and its consequences. What follows is some of what I have found from my qualitative, phenomenological research into intimacy, "the experience of self as part of nature" (Beyer, 1999, 133). I will offer

begin the psychological work involved in putting itself in a position to relate more intimately.

It's a sunny midsummer evening as I walk along a path in the park. At first I walk quickly, habitually maintaining the pace of the day. Eventually I remind myself that I'm not going anywhere, that

insulating veil thawed to reveal that I was and had always been living within an extraordinarily rich sensory world — and that until now I had missed most of it.

This is the second point: We often discover most poignantly how disconnected and muted our habitual sense of self is only as its grip is relinquished and as we awaken into greater levels of intimate relating. For better or worse, the habitual sense of self is recognized as such most thematically in retrospect, from within the experience of intimate relating, as the thick and frozen shell of the habitual sense of self is thawing and being shed. In other words, it is when I am most numbed and insulated that I am most likely to be unaware of that fact; and, conversely, it is when I am relating most intimately that I most clearly realize that I habitually am not. It is easy to see why, in the absence of intimate relating, one could easily forget that any other way of being in relation is possible, easy to forget that one is habitually relatively numbed and cut off from the fullness of experience.

We are now condemned to experience the precious moments of everyday life with a relative shallowness, with an unnecessary impoverishment, like experiencing life with all the clarity of listening to a Beethoven symphony through a cheap transistor radio and with cotton in our ears.

a brief description of such an experience along with just a few of the main constituents from my research of the unfolding structure of the experience.

One day, a while back, I felt a strong inclination to get out of the office and take a walk. I delighted myself with the idea that I would go to a nearby nature reserve after work. This is a common and unremarkable event so far — daydreaming at work — but I have come to recognize this kind of moment as psychologically extraordinary. I can summarize it this way: my habitual egoic sense of self (my day to day, usual way of being) is recognizing a request, or an invitation, from what will later be experienced as my larger, more expansive sense of self to put itself in a position to release its constricting grip on the whole of the self. In other words, my habitual sense of self is here renouncing (for the moment) its commitment to the barnacle identity and risking opening itself up to the experience of wholeness.

So, point number 1: The habitual egoic sense of self can and does recognize the need for genuine intimate relating, though often in the guise of some apparently benign activity (going for a walk) and not often recognized thematically for all that it is. The habitual egoic sense of self apparently knows how to

I'm just wanting to be here, and I find myself walking ever more slowly, finally coming to a stop at what would otherwise be an unremarkable spot along the trail. With no apparent deliberation or reflection, I sit, feeling only now the softness of the grass beneath me. As I sit I begin to notice more, begin to be aware of more. I hear a crescendo of sounds that were always there but which I did not notice before: the buzzing of bugs, the wind, traffic noise in the distance. I began to see more of what I had apparently been overlooking.

Notice that this is not experienced as just increased sensory excitation, as if the volume of my senses were simply being amplified. Rather, this is a shift in egoic functioning, a shift in the way I experience my self. Just prior to the experience of more intimate relating, my visual experience was skimming over my world like a stone skipping over the depths of the water, seeing only a portion of what was always there to see. Only now do I experience the colors in greater richness, the smell of the dirt, the textured aromas of living earth, the reminiscent smell of sunlight on grass. The previously experienced numbness of not-feeling, not-hearing, not-seeing, and not-smelling, the pervasive experience of my habitual sense of self — this

As I experience my senses come alive in the relating, I find myself letting go of my ordinary sense of the passing of time, experience myself being given over to a sense of time based on the emerging rhythm of the flow of the relating rather than on standardized clock time. The gradually increasing sense of the back and forth, reciprocal flow of the experience feels as if I am transitioning, like from a wrestling match to a kind of dance. I experience a gradual letting go of my posture of mastery and purposefulness, a letting go of my previous inclination to be exclusively controlling or productive, "as if I needed to get somewhere" Instead of "working at a task," I join more receptively and playfully with the emerging flow of the unfolding engagement with nature, letting it be what it is as it emerges in the relating. I am no longer doing something in or to nature, but rather now I am doing something "with" nature, experiencing my self relatively less as a doing-being and relatively more as a being-being.

Point number 3: The habitual egoic self here is not just acting in its usual capacity and primary role as executor and maintainer of a fixed identity, but it is rather recognizing that it needs to abdicate, if only for a while, and makes preparations to do so. With respect to the habitual barnacle aspirations, the habitual egoic self is doing a complete about face. The egoic self defers to the whole of the self; or, the whole self becomes aware of the need to relinquish its exclusive identification with the constricted and impermeable egoic sense of self, and the egoic self takes steps to put itself in a position to become more permeable and expansive. The habitual egoic self lets go of exclusive identification with the encapsulated, skin bounded, biographical sense of self — it is now experienced as all of that and more: the expansive and permeable sense of self transcends the habitual and includes it simultaneously. The remarkable thing is that the habitual egoic self is operating here in the service of the whole of the self rather than in the supposed interest of a smaller fragment, moving from a lived sense of alienation to an experience of wholeness and connectedness.

My emerging openness is experienced as a self-accepting, relaxed, comfortable, consonant sense of embracing presence to whatever emerges into my awareness. I begin to feel free of any personal concerns outside of this moment, free of the weighty grip of my usual psychological

sensual experiences, leading to greater levels of openness, and so on. It is the mutually enhancing interplay of a sense of trust and safety and progressively more permeable self boundaries.

Point number 4: Intimate relating involves the experience of relative permeability of self boundaries. As I enter into the rhythm that emerges in my engagement with the nature around me, becoming progressively more absorbed in my being present in the relating, I experience my awareness flowing into and through my body and senses, experiencing a pronounced ease of being. I feel filled up, renewed, nourished. I experience a releasement from an exclusive identification with my habitual sense of self, my sense of self extending outward beyond my habitual self boundaries toward and into the nature around me. I look toward a clearing and feel myself being drawn outward, pulled into the clearing, as if my sensory experience itself has become saturated with

ence myself leaving my body — it is not a dissociative experience. One's sense of self is not being vacated, it is being re-inhabited. Nor do I feel I am the same as I was before, just larger and just filling up more space; it is not a self-aggrandizing expansion. What I live as self expands to include what feels like genuine but formerly disowned aspects of my habitual self and the nature around me. The sense of self itself is transformed as the boundaries are experienced as more permeable and expansive.

My hand moves toward a leaf with a little bug on it. I touch the leaf. I feel a poignant sense of care, compassion, and oneness, as if it is part of me and I am part of it. This is Point number 6: Intimate relating involves an experience of identification with the permeable and expansive sense of self, a sentiment which comes to me with a pronounced clarity of awareness and presence to my own being. I experience a profound sense of being who I most truly am in this more expansive, permeable, and inclusive wholeness. It is an experience of the process of psychological identification: "At this moment I am being who I really am, and my previous sense of self was illusory." I identify with the full immersion into the whole of myself, a more unified self relatively free of impermeable barriers or divisions, experiencing a harmonious and contented sense of at-homeness-in-nature.

My hand moves slowly away from the leaf, I stand, slowly moving again down the path, now with a greater sense of calm and presence, and the mundane issues of the day start to again enter my awareness. My pace quickens as I begin to experience the return of the barnacle self, but for a while I feel in some way transformed, the effects of this experience lingering as I re-enter my usual habitual mode.

To summarize: The experience begins from an ongoing habitual sense of self characterized by living oneself in a rela-

Ours is a culture in which people talk very little about relating at all, much less about intimate relating.

In this moment of utter clarity of awareness one discovers a wholeness of self in one of its most expanded, connected and harmonious moments, and the message is delivered thoroughly saturated with a sense of complete self acceptance.

investments. I now feel that I am entering into a safe and special way of being my self, safe with respect to dangers from within (what was previously experienced as) my interior, my own psychological dangers, and safe with respect to dangers from the nature around me. The experience of safety allows for progressively greater levels of openness, which are then met with generally enlivening

a sense of self. I feel myself flowing outward into nature and nature flowing into me, nature and me saturating each other in our intermingling and flowing connectedness. I experience a dissolution of separateness and simultaneously a profoundly clear sense of self.

Point number 5: Intimate relating involves the experience of an expansive sense of self. Note that I do not experi-

tively constricted and impermeable way, moving through a period of relative permeability and expansiveness of self, and then returning to a somehow revised sense of the more constricted and impermeable, habitual sense of self. Through the unfolding of this experience the grip of exclusive identification with one's habitual sense of self is relaxed, allowing one's awareness to re-emerge from its supposed separateness and extend its relatedness out into nature, thus to re-inhabit vacated but genuine regions of self. In this moment of utter clarity of awareness one discovers a wholeness of self in one of its most expanded, connected and harmonious moments, and the message is delivered thoroughly saturated with a sense of complete self acceptance. The experience is one of transcendence, connectedness, and identification. It appears that intimate experience with nature can be a very important part of human psychological well being.

Moreover, we can see here a promising basis for a truly effective environmentalism. This experience involves a deeply felt recognition of one's complete embeddedness in and appreciation and respect for the rest of nature, a relatively unimpeded flow of care and compassion toward the rest of the natural world, as if nature was part of one's self — a more ecocentric, as opposed to anthropocentric awareness and identity develops. A more ecocentric sense of self naturally inclines one to relate with nature in a more caring and responsible way. This, of course, is the main thrust of deep ecology: that the well being of humans and that of the rest of nature are inextricably intertwined.

At issue is the quality of the relating and how that experience does or does not get integrated into our psychological and social worlds. For a long time we've tried barnacle mimicry as a goal worthy of our aspirations; the results are not so good, and its premise of sep-arateness from nature has gone mostly unquestioned and runs counter to direct experience. Perhaps it would be better if we aspire instead — in our relationships with each other and with the rest of nature — to genuine intimate relating.

References

Adams, W. (1996). Discovering the sacred in everyday life: An empirical phenomenological study. *The Humanistic Psychologist, 24*: 28-54.

Beyer, J. (1999). Experiencing the self as being part of nature: A phenomenological-hermeneutical investigation into the discovery of the self in and as the flesh of the earth. PhD diss., Duquesne University.

Fox, W. (1995). *Toward a transpersonal ecology: Developing new foundations for environmentalism*. Albany, NY: State University of New York Press.

Glendinning, C. (1994). *My name is Chellis and I'm in recovery from Western civilization*. Boston: Shambhala.

Maslow, A. (1971). *The farther reaches of human nature*. New York: The Viking Press.

Photo: Glenn McCrea, www.dewdropworld.com

Earth is Not My Mother

Toward Contemporary Styles of Earthly Discourse

Craig Chalquist

E copsychology crystallized as a critical edge of the environmental movement sharpened by deep psychology. Will that edge be blunted by a self-limiting fear of change, or can it sculpt a vocabulary appropriate for our troubled time?

Ecopsychology: A Project Initially Ignored

The word "ecopsychology" began to float in the mid-1990s as a name under which various environmental and psychological approaches to the accelerating crisis of our relationship to the natural world began to find a home.

Bypassing environmental psychology's lucrative preoccupation with ergonomics, retail architecture, and other promotions of mass consumption, ecopsychology has favored the bioregional emphasis on making our communities conform to the features of their lands,

Craig Chalquist, MS PhD is a core faculty member of the School of Holistic Studies at John F. Kennedy University. An author of four books and various articles and book chapters, he is co-editor with Linda Buzzell, MFT, of Ecotherapy: Healing with Nature in Mind (Sierra Club Books, 2009). He is also a Master Gardener through a partnership of the University of California with the U.S. Department of Agriculture. Visit his home page at http://www.chalquist.com. Contact: 654 Center Street, Walnut Creek, CA 94595, www.chalquist.com, craig@chalquist.com.

the ecofeminist analysis of hierarchy and patriarchy, the activist emphasis on social justice, the Deep Ecology critique of exclusively human-centered values aloof to other species and to Earth itself, and various indigenous modes of experiencing the land as vital and worthy of rituals of reconnection. Participants danced and meditated, lived simply to fight consumerism and its wastes, gar-

> # Thank Fortune, we are not rooted to the soil, and here is not all the world.
>
> ## (Thoreau, 1962, p. 12)

dened organically, beat drums, hoisted prayer flags. To many the movement stood excitingly on the verge of working its way into a public consciousness in dire need of ecological grounding.

The public failed to notice. Politicians ignored the movement, as did the medical and psychology industries. Mainstream scientists of the type who frequent laboratories regarded it as softheaded. As for the public, it went its

merry First World way shopping the planet to death.

The disappointment of many early ecopsychology advocates remains palpable a decade later. What happened? some wonder. Why didn't it catch on? Why were so many splendid solutions to the placelessness, anomie, anxiety, and stress of our day ignored by the very people who might have benefited? Why so little sustained challenge to corporations and governments that are directly and demonstrably responsible for abetting global warming, resource depletion, mass extinction, and ongoing misery and death for countless humans and nonhumans?

Those who work in this movement—and it continues today, still flowing in the cultural underground—are well aware of the surface obstacles, such as the trillions spent by government and big business to keep us all distracted, entertained, and chained to desks and cubicles and assembly lines. The juvenile level of American political discourse is enough all by itself to make voting seem hopeless. Comparisons to the fate of Imperial Rome abound, as when Lewis Mumford wrote that when the barbarian hordes invaded Hippo, a Roman city in Africa, the first sound they heard was the roaring of crowds more focused on the circus than on their own personal safety (Mumford, 1997).

Many in the ecopsychology movement were and are activists, and activism by necessity tends to focus on the success or failure of one campaign at a time, especially when the goal is to wake up "the sense of men asleep" as Thoreau referred to mainstream consciousness (Thoreau, 2005, p. 149). This can make it difficult to remain in a psychological lence, if only at one gladiatorial remove. "Life has an inner dynamism of its own," wrote psychoanalyst Erich Fromm; "it tends to grow, to be expressed, to be lived. It seems that if this tendency is thwarted the energy directed toward life undergoes a process of decomposition and changes into energies directed toward destruction. Destructiveness is through traditional small-scale farming. Paul Shepard (1996) and Chellis Glendinning (1994) have cataloged the health and wisdom of indigenous ways of eco-friendly living. Starhawk (1999) likes neopagan approaches and Leslie Gray (Roszak, Gomes, and Kanner, 1995) espouses shamanism. Not all of the above are ecopsychologists, but all share its urgency for profound reengagement with what's left of the living world. All seek to widen the range of embodied experience into earthly realms partially or entirely repressed by a public awareness colonized by fragmentation, manpower, hardware, and haste.

Will ecopsychology's edge be blunted by a self-limiting fear of change, or can it sculpt a vocabulary appropriate for our troubled time?

space of permanent revolution, or rather evolution, with activism of the more reflective sort embraced as a way of life. As for rerouting the mainstream, what might not have been apparent even a decade ago looks more and more likely now: that only some profound shock, some deep dark night of the collective soul, can rouse those who sleepwalk from within the comforts and routines paid for by the exploitation of other landscapes and cultures. Societies so insulated from what is required to keep them materially afloat tend not to pierce the bubble on their own until the effects reach far enough homeward to collapse it. The citizens of Rome had no real idea of the fabulous costs of supporting their empire until the flooding of key silver mines wrecked their economy. Even the capture and sacking of the capitol itself did not alert the majority of Romans that the Western Empire was falling.

To carry the analysis farther: it may be that proponents of ecopsychology have underestimated either the prevalence or intensity of a culturally embedded hatred of Earth. As Alan Watts pointed out long ago, it is inaccurate to think of Westerners as materialists (Watts, 1968). "Material" strivings for money, power, or territory actually serve intangible cravings for purity, perfection, status, and control. Dematerialists filled with thwarted needs for relationship, belonging, sovereignty, and meaning of the kind inherent in an organic connection to the world find themselves drawn toward death and vio-

the outcome of unlived life" (Fromm, 1994, p. 182). We have only to think of global warming, the unrestrained outcome of perpetual internal combustion exploding every day into smoggy literality.

Ultimately, however, the new/ancient field's inability to catch on might have originated within ecopsychology itself.

Green Conservatism

For the most part the reaction of the ecopsychological thinkers, doers, and activists to the delusional separation of self from planet and society from nature has been to call for a return to sensibilities described as indigenous, natural, aboriginal, land-based, undomesticated, or rural. Tracking Muir (1997) and Thoreau (2005), Robert Greenway (in Roszak, Gomes, and Kanner, 1995) has documented the restorative ecstasy of going out in the wild, and Naess (1993) an expanded selfhood that merges with one's natural surroundings. Wes Jackson (1996), Aldo Leopold (2001), Wendell Berry (2002), and Gene Logsdon (1995) have written about feeling closer to place

At least two important things happen when an evolutionary movement emerges from the murky waters of collective consciousness, turns, and thrusts back against them. The first is that it carries within it some elements of the turbidity of its source. The second is that it reacts against other elements by deemphasizing or excluding them. Often these happen together.

James Hillman has alerted us to what he calls unconscious Christianity: hidden religious assumptions that have burrowed into psychology (Hillman 1983). This legacy includes the traditionally Christian emphasis on individuality, self-control, unity of personality, personal redemption, will power, literal interpretation of stories and images, and valo-

It may be that proponents of ecopsychology have underestimated either the prevalence or intensity of a culturally embedded hatred of Earth.

rization of what it considers the higher, purer, and brighter side of human nature over coming to grips with its shadowy aspects. Under the influence of the monotheistic preoccupation with literalism, for example, mainstream psychology lacks a capacity for hearing deeply into symbols, motifs, and metaphors, confining itself instead to whatever can be measured and verified against some external standard of validity. Very often psychology's practitioners lack even a rudimentary awareness that what they pin down on charts and tests reflects only the grossest aspects of the mercurial shifts and flows that characterize a reasonably alive human consciousness.

An environmental parallel to this unconscious Christianity (not to be confused with conscious Christianity as a spiritual system) surfaces in the unconscious conservatism of the deep ecologies and ecopsychologies, a conservatism that prizes the ancient while disregarding a spectrum of present knowledge sources.

Various dictionaries identify "conservatism" as

1. Favoring traditional views and values; tending to oppose change.

2. Traditional or restrained in style.

3. Moderate; cautious.

And so Wendell Berry links health and happiness with wood-smoked Christian values and a cultivatable plot of good land; his country-doctor prescription includes family, faith, and farming, as though the oppressive shadow of these had never been amply demonstrated and analyzed. Paul Shepard wanted to do away with civilization itself. Derrick Jensen wants to blow it up (2006). Other proposed curatives for the ecologically damaged present include abandoning the city to head for the treeline, chanting around campfires, visionquesting, mask-making, shamanizing, sageing, meditating, and singing "Kumbaya" at city council meetings.

However valuable in their place, such practices when considered together share a wistful gaze locked onto an imagined pastoral or indigenous past. All cling to archaic imagery relevant to a different time. All ply the modern Western fantasy of what deep roots and Earth-based spirituality should have looked like while ignoring how some of these practices and symbols arrived on the scene as cultural and spiritual transplants dug up from outside the Western heritage but glimpsed through a Western glass darkly. Most stay safely in the wide lap of what Jung would have identified as old myth: antique symbol

systems in need of renewal (Jung, 1981). Instead, they undergo imitation by rootless people understandably hungry for a sense of place, belonging, and embodiment.

It may be that ecopsychology's inability to catch on might have originated within ecopsychology itself.

The question is not whether the old myth—a kind of Demeter view of land-based living—should or should not constitute an approach to being in touch with the world. Obviously some find it meaningful, particularly those raised within the original traditions. Its practices work; its value is time-tried and tested. The question is: What about people for whom the old myth does not work? Those for whom prayer flags or dream catchers, Kuan Yin or Black Elk contain no more numinosity, no more power

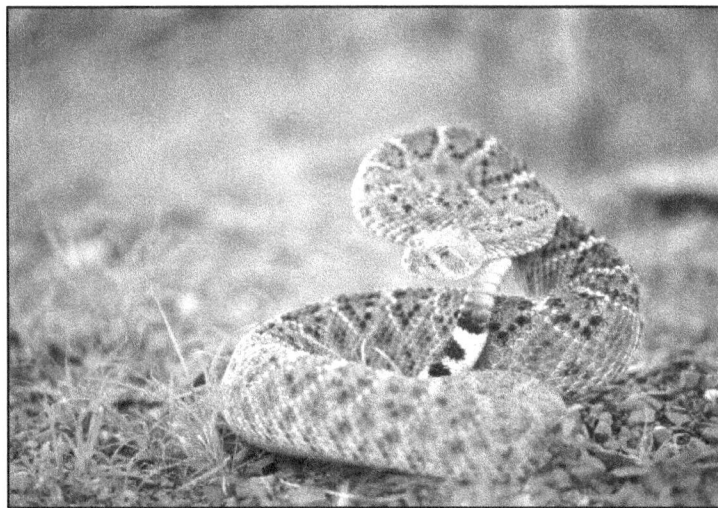

Photo: Glenn McCrea, www.dewdropworld.com

to enchant, than do the cross or Christmas? Retreating like soon-to-be-rooted Daphne from the outstretched arms of an Apollo future is not an option that feeds their souls. Yet neither do they wish to swim any longer in industrially contaminated mainstream currents.

Dreaming the Myth Onward

For some years now I've experimented with a three-phase alternative to

either regressive romanticism or pseudo-progressive technologism: Exploring what my ancestry has to offer of image and history and myth, translating it into contemporary language, and seeing where my story finds inclusion in the geographically framed story of wherever I happen to live. This represents an attempt at what Jung refers to as dreaming the myth onward (Jung, 1981), with emphasis on the "onward." *

I share, for example, the indigenous view of the world as animated and the ancestors as ever-present. This was the view of my indigenous ancestors, some of whom celebrated Samhain as the time when this world and the Otherworld come into closest spiritual proximity. But I hold this view as a set of metaphors that celebrate a deep psychic fact that resurfaces in panpsychism, systems theory, and depth psychology. Passing up the chance to toss the bloody bones of butchered cattle onto roaring bonfires, I light candles instead, open a bottle of locally harvested wine, and spend silent time greeting the imaginal presence of those who came before me. This observance of today makes me feel close to them, those souls who saw the world in such different terms than my own, and offers a fulfilling sense of restored continuity.

On my desk sits a pendant shaped like what my aboriginal Norse ancestors would have recognized as Mjöllnir ("MULE-ner"), the lightning hammer of Thor. He used it to deadly effect on presumptuous

* Jung is sometimes co-opted by programs and practitioners who use his teachings to defend academic or ceremonialized evocations of pre-industrial modes of consciousness. Nothing could be farther from Jung's own project, which drew on ancient ritual and myth in order to give them new psychological life in the present. Jung himself was an example of a man for whom the old creeds and myths no longer provided psychic containment for his inner experiences, a fact he realized while still in his youth and which he never lost sight of.

giants. When he threw it, the crackling equalizer always returned faithfully to his practiced hand. What the monastery-sacking Vikings took into battle as a literal war hammer I understand psychologically as the flashing, pounding, flying insight that flattens giantism, the inflationary state of anything human that gets too far beyond its natural boundaries. Some say the giants went away or never existed, but they roam the land today in the bulky guise of huge corporations, totalitarian ideologies, vast empires of money and matter, gigantic towers and machines oppressing bodies and souls alike. I wear this pendant not because I believe it holds magical powers that keep me safe, but as an ancestrally flavored reminder that "Mjöllnir" means "mealer" in the sense of a powerful grindstone, with giantism providing grist for the patient mill of ever-present ecological powers demanding their rightful due.

Dreaming the myth onward also means tracing where ancestral stories and images remain incomplete, their cultural continuity broken. It is true that many of my Anglo-Celtic forefathers were conquerors, but also true that they were conquered too, from the Huns who pushed out the Angles, Saxons, Frisians, and Jutes to the Romans who warred on the Celts across Europe. The will to conquest rages like a contagion from region to region and culture to culture; the displaced are particularly susceptible to it. Their descendants are left with puzzle pieces for a heritage: a Celtic knot, a Saxon white horse, some

The unconscious conservatism of the deep ecologies and eco-psychologies prizes the ancient while disregarding a spectrum of present knowledge sources.

phrases in Gaelic, the spear and the cauldron, runes and obscure scripts...and perhaps an unpleasant measure of ancestral guilt.

Sometimes puzzle pieces are enough. In the final chapters of Roots, Alex Haley describes the remarkable series of journeys that led him from a garbled place name handed down through generations of his family to the village in Africa where his ancestor Kunta Kinte had been captured by slave traders and forced aboard a ship for the terrible Middle Passage. Haley went to the village in person to meet kin, to heal, and to close the circle: a ruptured story finally dreamed forward (Haley, 1974).

For some, recovering ancestral symbols and tales involves exploring Western sources of spiritual expression long overshadowed by Christianism and

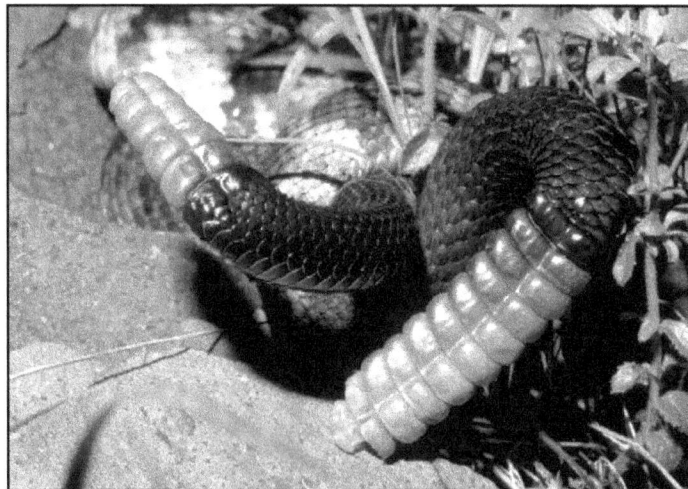
Photo: Glenn McCrea, www.dewdropworld.com

scientism. The seeker who turns away from the West to embrace the East overlooks many lore-rich treasures waiting to be dreamed forward. We too have our practices of egoless contemplation: phenomenology, Goethean science, the *vera imaginatio* ("true imagination") of alchemy. We too have our I Ching counterparts, including geomancy and the reading of runes. Our ancient meditative practices were called *theoria* by

the ancient Greeks: a faculty for contemplating beauty, meaning, and even the world. Circumambulating a prayer wheel tied with colorful scarves looks to us like dancing around the May Pole. Our ancient traditions reach so deeply into Christendom itself thanks to its systematic programs of cultural appropriation that some believe the Dionysian celebrant Jesus and his original followers to have been more pagan (from a word for "peasant" and "peace") than Christian. One could even argue that the early Christians were seeking to restore indigenous values to the failing heart of the urbanizing Roman Empire. Consider the lilies of the field.

For those of us not living in the lands of our ancestors, dreaming the myth onward invites deeply meaningful explorations into how our stories—both personal and ancient—line up with the stories now around us. The land possesses a mysterious and potent capacity for reaching out to its inhabitants through their own imagery. I'm remembering Sebastopol, a small town in Northern California, and its penchant for showing up in my dreams as a woman named Evie (Eve) addressing me as Cain. At that time my large circular birthmark and I were living on the property of a local butcher who stood in for Abel. Leaving that lovely place to move closer to work felt like a departure from Eden.

Here we must be more careful than our rapacious forefathers were. Native Northern Californians say that a huge snake swims in from the Pacific to visit the coastal rivers and test young men into adulthood. The dragons fought by British knights come to mind. Rather than impose European names and categories onto the local ones, however, as was done so often in times of colonization and conquest, we can hold these as different imaginings of some local spirit of place while bearing in mind that people who have lived there for millennia know the place much more intimately than we do. In contemporary language we can appreciate the snaky being as the psychically animated presence of currents and eddies sweeping inland as intelligent ocean greets sentient river and makes its periodic visit.

Holding things this way also bypasses the unconscious conservatism of mis-translating indigenous terminology. Where Native Americans describe Earth as mother, for example, the rest of us have pushed the metaphor literally and been captured by it, from sucking the

The seeker who turns away from the West to embrace the East overlooks many lore-rich treasures waiting to be dreamed forward.

planet's resources like milk from an exhausted breast to leaving our waste around for Mom to pick up to putting her on so high a pedestal that we send children out of the city to learn about "nature" somewhere else. To a developmentally attuned ear, the wearying overemphasis on forests and wilderness begins to sound after a while like a defensive idealization of Mom's purity and chastity. To cling to the ceremonial, the native, the rural, the "natural," or the agrarian without regard for other kinds of relationship to place is to remain perched insecurely on Gaia's leaf-draped knee, apparently safe from the arduous task of strengthening our terrestrial bonds through refashionings of contemporary language.

Should we not protect the forests, then? Of course we should, but the world has given us more than forests: Technologies and sciences ultimately come from it too, as nonhuman animals demonstrate every time they use tools, plan for the future, leave funerary twigs and leaves for lost companions, and store up food for the winter. A city dweller who eats

from a small balcony garden, composts with a worm box, rides a bicycle, and stays warm with a solar panel hung from a window depends that much less on distant sources of food and energy. What he needs but seldom finds, however, is a language of connection and interiority suitable for cultivating his sense of emplacement. He needs a current vernacular for ensouled buildings and suffering landscapes, regenerated neighborhoods and home-grown crops, because the language of "nature spirits" and "yin/yang energies" does not nourish his present-day sense of these things as potentially or actually alive. A current perspective should respect the ancient terminology enough to examine which aspects of it invite reimagining.

Imagining a Terrapsychology

"Terrapsychological" work with story, psyche and place began when a small group of us appreciatively began blending ecopsychology with depth psychology and systems theory and other evolving frames of reference to fashion an updated vocabulary for describing and exploring the world's uncanny animation. For example, Matthew Cochran

geography" tracks the stratification and meandering, folding and weathering of the naturally emplaced psyche. Local "ecological complexes" (Chalquist, 2009) recur as themes or images, like the Eden echo in Sebastopol. Assessing these key us in on aspects of what the Romans knew as the *genius loci* or "spirit (or soul) of place." They show us its psychic face.

Terrapsychology is a multidisciplinary approach to investigating the deep connections between people and places (Chalquist, 2007). As such it attempts to dream up a "new myth" to transform our relationship to our homeworld one living location at a time.

If we are ever to put in place the kinds of Earth-based communities that match our needs and deepest desires, we will likely require an ongoing and collective cultivation of a truly planetary psychology, one that can grow meaningfully updated visions of where we belong in the world and how we can live with it and with each other. The work of Aviva Joseph provides an example of holding together social justice and terrapsychological transformation while building homes for displaced Bedouins outside Jerusalem, a divided city of many active fault lines (Joseph, 2007).

By "new myth" I mean a new collective story. Story is unique in its capacity to pull together many strands—subjective and objective, lore and fact, naturalism and ecosystem--into a coherent picture that stirs the imaginative facul-

Whether ecopsychology will prove viable depends on how its practitioners summon the courage to push beyond the confines of unconscious conservatism to speak to a wider audience in a comprehensible tongue while resisting being co-opted and diluted by dominant hegemonic and economic forces.

(2005) and Laura Mitchell (2005) have coined the term "nomadic awareness" for a particularly sensitized non-possessive listening in on what the ground underfoot has to say to the wandering visitor. Cochran's poetic "archetypal

ties of the listener. Story goes straight to the heart of the matter. A deep psychological shift occurs when your story joins you intimately to where you live. The place becomes part of your psyche, and you experience yours as part of the place's wider and deeper intelligence. The lonely sense of rootlessness gives way to a sense of belonging. Likewise, so do many of the discomforts we mistake for permanent or solely internal: alienation, anomie, facelessness, disconnection, depression, psychic numbness, and the anxiety of psychological exile from the world. When we align our story with that of our time and place, newly situating ourselves in nested, animate ecologies, the symptoms of chronic disengagement give way to feeling at home in the cosmos.

This in turn creates a sense of humility and protectiveness toward the land. At

Terrapsychology investigates deep connections between people and places. It attempts to dream up a "new myth" to transform our relationship to our homeworld one living location at a time.

such close range it becomes emotionally obvious how its interests and needs are also our own.

Ecopsychology has accurately critiqued the knee-jerk application of "natural" science methods as anthropocentric, tyrannical, and psychologically distancing, but we sometimes forget that science too is a contemporary language, its findings capable of reimagining as geo-psychic metaphors. That the devilishly themed Rancho del Diablo Rincon in Southern California sold in the 1800s for a measurable quantity of money remains an empirical fact, but when understood as a resonant image locally embedded, the amount reveals its storied sense: $666.66. Developers have unconsciously repeated a local motif at Point Conception, which the native Chumash believe to be a gateway to another realm, by pushing to build a spaceport there.

A truly planetary psychology will have to be more flexible than comprehensive. Conceptual schemata that purport to explain everything perpetuate an unhelpful legacy of colonial-imperial expansionism. They also harbor an idealizing ambition of enthroning the lone genius who invents the latest and largest explanation. Given the uncountable variety of people, places, creatures, and things, each with its own constantly shifting needs and relationships, a framework of theory and practice capable of picking up and putting down whatever tools the terrain requires at the moment should serve us and Earth better than the inherently competitive one-size-fits-all approach left over from the weary Age of Empires.

Instead of indulging the omnipotent fantasy of a grand explanatory scheme that calls itself "meta-" to validate itself, why not pool energies for a second great mapping of the globe underfoot, a project of psychocartography to correct destructive colonial designs by cataloging the moods, the wildlife, the lore, the history, and even the dreams of each living place encounter by deeply lived encounter?

Whether ecopsychology will prove viable depends on how its practitioners summon the courage to push beyond the confines of unconscious conservatism to speak to a wider audience in a comprehensible tongue while resisting being co-opted and diluted by dominant hegemonic and economic forces. Ecopsychologists certainly need not restrict themselves to the Western heritage, but like all of us in search of grounding and homecoming, they will need a clear sense of purpose in the present, in the service of new myth, before their steps can pass beyond those inscribed by their sure-footed forbears.

References

Berry, W. (2002). *The art of the commonplace*. Emeryville, CA: Shoemaker & Hoard.

Chalquist, C. (2007). *Terrapsychology: Re-engaging the soul of place*. New Orleans: Spring Journal Books.

Chalquist, C. (2009). *The tears of Llorona: A Californian odyssey of place, myth, and homecoming*. Walnut Creek: World Soul Press.

Cochran, M. (2010). The Eros of Erosion: Revealing Archetypal Geology. ReVision, *31*(3&4), 36-41. doi:10.4298/REVN.31.3.4.36-41

Fromm, E. (1994). *Escape from freedom*. New York: Holt.

Glendinning, C. (1994). *My name is Chellis & I'm in recovery from Western civilization*. Boston: Shambhala.

Haley, A. (1974). *Roots: The saga of an American family*. New York: Dell.

Hillman, J. (1983). *Inter views*. Woodstock: Spring.

Jackson, W. (1996). *Becoming native to this place*. Berkeley: Counterpoint.

Jensen, D. (2006). *Endgame: The problem of civilization* (Vol. 1). New York: Seven Stories Press.

Joseph, A. (2007). Personal communication.

Jung, C. G. (1981). *The archetypes and the collective unconscious*. Princeton: Princeton University Press.

Leopold, A. (2001). *A Sand County almanac*. New York: Oxford University Press.

Logsdon, G. (1995). *The contrary farmer*. White River Junction, VT: Chelsea Green.

Mitchell, L. (2005). The eco-imaginal underpinnings of community identity in Harmony Grove Valley: Unbinding the ecological imagination. Unpublished doctoral dissertation at the Pacifica Graduate Institute.

Muir, J. (1997). *John Muir: Nature writings*. New York: Library of America.

Mumford, L. (1997). *The city in history: Its origins, its transformations, and its prospects*. New York: MJF Books.

Naess, A. (1993). *Ecology, community, and lifestyle: Outline of an ecosophy*. Cambridge: Cambridge University Press.

Roszak, T., Gomes, M., & Kanner, A. (Eds.). (1995). *Ecopsychology: Restoring the earth, healing the mind*. San Francisco: Sierra Club Books.

Shepard, P. (1996). *The only world we've got*. San Francisco: Sierra Club Books.

Starhawk. (1999). *The spiral dance: A rebirth of the ancient religion of the Goddess*. New York: HarperOne.

Thoreau, H. (1962). *The journal of Henry D. Thoreau*. Mineola, NY: Dover.

Thoreau, H. (2005). *Walden*. Lawrence, KS: Digireads.

Watts, A. (1968). *The wisdom of insecurity*. New York: Vintage.

Diamond in the Rough

Primitive Ecopsychology, the Diamond Approach, and Transpersonal Ecopsychology

John Davis

This article describes a confluence of two paths, the Diamond Approach and primitive ecopsychology, using the example of wilderness retreats I call "Diamond in the Rough." This integration can expand the field of ecopsychology into a more precise and useful understanding of its overlap with spirituality or transpersonal ecopsychology.[1]

Ecopsychology

Enduring psychological and spiritual questions—who we are, how we grow, why we suffer, how we heal—are intimately connected to our relationships with the physical world. Similarly, the over-riding environmental questions of our time — the sources of, consequences of, and solutions to environmental disaster — are rooted in our images of self

John Davis, Ph.D., is a professor at Naropa University where he directs the M. A. program in Transpersonal Psychology and its Ecopsychology concentration. He has been an ordained teacher of the Diamond Approach since 1983, and he is the author of *The Diamond Approach: An Introduction to the Teachings of A. H. Almaas* (Shambhala). John is also on the staff of the School of Lost Borders where he leads wilderness trips and trains wilderness rites of passage guides. For more information, visit www.johnvdavis.com. Contact: jdavis@naropa.edu, 2130 Arapahoe Av, Boulder, CO 80302, 303-245-4654.

and nature and the behaviors which stem from them. Ecopsychology integrates ecology and psychology in responding to both sets of questions. Among its contributions are shifting the basis for environmental action from anxiety, blame, and coercion to devotion, joy, and invitation (Roszak, 2001); bringing the natural world and ecological thinking to psychotherapy and personal growth (Conn, 1998; Swanson, 2001); and fostering ways of living which are both ecologically and psychologically healthy and sustainable (Fisher, 2002).

One of a number of areas studying human-nature relationships (such as environmental psychology, ecospirituality, and environmental education), ecopsychology is founded on three insights. (1) There is a deeply bonded relationship between humans and nature. (2) The dissociation of humans and nature leads to suffering both for the environment (ecological devastation) and for humans (arrested human development, grief, despair, anxiety, or alienation). (3) Realizing and deepening the connection between humans and nature is healing for both. This reconnection expresses itself in ecotherapy, work on grief and despair about environmental destruc-

tion, integration of the interlocking projects of environmental action and social justice, and support for more effective and sustainable environmental action and lifestyles based on positive motivations such as joy, compassion, and love.

Primitive Ecopsychology

For many years, I have had a deep and abiding passion for wild nature, finding support, challenge, insight, and growth in the natural world and especially its wilder places. This passion found a home in ecopsychology as a vehicle for exploring the confluence of nature, psyche, and spirit (Davis, 1998), and it deepened when I participated in a wilderness rite of passage, or "vision fast," based on the work of Steven Foster and Meredith Little (Foster & Little, 1988; Davis, 2005). I began an apprenticeship with one of their first students, and a few years later, I met and trained with Steven and Meredith at their School of Lost Borders. In addition to the personal impact of the vision fast ceremony, I was drawn to the combination of their straightforward, generous teaching style and their thoughtful articulation of the conceptual underpinnings of their work. I have now led vision fasts for 20 years, I train wilderness guides, and I am on the staff of the School of Lost Borders.

Foster, at one-time a professor of literature and poetry, often experimented

---

[1] Thanks to Ann DeBaldo, who made suggestions on an earlier draft of this chapter, to my partners in this work, and to my teachers.

with the best language to describe his work. He was one of the first to use the term ecopsychology and, at some point, began using the term "primitive ecopsy-

Primitive ecopsychology may be seen as a branch of the larger field of ecopsychology, one firmly oriented to encountering the wild Earth directly.

chology" for the work of the School of Lost Borders. Here, the word "primitive" suggests two things. First, it points us to the wild world — undeveloped, untamed, and unaltered by humans — as a means of healing, maturation, and self-realization. Touching the wild, whether in an extended wilderness excursion, a nearby park, or even in our own bodies in this moment, wakes us up, makes us more whole, and transforms us. (At the same time, Foster was not one to romanticize nature. He respected its raw power and saw the importance of preparation, support, context-setting, and integration of nature experiences.) In a second sense, "primitive" suggests that which is primary, original, or first. It points us to direct and immediate contact with the natural world before emotional reactions or intellectual analysis. Thus, primitive ecopsychology may be seen as a branch of the larger field of ecopsychology, one firmly oriented to encountering the wild Earth directly.

I see three key elements in primitive ecopsychology. The first is the value of direct, immediate contact with the natural world. The paradigm of primitive ecopsychology centers on wilderness experiences, but it is by no means limited to wilderness. Looking closely at wilderness experience, we will find it to be more of an attitude than an absolute.

Most of the places we use for the Diamond in the Rough trips are wilder but not, strictly speaking, wilderness. Signs of human intervention are never far away. How wild does the wilderness need to be for the purposes of primitive ecopsychology? Not very. The key is to encounter the natural world directly and openly with less of the insulation of modern life.

The second element of primitive ecopsychology is the model of the vision fast, Foster and Little's first work. With a deep structure reflecting the three stages of a rite of passage (van Gennep, 1961), the vision fast is essentially a threshold-

Photo: Glenn McCrea, www.dewdropworld.com

crossing ceremony. Following preparation and severance from the familiar, the participant crosses a threshold into a liminal space, and then returns. While the specific purpose of a rite of passage is generally the confirmation of a change is status or a life transition, Foster and Little designed a wide range of practices with a similar structure (Foster & Little, 1989). It is not uncommon for participants to associate the vision fast model and its associated teachings

with Native American Indian spirituality. Indeed, it draws from the same archetypal roots. The orientation of the School of Lost Borders' work has always been to respect those who have developed and kept alive such practices and, at the same time, not to appropriate them. Drawing from the deep, pan-cultural roots of all rites of passage, Foster and Little sought to re-create forms relevant to our time, place, and culture.

The third element of primitive ecopsychology is the use of a particular four-fold model of nature, including human nature (Foster & Little, 1998). This Four Shields model is featured as a specific teaching by the School of Lost Border and included in virtually all of its courses. It describes four cardinal directions, times of day, seasons, ways of being, ways of knowing, ways of loving, and so on. Its specific origins appear to be Mayan, but its basic outlines are found in many cultures around the world. While our particulars fit the northern temperate zone, remarkably similar four-fold models can be found in teachings of Native American Indians, Africans, Jungian psychology, and many others (Foster & Little, 1998). This model of human nature stems equally from natural cycles, human life cycles, and a wide variety of dimensions of human action and experience. It is a basis for ecopsychology inasmuch as the Four Shields model derives from our understanding of natural processes.

Each of these three elements of primitive ecopsychology are important in the Diamond in the Rough retreats. First and foremost, these retreats encourage direct contact with the natural world and support participants in opening, listening, engaging, and learning from it. Drawing from the vision fast model, this encounter takes the form of daily solo experiences, each a threshold crossing, along with a longer 24-hour solo. Finally, the

Four Shields model gives these retreats their basic shape and is a part of its core teaching.

The Diamond Approach

The Diamond Approach is a thorough, coherent, and precise articulation of human nature and a path for living an authentic, realized life in the world. It is a mystical path in the sense that its ultimate foundation is the pure non-conceptual ground of being. At the same time, it values living in the world, relating to others, and functioning as means to, and expressions of, self-realization. The Diamond Approach blends both the personal and the transpersonal aspects of full human development. The Diamond Approach has been developed and described extensively by A. H. Almaas (e.g., Almaas, 1998, 2004; Davis, 1999). It provides a detailed, inclusive, and thorough map and path through the depths of human consciousness. I met Almaas is 1975, and I have been studying with him since as a student and one of the first teachers he trained in the Diamond Approach. The Diamond Approach is typically taught in group and individual sessions. Its methods incorporate individual practices (such as meditation and contemplation), small process groups, and large group teachings blending conceptual and experiential knowledge. While the Diamond Approach incorporates insights and findings from modern psychology, neuroscience, and a variety of spiritual disciplines, the Diamond Approach is an original system with its own mature, unique logos.

Among its many elements, two have been especially relevant on the Diamond in the Rough retreats: its main method, the practice of inquiry, and one of its central concepts, the soul. The Diamond Approach is based on the practice of inquiry, an engaged, open, and open-ended exploration of one's immediate experience (Almaas, 2002). Inquiry follows the thread of one's experience, revealing the inner nature of the experience and supporting the transformation of consciousness. Along the way, inquiry exposes resistances, distortions, fixa-

tions, and other barriers to the freedom of experience. This exploration of immediate experience leads to understanding, which in the Diamond Approach is taken to mean fully-lived experience which includes the knowing of the experience. Experiencing, knowing, and realization are not separate.

The soul is the organ of consciousness or being itself, the means by which being knows itself and the means through which being functions.

In this view, the soul is not an enduring or permanent object. Consistent with the original meaning of soul in Western spiritual and philosophical disciplines, it is the organ of consciousness or being itself, the means by which being knows itself, and the means through which being functions. As an organ of being, the soul is the locus of individual perception, action, and development. It is the soul which is transformed by experience and which matures. We can say it is the soul which is truly alive in a person. More succinctly, the soul is the individual consciousness.

The soul's inherent aliveness is generally deadened, dulled, or contracted by patterns of avoidance and defense based on the past. The residue of undigested experiences, conditioning, defenses, and resulting ego structures such as self-images and identifications shape the soul, binding, distorting, and restricting its aliveness. These structures may be temporarily useful to the developing soul, and they are approximations of the soul's true nature, not mistakes of development. However, unless they are metabolized by the soul, these structures become barriers to inner freedom and full expression. Consequently, the Diamond Approach distinguishes a soul which is restricted from a soul which is free and realized. The more free the soul, the more apparent are its inherent qualities and the more transparent it is to its

essential nature as aliveness, presence, emptiness, and depth.

The Diamond in the Rough retreats focus on certain inherent qualities of the soul: its dynamism, its exquisitely tender sensitivity, its impressionability which gives it the capacity to be influenced by experience and to mature, and its intrinsic freedom and potentiality. The integration of these qualities of the individual consciousness or soul reveal its essential presence and aliveness. These wilderness-based retreats provide the opportunity for participants' focused inquiries in nature to reveal and deepen these qualities.

Common Ground for a Wilderness-based Retreat

Both the Diamond Approach and primitive ecopsychology aim to expand and deepen experience and bring us more fully into the present moment. Both draw us into direct and immediate contact with the totality of the body, heart, mind, and spirit. They express a genuinely optimistic view of human nature, along with a respectful, compassionate, and unflinching recognition of the obstacles to the full realization of our potential. Each appreciates the maturation of the human being as an ongoing and open-ended process. Finally, both the Diamond Approach and primitive ecopsychology are deeply committed to living in the world, this world, not transcending it.

Here, I will outline the general structure of the teachings on these retreats. We set up a basecamp in a natural wild area and practice safe, Leave-No-Trace camping techniques. Most days follow a similar format. We gather early in the morning for a period of mindfulness meditation followed by a brief teaching. The teaching leads to a focus for the day's solo. Participants are on their own for the rest of the morning and most of the afternoon, free to wander from base camp as they wish. The areas we use for these retreats offer a variety of directions and terrains to explore in solitude. Sometimes participants choose a particular landscape which matches their inner state; other times, they allow spontaneity and synchronicity to guide them. At the end of the day, we gather for a brief check-in and communal dinner, followed by a more thorough debriefing and exploration of the experiences of the day.

The South Shield and the Soul's Dynamism

The teaching begins with the south shield, the place of summer, high noon, the child, and the body. Entering the new environment of the wilderness invokes a sense of childhood with both excitement and fear. The child is raw, playful, and innocent to long-term impacts. The south shield invokes the body, physicality, and raw sensations. These are times of instinctual fight and flight, and summer is a time of high energy, vitality, vigor, and expansion.

One aspect of the Diamond Approach's teachings on the soul mirrors the south shield well. When we first turn our attention to our consciousness, we find it is continually in change. The soul is constantly morphing, revealing its fundamental dynamism and flow. In a soul which is more free, such dynamism is unfettered. The impacts of the ego-self, on the other hand, contract and rigidify the soul, restricting its flow and dampening its dynamism. This flow may be more coherent or more fragmented, its pacing languid or frantic, its tone loud or quiet. So, it is with the body, the child, and the energy of summer. From boisterous play and splashing in the water, we summer-children lay down in the shade and drift into reverie chewing on a piece of grass, only to be stung by a bee, awakened to our physicality, and shocked into terror and rage.

On the Diamond in the Rough, the task for this phase focuses participants on the soul's dynamic flow. We invite participants to go into nature and focus on movement and flow. How does your body move across the land; where do you see nature's dynamism; how do you experience your aliveness?

The West Shield and the Soul's Sensitivity

Summer eventually gives way to fall; shadows lengthen, and the child cannot stay forever a child. The rambunctious child matures into an adolescent. Playfulness slows and reflects; anger grows into recognition of its impacts;

fear quiets into awareness of our vulnerability. The child is not gone, but the adolescent takes center stage. This is the territory of the west shield: autumn, dusk, adolescence, and the heart. Here, the adolescent begins to notice herself or himself as a distinct individual, and the inner life becomes more dramatic. Feelings unknown to the child appear: doubt, worry, grief, shame. Indeed, the adolescent is, as much as anything, a creature of introspection and self-reflection. The west shield is such a place of doubt, ambivalence, suffering, and heartfelt tenderness. This is also the place of the shadow. While the archetypal child is blissfully unaware of ambiguity, guilt,

> ## How does your body move across the land; where do you see nature's dynamism; how do you experience your aliveness?

shame, and other elements of the psychic shadow world, the archetypal adolescent seems to live in the shadows as much as the light. It is a bittersweet and sensitive time.

Drawing on the Diamond Approach, we recognize the soul's sensitivity to all that touches it, whether from internal or external sources. Joy and pain impact the soul, as do cruelty and kindness. The more free the soul, the more sensitive it is; the less free the soul, the more dulled it is. Whereas the obstacles of the south shield dampen the soul's vitality and dynamism, those of the west shield entangle the soul in self-consciousness and suffering. The soul becomes thick and obscured, and the inner light infusing the soul dims a bit.

This sensitivity in the soul means it has the potential to be wounded. Yet, there is a depth of personal presence and authenticity which develops through such sensitivity and vulnerability. The focus of the solo in this phase of the

retreat draws on this wisdom. To encourage participants to open the soul to all its experience, we encourage them to relate directly to their wounds and to the wounds they encounter in nature. "Find a wounded place in nature, and be with it," we suggest, or they may engage nature as a therapist, choosing a tree or rock (the ultimate "non-directive therapist") and telling their wounds to that natural object. By going into our wounds, rather than avoiding them, we re-engage the soul's sensitivity and develop its presence.

The North Shield and the Soul's Maturation

The shadows of fall deepen into long nights, bringing new challenges and calling for new capacities. Cold winds blow in from the north, and winter is upon us. If we are to survive — if our people are to survive — we need to be more thoughtful and analytic, planning, organizing, and delaying our own gratification for the good of the community. The adolescent matures into adulthood and exercises newly developed capacities for willpower, responsibility, intention, self-control, directed action, structure, and consideration for others. Where the south shield was primarily about the body and the west shield about the heart, the north shield is about the mind. Again, the child and the adolescent are not rejected or left behind. Rather, their views of the world are incorporated into the adult who can play and feel without being deterred from the work that needs to be done. Thus, this shield is the place of winter, night, adulthood, and the mind. Its gifts include rationality, will, and the creation of enduring structures.

Through the Diamond Approach, we find something else to be true about the soul. The soul not only registers the impacts of its experiences; it records them. These imprints and impressions allow the soul to mature, individuating and developing greater capacities for knowing, understanding, and expression. With these come the capacity for effective action and thoughtful generosity.

While the focus for this phase of the retreat could go several directions, including exploration of the laws of nature, both within and outside us, we often focus on a personal exploration of our human-nature relationships. Participants are encouraged to look at the patterns in their views of their relationship with the natural world and the impacts these patterns have on their souls. How mature, realistic, and confident are these views of nature? Are they based on fear of nature, objectification, and use of nature, or a kinship with the natural world? This is an exercise in sincere and mature self-understanding, not self-criticism, self-inflation, or intellectualization. Suspending both judgment and theoretical analysis are important for this solo.

The East Shield and the Soul's Potentiality

At this point in the retreat, we shift our pattern of mid-day solos and morning and evening gatherings, and we invite participants to a 24-hour solo. We do very little discussion of the east shield prior to this solo. Since the nature of the east shield often transcends ordinary discourse, we keep explanations to a minimum at this point, and instead, we reinforce the solo as a chance to go beyond expectations. It is an extended inquiry into one's immediate experience beyond conceptual frameworks and an opportunity for direct encounter with the soul and its potential.

The evening before the solo includes simple ceremony, reflecting the mode of this shield. Simple actions are given deeper significance. Crossing a threshold can signify to the unconscious, as well as the community, that one is willing to enter a world with fewer rules and roles and greater possibilities — a sacred space. The next morning, participants do cross a ceremonial threshold at dawn, symbolically leaving the familiar world and entering a world of unknown potential. They return shortly after dawn on the following day.

In the twenty-four-hour cycle, the east shield corresponds to the dawn. As the Earth turns, what becomes of the night? The sky lightens slowly in the east. First, we are fooled a bit by false dawn, and then, the sun! Illumination, revelation,

vision, joy, delight! Realization and release. Unearned grace. The sun illuminates our world; a brighter light illumines our souls. As spring arrives, what becomes of winter? One day, we discover that the buds on the trees have begun to swell, and a blossom appears on an apparently dead branch. The world is alive with potential once more, and naturally, we feel this is a time to celebrate this rebirth. And what becomes of the winter shield's adult? As the adult steps through the veils between life and death, a life is completed and a soul returns to formlessness. At the same time, new life crosses the veils between death and life; a new life begins. The spring shield is a

Photo: Glenn McCrea, www.dewdropworld.com

place where death and birth co-emerge. Similarly, this is the place of paradox, mystery, and the joker, jester, and trickster, overturning our structures so they can come alive again, infused with space and light and ready for the vigor of the south shield.

Through the lens of the Diamond Approach, these qualities of the east shield are reflected in the soul's inherent freedom and potentiality. In its most pure manifestation, the soul's realization is free and never-ending. The soul is transparent to its divine nature and open to transformation; not just expansion in a horizontal dimension to a broader range of experience, but a vertical shift in its identity and its relationship to its source or ground.

The Diamond in the Rough retreats typically emphasize the soul's potential, the possibility of its transformation, and its ultimate transparency to being. Unoccluded by structures based on defens-

es and the past, the soul perceives and expresses its depth. While most participants do not articulate their east shield experiences this way, we see it in the joyful faces returning from the solo, a deeper sense of peace and contentment, a more open presence, a lightness in their steps and voices, and a taste of the mystery.

With regard to the Four Shields, the cycle does not stop in the spring. Spring is followed by summer. So, the transcendence and illumination of the east shield is followed by a turn to the south shield once more. Our visions must become physical, embodied, and dynamic, or else, carried off by visionary bliss, we stub our toes or sit on a cactus, reminding us in no uncertain terms that we are embodied. Therefore, we focus part of the last day on the return from our wilderness basecamp to our homes.

Toward a Transpersonal Ecopsychology

What can this work contribute to the discourse on human-nature relationships and ecopsychology? While the aspirations of ecopsychology for personal healing and environmental sustainability are vital to the future of human beings and the Earth, I have also been interested in the possibilities of ecopsychology as a basis for self-realization and full human development. Ecopsychology often has qualities or sensibilities associated with spiritual wisdom traditions. Yet, these qualities are more often alluded to than examined or practiced. Ecopsychology has not articulated clearly and robustly the connections between psyche, nature, and spirit, in large part, I believe, because it has not had the language to do so. This inquiry has led me to the interface of ecopsychology and transpersonal psychology. Along with the Diamond Approach, transpersonal psychology can provide such a language (Davis, 2003).

I propose that ecopsychology be extended to a view that both includes and transcends its nature-as-family and nature-as-self metaphors to a narrative in which both nature and psyche flow as expressions of the same ground. This is not simply a reciprocity between humans and nature nor merely a broadening of the self to include the natural world, though it includes both. In this view, maturation continues beyond identification with the individual self as a separate entity interacting with nature to an identification with being, spirit, or the ground of being which gives rise to all manifestations, human and nature. Nature and human are relative discriminations, useful in some contexts but not final. Transpersonal ecopsychology values all expressions of being, natural and human. Environmental action is revealed as a caring reflex, the Earth caring for itself.

The Diamond in the Rough retreats are one expression of this work, integrating the full circle of nature (summer, fall, winter, spring; day, dusk, night, dawn), human nature (child, adolescent, adult, death/birth; body, heart, mind, and spirit), and the totality of the human soul's aliveness (including its dynamism, sensitivity, maturation, and potential). Ecopsychology has developed its south, west, and north shields; transpersonal ecopsychology completes this view, representing its east shield, and enriching ecopsychology as a path for self-realization and on-going maturation of the soul.

References

Almaas, A. H. (1998). *Essence: The Diamond Approach to inner realization.* Newburyport, MA: Weiser Books.

Almaas, A. H. (2002). *Spacecruiser inquiry: True guidance for the inner journey.* Boston: Shambhala Publications.

Almaas, A. H. (2004). *The inner journey home: Soul's realization of the unity of reality.* Boston: Shambhala Publications.

Conn, S. (1998). Living in the Earth: Ecopsychology, health, and psychotherapy. *The Humanistic Psychologist 26,* 179-198.

Davis, J. (1998). The transpersonal dimensions of ecopsychology: Nature, nonduality, and spiritual practice. *The Humanistic Psychologist 26*(1-3), 69-100.

Davis, J. (1999). *The Diamond Approach: An introduction to the teachings of A. H. Almaas.* Boston: Shambhala Publications.

Davis, J. (2003). An overview of transpersonal psychology. *The Humanistic Psychologist 31*(1-3): 6-21.

Davis, J. (2005). Wilderness rites of passage. In B. Taylor (Ed.), *Encyclopedia of Religion and Nature* (pp. 1150-1151). London: Thoemmes Continuum International.

Fisher, A. (2002). *Radical ecopsychology: Psychology in the service of life.* Albany, NY: State University of New York Press.

Foster, S., & Little, M. (1988). *The book of the vision quest: Personal transformation in the wilderness.* NY: Prentice Hall.

Foster, S., & Little, M. (1989). *The roaring of the sacred river: The wilderness quest for vision and self-healing.* Big Pine, CA: Lost Borders Press.

Foster, S., & Little, M. (1998). *The four shields: The initiatory seasons of human nature.* Big Pine, CA: Lost Borders Press.

Roszak, T. (2001). *The voice of the earth: An exploration of ecopsychology* (2nd edition). Grand Rapids, MI: Phanes Press.

Swanson, J. (2001). *Communing with nature: A guidebook for enhancing your relationship with the living earth.* Bloomington, IN: Authorhouse.

Van Gennep, A. (1961). *The rites of passage.* Trans. M. Vizedon & G. Caffee. Chicago: University of Chicago Press.

On Building a Personal Relationship with Nature

Cynthia Oei

Tilden Park is a large regional park in Berkeley, filled with Coast Live Oak, California Laurel and Blue Gum Eucalyptus. Sometimes, when it's really warm or just after a rain, you can smell the Eucalyptus — its scent becomes the air you breathe. My favorite time to go is on these warm days, when the honey hued light is rich and golden, and when a flutter of wind dances through the grass and also through your hair. My favorite place is on top of a small hill where a large Blue Gum rests amidst a grove of others. I've been coming to this same spot for the last three years now, and when I am here and lean my back against this tree, it is always a homecoming. I love this place and feel that because I have a small piece of earth to come home to, it is easy to forget about the peril the rest of the planet faces. However, since becoming more and more aware of ecological and social issues this past year, I have been awakened to the dangerous ecological tipping point our planet faces. For the first time I am able to see just how connected this fine line between environmental equilibrium and disaster is to our hypermodern culture, a culture which also seems to be teetering on some precarious edge. As "modernity" is reflected socially, economically, politically and spiritually,

Cynthia Oei is a clinical psychology doctoral student at the California Institute of Integral Studies. She currently lives in Los Osos, CA, where she is writing her dissertation about the Wilderness Awareness School's Kamana Naturalist Training Program. She is interested in the practical aspects of applied ecopsychology and in her spare time enjoys practicing wilderness survival skills. She may be contacted at cynthiaoei@yahoo.com, or by calling (510)701-9615.

which may transform into a greater care for ourselves and the larger community within which we live.

Ecopsychology

The foundation of ecopsychology rests on the understanding that we are of the earth. As in Gaia Theory, the earth is

> **As dire as this current planetary situation is, the upside to recognizing our intimate connection to the earth is the realization that within this connection there lies a key that may be used to turn things around for the better.**

the ailing environment also mirrors our narcissistic, ego-driven culture, going so far as to reveal an "opposition to nature" (Spretnak, 1997, p. 41). As dire as this current planetary situation is, the upside to recognizing our intimate connection to the earth is the realization that within this connection there lies a key that may be used to turn things around for the better. In learning how to foster a personal relationship with the earth, we may actually come to care for it,

seen not as an inert planet, but as an animate organism that lives and that we are directly connected to. This bond may be characterized as a relationship of reciprocity — we are of the earth and it is of us. Instead of a dualistic perspective that separates humans from what surrounds them, people are recognized as being integral to, part of, or at one with the planet. Hillman (1995, p. xix) says, "The cut between self and the natural world is arbitrary, we can make it at the skin or we can take it as far out as you like — to the deep oceans and distant stars." If one has had the opportunity to spend lengths of time in nature, this statement may not be difficult to imagine. On a gross level, it may be that after a time one's sleeping rhythm syncs with the rise and setting of the sun. On a finer level, one may notice that when collecting from the wild for food or for fire, the characteristics and personality of the plant or tree that was harvested from becomes more and more apparent. On a more intrinsic, intuitive level, one may then begin to feel the bond that exists between the self and these other natural elements, over time perhaps even feeling as if this plant or tree speaks in certain ways. It becomes as if a common language between the self and the natural world begins to form. Of this, Metzner (1999, p. 32) notes, "According to alchemical philosophers such as Paracelsus, as well as the primal worldview of tribal cultures, the elements are not only the major structural divisions of the organism … they are also living, intelligent, autonomous, spiritual forces, with modes of expression on many levels. To the ancient seers and philosophers of nature, each element was a field of expression of an intelligent, conscious being".

Embedded within the relationship of the earth and the self are deeper underpinnings that provide the basis for the bond. From a psychological point of view, we are connected to nature simply because we are beings that have arisen from within it. The fact that we have opposable thumbs speaks to eons of intricate evolutionary interplay between ourselves and the natural world. As a result, the development of a connection so intimate it may even be impercep-

tible, emerges in the same way a bond develops between parent and child. As such, "ecopsychology proceeds from the assumption that at its deepest level the psyche remains sympathetically bonded to the Earth that mothered us into existence" (Roszak, 1995, p. 5). Intriguingly, Louv (2005, p. 156) takes this idea one

Photo: Glenn McCrea, www.dewdropworld.com

step further and proposes that without a positive attachment to nature, our development as competent human beings may in fact be stunted. He says that "in the world of child development, attachment theory posits that the creation of a deep bond between child and parent is a complex psychological, biological, and spiritual process, and that without this attachment a child is lost, vulnerable to all manner of later pathologies. I believe that a similar process can bind adults to a place and give them a sense of belonging and meaning. Without a deep attachment to place, an adult can also feel lost."

Reflecting on my own experience with a deep attachment to a place, I remember how I first came to know my own special spot under the shade of the Blue Gum in Tilden Park. I had just begun my first year doing therapeutic work within the clinical psychology doctoral program of the California Institute of Integral Studies (CIIS), and as prepared as I thought I was, I quickly became

overwhelmed having to deal with a host of countertransference issues and insecurities that arose from working with clients. On top of all this, I also had to juggle the rigors of my academic load, and with all these things piled up I found myself really struggling emotionally and mentally just to keep up. With so much intrapersonal upheaval to contend with, what ended up happening is that I found myself in the woods a lot … sometimes every day. I have always gravitated toward nature and so it seemed like the perfect place to unwind. I would just walk, sometimes go on a run, but more often than not I found myself at my spot just sitting with the Blue Gum. What I came to find was that every time, even when I thought that what I had on my plate was just too much, I would feel better. Being in nature and connecting in with this one particular tree allowed me to find center, decompress, reconnect with myself and become recharged … every time. As the months drew on, I began to feel deeply connected to this place and to this tree and every time I was at Tilden I couldn't walk by my spot without stopping and saying hello. As much as I felt a draw within myself pulling me there, somehow, I also felt a draw coming from the land itself. Even though this feeling could not be explained rationally, it was also so powerful that it became undeniable, and so began my relationship with a little patch of earth and a tree.

Little did I know at the time that in addition to building a connection with elements of the natural world, I was also learning to foster a richer relationship with my deeper self. According to Hillman (1995, p. xix), "Adaptation of the deep self to the collective unconscious and to the id is simply adaptation to the

To the ancient seers and philosophers of nature, each element was a field of expression of an intelligent, conscious being.

Creating a relationship with nature is possible regardless of where one lives.

natural world, organic and inorganic. Moreover, an individual's harmony with his or her own deep self requires not merely a journey to the interior but a harmonizing with the environmental world." Indeed, as I continued to come to my spot to unwind, connect in, and build on my relationship with the natural world, what I also began to notice was that I was becoming more and more adept at connecting in with a part of myself that I had not ever been acquainted with before. I was able to touch a quiet center within myself, a part of me that was untainted by all my thoughts, stresses, and obligations. Even after leaving my spot, I could carry this new awareness with me, and learn to use it within my life when I was feeling anxious or unsettled. Harper (1995, p. 185) states, "when we are truly willing to step into the looking glass of nature and contact wilderness, we uncover a wisdom much larger than our small everyday selves". If it is true that alongside the physical world of the earth there lies a deeper wisdom, then I believe that by connecting in with nature I was able to tap into it and find resonance between it and my own psyche, my own inner world, and in turn it has helped me by strengthening my own sense of self.

Creating a Connection to Nature

As powerful as my earlier experiences in Tilden Park were, eventually I had moved to San Francisco, and due to the limiting factors of time, energy, and interbay traffic, I was unable to get to my spot as frequently as I would have liked. I remember that I often felt trapped, stuck in a labyrinth of cars, concrete, and pollution. I was in the epicenter of modern life and felt lost without the ability to access nature in the way I was used to. Very quickly, I realized that I was facing a problem that many people had. Although ecopsychology seemed effective and could be readily practiced when the woods were at your fingertips, what could be done when the closest wilderness was forty-five minutes away? How does one create a relationship with nature when nature seems to be nowhere around? Although a fair amount of literature about the efficacy of ecopsychology seems to exist, there are few resources that discuss how to apply this theory in everyday life. Presented with this situation, I soon began to look into and explore various naturalist, permaculture, and nature awareness workshops and programs in the Bay Area to see if I could learn something that would help me with my problem.

Of all the things I learned in these workshops, the greatest thing was to realize that nature was all around me. Although an urban environment is not the quintessential "natural" environ-

Photo: Glenn McCrea, www.dewdropworld.com

ment, it too is embedded within the natural world, and therefore is home to many elements of the wild. Within the city one can find dozens of native plants, trees, and birds. Furthermore, as in the woods, in the city it is also possible to experience the change of the seasons, the rising

of the moon, the flux of the weather and the temperament of the wind. It is possible to note which neighborhood birds are resident birds and which are migratory birds, it is possible to notice how many degrees the sun moves north in the summertime, and it is also possible to detect changes of humidity and temperature in the air. Although it may not be readily apparent, a city may contain much more nature that one might think. It is because of this that creating a relationship with nature is possible regardless of where one lives. Realizing however, that it may be more challenging and require more effort to connect with nature in urbanized areas, one avenue of approach that may help in any environment is through engaging the senses.

Jon Young, a well known naturalist and tracker, suggests that one way a person may connect with their surroundings is through sensory awareness, which is simply the act of actively utilizing the five primary senses of perception. Through the integrated use of vision, hearing, touch, smell, and taste, perceptual tools we were born with to engage with the our environment, it is possible to create a relationship with the natural world. As humans, not only do we have a capacity for this relationship, but we are in fact designed to relate to nature; we are meant to interact with our environment all the time. Unfortunately as the development of our fast-paced, technological, and hyper-modern culture continues to grow, our reliance on our senses has diminished. Our need for comfort and our reliance on technology has created a way of being that significantly reduces the need to look up from a computer screen, or to pay attention to anything while walking down the street. Louv (2005, pp. 58-59) comments on this price of progress by saying, "It doesn't take an encounter with a lion for us to recognize

We are in fact designed to relate to nature.

that our sensory world has shrunk," and as a result, even "our indoor life feels downsized, as if it's lost a dimension or two." If we have gained a degree of convenience through our technological age, then the price we have paid for it is a numbing of how we experience life. However, by reactivating our senses, we can again live and experience the richness of the world.

Sewall (1999, p. 14), a perceptual eco-psychologist, says, "It is only through the senses that we experience what it means to be fully human. It is only through the engaged senses that we are able to feel wholly, utterly in the world." So then, if "perception is the energetic movement between what is inside of us and what is out there in the world" (Sewall, 1999, pp. 17-18) then sensory awareness is the only way to begin building the bridge between our selves and the natural world, becoming the first step to create a relationship with nature. What is even more alluring about this idea is that reawakening the senses can be done anywhere and translates into numerous activities that can be done within one's day-to-day life. As mentioned earlier, some basic exercises one can try are to begin noticing what time the sun rises and sets, or what kind of bird makes the calls you hear outside your home. Other activities may include actually being attentive to what you see and to make a point of noticing details, or to begin registering the direction of the wind by sensing where you feel it on your body. The number of ways to take in one's natural environment is infinite, and even if only a couple of them are regularly practiced, the experience of living has no choice but to become enlivened.

One of the first practices I attempted to do along the road of engaging my senses was to find another special spot that I could access from home. Having been

used to the rustic beauty of the woods, I somewhat begrudgingly decided that I would make my 3-foot by 4-foot back porch this place. It was not anything you would see on National Geographic, but it was close by and therefore convenient to go to anytime I wanted. At first I would sit on this porch and try to take in what I saw, and heard, and smelled. Although I didn't feel instantly "enlivened" as I did when I went to my spot in Tilden, it was a peaceful practice so I continued to try working with my senses. Over time (it has been two years since I began this exercise), what began to happen is that I began to see that nature really did exist in the city. After visiting my porch as often as I did, I became acquainted with the hummingbird that perches on the neighborhood's pine tree, I learned to identify the trees I could see in the

Because I had learned to pay attention, it was as if the nature that once seemed hidden came to life.

surrounding backyards, I was able to notice trends in the weather, and I was able to witness robins nesting in a nearby avocado tree. As more time passed, I was able to hone my senses to detect finer movements within the landscape and to detect sounds I would have tuned out in the past. I was becoming more and more able to tap into the rhythm and flow of that tiny spot, not just the comings and goings of wind and birds but the general feeling of the area. It was as if the use of my senses helped me out of my mind and allowed me to become synced into the world around me. I found that even as I walked down the busy streets to and from CIIS, I was able to take the relationship I had created on the porch out into the larger world. Because I had learned to pay attention, it was as if the nature that once seemed hidden came to life. And because I was able to engage with my outside world in a new way, my inner world also benefited, no longer defaulting to a tuned-out state every time

I left the house. Looking back on this experience, I am amused by my initial regard of my back porch as a second-rate nature spot that would have little to offer, or even by my feelings of being trapped by the lifeless confines of San Francisco. Little did I know that the key to bringing more of the natural world into my life was to use my senses to engage with the nature that was sitting right in front of me.

Nurturing a Relationship to Nature

As with all relationships, one that is created with the natural world must be nurtured and cared for. Accustomed to doing things outside of the daily context of life such as attending a workshop, or even going to therapy once a week, in order to achieve greater fulfillment in life is unfortunately the most that many are willing to do to get there. The problem that usually arises because of this is that without regular attention, that which is gained from these sporadic encounters will often be lost. To this Roszak (1992, p. 310) says, "my guess would be that by the time most clients have fought their way home on the freeway, whatever good was achieved during their psychiatric hour has been undone. They are sunk once more in the collusive madness that they never left behind." The only way to sustain anything that is learned is to integrate it into one's everyday existence. In this way, the learning becomes part of one's own baseline instead of an external remedy that must be sought outside the self.

As such, the only way to nurture a relationship with the natural world in a way that allows it to grow and develop is

As with all relationships, one that is created with the natural world must be nurtured and cared for.

to integrate a practice of connecting with nature within life. Fortunately, because sensory awareness can be done while walking down any street, looking out a window, or even sitting on a back porch, maintaining a relationship in this way is possible anywhere one may be at any time. The only hardship that may arise is to remember to do it.

In due time, with regular practice of course, what occurs is that due to brain patterning, the act of remembering to pay attention to the senses does not need to happen so explicitly. "If you repeat an activity, image or idea over a period of time, then your brain's neurological pathways form a shortcut so you don't need to think about it" (Young, Haas & McGown, 2008, pp. 15-16). One's connection with nature not only begins to form a foundation within the greater aspects of life, but within the self as well. Just as one might feel that their partner is part of them, nature can also be

By the time most clients have fought their way home on the freeway, whatever good was achieved during their psychiatric hour has been undone.

found within. A communion between the self and the sky becomes implicit.

What Needs to Happen

With all the merits that ecopsychology entails, it is still new within the discipline of psychology and therefore, is often left on the shelf with many other psychological theories because of the lack of resources that discuss how to apply it. This is unfortunate because as people are waking up to the strains of their modern lifestyles and begin to seek, crave even, deeper connections with their selves and the earth, they most likely grasp onto the first opportunity to "find themselves" and to "find nature." In the San Francisco Bay Area at least, vision quests, day quests, outdoor intensives, and wilderness therapies that last anywhere between a day and a week are everywhere to be found. They promise renewal, connection with the natural world, and deep inner awakening, and no doubt, many of these activities are likely very powerful. What I have found in speaking to those who have explored these avenues is that because their experience was so out of context with their lives, it becomes very difficult to figure out how to bring to their everyday life what they've learned! So it too sits on the shelf.

What needs to happen within the field of ecopsychology is a discussion about how to bring its theories off the shelf and into practice. Moreover, ideas about how to open up the world of nature to those who live nowhere near a forest or stream should also be included in the discussion. Learning to connect with and build a relationship with nature through engaging the senses may be one way that anyone living anywhere can create such a connection. And as we on the ecological, social and ecopsychological front are discovering, fostering this connection is becoming imperative. The quality of care that we have in our relationship with our planet is becoming essential to our survival. We need to care for the earth, and we need to start somewhere.

References

Harper, S. (1995). "The way of the wilderness." In T. Rozak, M. E. Gomes, & A. D. Kanner (Eds.), *Ecosychology: Restoring the Earth, healing the mind* (pp. 183-200). San Francisco: Sierra Club Books.

Hillman, J. (1995). "A psyche the size of the earth: A psychological forward." In T. Rozak, M. E. Gomes, & A. D. Kanner (Eds.), *Ecosychology: Restoring the Earth, healing the mind* (pp. xvii-xxiii). San Francisco: Sierra Club Books.

Louv, R. (2005). *Last child in the woods*. Chapel Hill: Algonquin Books.

Metzner, R. (1999). *Green psychology: Transforming our relationship to the Earth*. Rochester, NY: Park Street Press.

Roszak, T. (1995). "Where psyche meets gaia". In T. Rozak, M. E. Gomes, & A. D. Kanner (Eds.), *Ecosychology: Restoring the Earth, healing the mind* (pp. 1-17). San Francisco: Sierra Club Books.

Roszak, T. (1992). *The voice of the earth*. New York: Touchstone.

Sewall, L. (1999). *Sight and sensibility: The ecopsychology of perception*. New York: Penguin Putnam Inc.

Young, J., Haas, E., & Mcgown, E. (2008). *Coyote's guide to connecting with nature*. Shelton: OWLink Media.

Spretnak, C. (1997). *The resurgence of the real: Body, nature, and place in a hypermodern world*. Menlo Park: Addison-Wesley Publishing Company, Inc.

Natural Presence

Teaching to recover our love of nature

Trileigh Tucker

My college students tell me at the beginning of every term in almost exactly these words, "I'm not a science person." But just a few years earlier, these same young people, as children, loved learning about the natural world, spending long hours investigating butterflies, worms, rocks, and creeks.

They're in my class because they have to be. Universities' rationale for a science requirement often emphasizes science's importance in contemporary society and its critical thinking and rationality. At least at the undergraduate level, science is often presented as a collection of facts and processes that are defined, known, and accepted. To students, scientists are the ones who fig-

Trileigh Tucker is Associate Professor of Environmental Studies at Seattle University. She holds a Ph.D. in geology from the University of North Carolina-Chapel Hill. Her interdisciplinary teaching and research interests include science and religion; natural history; environmental justice; sustainability; children and nature; and contemplative dimensions of science. She has served as Director of the Environmental Studies program and is a member of the Steering Committee of the Puget Sound-area Curriculum for the Bioregion. Dr. Tucker is currently working on a book called Natural Presence: Natural History, Contemplative Practice, and a New Vision for Science Education. Contact: Environmental Studies Program, Seattle University, 901 – 12th Avenue, Seattle, WA 98122, Phone: (206) 296-6492, Email: tri@seattleu.edu

ured out all these facts, methodically and working in the linear progression known as the "scientific method."

This view of the process of science is reinforced by students' textbooks, few of which evoke the role of intuition, creativity, coincidence, and accident in scientific discovery. Science courses typically don't invite us to develop a deeper intimacy with the earth, a more

> ## Science courses typically don't invite us to develop a deeper intimacy with the earth, a more finely attuned sense of beauty, a greater love for the natural world.

finely attuned sense of beauty, a greater love for the natural world that is the subject of these classes. Finding it difficult to identify with scientists, and having a narrow view of what science does, most students who aren't science majors — perhaps not surprisingly — choose not to learn more about the natural world except in their one or two required introductory science courses, taken reluctantly. We thus send into the world new citizens who not only don't know a lot about science, they often don't *want* to.

Science and Nature on a Societal Scale

We face a parallel, and I believe partly consequent, challenge at the societal level in our relationship to nature. There remains little doubt of the seriousness of the world's environmental problems, and "one of the greatest causes of the ecological crisis is the state of personal alienation from nature in which many people live. We lack a widespread intimacy with the natural world" (Pyle, 1993, p. 145). We are losing this intimacy on several scales.

We, and especially our children, are choosing to spend more of our life's moments inside and in relationship with electronic devices (Louv, 2006). Simultaneously, we face the prospect of the "extinction of experience" (discussed in Pyle, pp. 140-152) as we sacrifice to concrete and cinder blocks our neighborhood "wild spaces"—the in-between places, undeveloped city lots and marshy rivulets and abandoned plots that give us everyday glimpses of creatures living their lives.

On a larger scale, we are witnessing the irreversible loss of both species and landscapes. Anne Whiston Spirn (1998, p. 22) notes that "entire volumes of landscape literature are being lost and forgotten, whole libraries destroyed." Following Aquinas's characterization of the natural world as a sacred text, I have elsewhere made the argument that our destruction of species is the moral equivalent of knowingly destroying the last remaining copy of a religious tradition's most sacred scripture (Tucker, 2004).

The consequences of what Louv calls "nature-deficit disorder" are diverse and severe. Our lack of personal understanding of ecosystems' function and value means we are less likely to stop their destruction, and in addition our human physical health deteriorates with diminished time in nature, as does our joyful use of all of our physical senses in exploration. Psychologically, we lose our "native language of landscape" (Spirn, p. 15) along with one of our primordial intimate relationships. In losing our nature-connection, we also restrict our creative potential and the range of our imaginations: "A loss of language and loss of knowledge limits the celebration of landscape as a partnership between people, place, and other life and further reduces the capacity to understand and imagine possible human relationships with nonhuman nature" (Spirn, 1998, p. 23).

College students' required introductory science courses are often their very last formal interactions with the natural world. These classes thus provide a critical opportunity for reclaiming an authentic human presence with the earth, before it's too late.

Natural Presence: An Alternative

An alternative approach to science education, which I've termed Natural Presence, can meet traditional scientific educational goals while also engaging students' interest and enthusiasm and helping them to (re)build a meaningful relationship with the natural world. Natural Presence contextualizes science's intellectual inquiry in a holistic framework without splitting mind from heart. The term comprises three perspectives. First, Natural Presence explicitly allows the natural world to make itself present to us, as it is, on its own terms as far as possible. The term also notes that as children, we begin our lives "naturally" with this kind of holistic presence to nature. Third, this approach recognizes that the naturalist is present to nature in a special way that includes, literally embodies, her whole self.

Natural Presence does this by integrating the traditional discipline of natural history with contemplative practice. Through natural history, we engage not only our cognitive faculties, but also our physical and aesthetic senses, our creativity, our relationship with the transcendental. Contemplative practice honors our human need for reflective space as we build new information, ideas, intuitions into a framework of meaning. The broad tradition of natural history, and the science that is currently its dominant form, already contain many contemplative aspects, though these are typically unrecognized. Natural Presence elevates these meditative dimensions to conscious awareness and explicitly includes contemplative practice in courses.

Building on Parker Palmer's definition of teaching as "creating a space in which the community of truth is practiced" (Palmer, 1998, p. 90), Natural Presence engages both the external space of nature and the internal space of reflection, and it expands the community of truth to include the vast nonhuman world in which we are embraced.

Through engaging students as human creatures who evolved to learn in nature, and by engaging in an I-Thou relationship with the natural Other, we open the way to an authentic relationship with the natural world, in which we learn holistically, respectfully, and lovingly.

So Human: The Naturalist's Practice

> Here, indeed, is the tree-lover's paradise, the woods, dry and wholesome, letting in the light in shimmering masses half sunshine, half shade, the air indescribably spicy and exhilarating, plushy fir boughs for beds, and cascades to sing us asleep as we gaze through the trees to the stars. (Muir, 1890, pp. 9-10)

This is the naturalist at home, in his element, all his senses alive, intimate with place and creatures. John Muir perceives both precisely and broadly, with delight and affection, typifying the naturalist's presence. "That's so *human*," said one of my students' roommates upon hearing that he was keeping a nature journal. What does his comment tell us about our typical approach to science education?

Natural history is a tradition of inquiry dating back to ancient Greece, but today may need some introduction. To understand the human-nature relationship embodied in natural history, let us briefly examine its commonalities with and differences from contemporary science, and its shared characteristics with meditative practice.

> In losing our nature-connection, we also restrict our creative potential and the range of our imaginations.

> College science classes provide a critical opportunity for reclaiming an authentic human presence with the earth, before it's too late.

Places of Inquiry: Laboratory vs. Field

The venue for conventional science is the laboratory, a carefully contained room that may include controls on temperature, humidity, light, and even air pressure. The standardization of the laboratory's features intentionally renders its results universal rather than local; "it is precisely the stripped-down simplicity and invariability of labs—their placelessness—that gives them their credibility" (Kohler, 2002, p. 7).

Natural history, on the other hand, starts in a *place* with its uniqueness and local-ity. The naturalist goes into nature to learn about nature, encountering nature where it lives. Instead of addressing narrow questions in a controlled setting, naturalists consider complex questions in a rich environment. Natural history is democratic instead of elitist: anyone can be an excellent naturalist without specialized equipment or an advanced degree—as long as she is willing to pay thoughtful attention. Our environments' perceived richness is limited largely by the paucity of our attention.

As we become familiar with the natural history of a place, we become dwellers in it, not perched precariously on its surface but interwoven with it, with our natural neighbors, their lives, their relationships, their fates. The naturalist becomes part of a place as it becomes part of him; natural history brings us back home. The beauty of natural history's venue is that with enough commitment, discernment, and imagination you can learn far more than in a laboratory setting about the whole creature, the whole place, the whole ecology.

Avenues of Perception in Laboratory Science and Natural History

Much laboratory science relies heavily on our visual sense. The researcher looks carefully at experiments: the color of liquid in a test tube, the elapsed time displayed on a chronometer, the microscope slide bearing thinly-sliced tissue. Other physical properties of natural creatures and substances—weight, sonic frequency, rhythmic patterns—are converted to precise measurements that are typically presented visually. We do use

Photo: Glenn McCrea, www.dewdropworld.com

our hands, of course, to enter data into a computer system or to move equipment, and our ears may tell us by the sound of a tone when part of an experiment is complete, but vision is the dominant sense in much of laboratory science.

As naturalists, though, we must use all our physical senses. The inconspicuous pink and white flowers of *Daphne odora* don't tend to catch our eyes as we hurry across campus thinking about our next class—but their sweet-lemony scent is one of the most lovely in nature. This sensory trigger goes straight to our limbic cortex and has a significant effect on our mood. We academics, students and faculty alike, walk across campus probably at least six times a day, but don't see or hear or smell where we are. I was walking with a colleague one day and had just remarked on something natural that caught my attention. She stopped, looked at me, and said she wondered if she was even alive on campus most of the time, given how rarely she noticed the world of nature around us here.

Like all animals, we were born to live

in the natural world. All of our evolutionary history has designed our bodies to see nature, smell it, taste it, hear it, feel it. Being alive in its fullest sense means being sensorily aware, attuned to where we are in its richness. Natural history is the form of inquiry about our home that reflects most completely who we are, as learners and as fully-alive creatures.

Observational Scales and Places

The naturalist, like all scientists, is motivated by a desire to know the non-human Other. In our efforts to know nature an sich, we try to suspend our preconceptions. Precision and measurement are ways to do this. (It's perhaps like knowing your spouse's shirt size and color preferences so that your gifts give more pleasure.)

Both natural history and conventional science include vastly different scales of observation, from the astronomical to the microscopic. However, in disciplinary science, most practitioners specialize in one scale of the natural world; for instance, the scale of minerals or plate tectonics. Natural historians typically study one place on different scales, scanning miles of a ridgeline and the millimeter variations of a spider's coloration. Naturalists strive in a place to see relationships we may miss when narrowly focused on one realm or scale. Because any place comprises animals, plants, landscape, water, soil, and other components, natural history is inevitably integrative across disciplines. The naturalist develops a sophisticated, broad environmental literacy. "To a person uninstructed in natural history, his country or seaside stroll is a walk through a gallery filled with wonderful works of art, nine-tenths of which have their faces turned to the wall." (Huxley, 1903, 91) Natural history turns these faces to our own.

Narrative and story are essential to natural history; as E.O. Wilson relates, "The most important evolutionary biologists are those who invent the most important questions. They look for the best stories

Like all animals, we were born to live in the natural world.

Nature has to tell us, because they are above all storytellers" (Wilson, 1994, p. 167). The story is the "meaning of the patterns [formed by the data]" (Wilson, p. 167). My urban university's landscape pmanager enraptured students by revealing the ever-evolving intra-bug dramas on our ornamental trees. We humans

A good naturalist sits in much the same way as a monk at prayer.

become psychologically engaged with individual creatures and their individual lives, more than with generalized species and their statistics. Offers will pour in from newspaper readers to adopt the animal featured in a story about a burning house, whereas budget cuts for animal shelters draw little attention. Conventional science helps us care by illuminating powerful generalities; natural history helps us care through stories of local places and individual creatures, which lead us to other places and creatures, and ultimately whole ecosystems and their living dynamics.

Objectivity, Subjectivity, and Humility

At its best, modern science represents an exercise in humility through requiring the "objective" measurement and replicability that kept in check the observer's ego. "The striving for objectivity is understood, phenomenologically, as a striving to achieve greater consensus among a plurality of subjects, rather than as an attempt to avoid subjectivity altogether" (Abram, 1996, p. 38). The measuring tools of modern science minimize an individual's mistakes and biases in communicating her or his observations to others. The expansion of that technology during the industrial and electronic revolutions, with its concomitant removal from the reach of individuals without sophisticated expertise and institutional support, worked to contravene the role of humility in scientific inquiry. Natural history, with its simplicity of approach and availability to anyone with senses

and curiosity, restores the possibility of humility as an essential element of compassionate scientific inquiry.

The Naturalist's Presence: Contemplative Dimensions

It is said that soon after his enlightenment the Buddha passed a man on the road who was struck by the Buddha's extraordinary radiance and peaceful presence. The man stopped and asked, "My friend, what are you? Are you a celestial being or a god?"

"No," said the Buddha.

"Well, then, are you some kind of magician or wizard?"

Again the Buddha answered, "No."

"Are you a man?"

"No."

"Well, my friend, then what are you?"

The Buddha replied, "I am awake."

(Traditional Buddhist story)

Natural Presence is about waking up, becoming alive once again to our world and our full humanness within it. Waking up requires pausing from our everydayness, recovery of the "no-thing-ness" and inner space that are an essential aspect of our human (way of) being. From atoms to the universe, the physical world overwhelmingly comprises space, not stuff. The emptiness of both physical and psychological space provides the elemental ground for change: growth, creativity, inspiration.

Contemplative practice creates the inner space that learning absolutely requires. This inner space is expressed physically, cognitively, and emotionally. Meditation has been shown, through rigorous scientific studies, to enhance brain function and increase cortical thickness in areas related to sensory processing and attention (Lazar et al., 2005; Lutz, Dunne, & Davidson, 2007), with corresponding behavioral changes (Jha, Krompinger, & Baime, 2007; Chambers, Lo, & Allen, 2008).

Natural history not only allows the expression of affect, but legitimizes and celebrates it, not experiencing emotion as a threat to analytical understanding

but as an aid to it. Rachel Carson noted that "if facts are the seeds that later produce knowledge and wisdom, then the emotions and the impressions of the senses are the fertile soil in which the seeds must grow." (Carson, 1956, p. 3) Affective benefits of contemplative time include reduced stress (Jain et al. 2008) and heightened brain activity that is associated with improved mood (Davidson et al., 2003) — which in turn enhances creativity and recall (Ashby, Isen, & Turken, 1999). All of these contemplative effects can contribute to improved learning as well as other forms of personal well-being.

A good naturalist sits in much the same way as a monk at prayer. She finds a comfortable spot and watches, witnessing the truth of what goes on around her. She is patient and both open and focused. She lets her ego get in the way as little as possible; when unrelated thoughts cross her mind that cause her to lose her attention to nature, she lets them go. She'll miss too much if she gets occupied with her "monkey-mind," so she centers herself instead into a Buddhist-like "focused attention." Heidegger noted that "meditative thinking ... must be able to bide its time, to await as does the farmer ..." (Heidegger, 1966, pp. 46-47): a perfect description of the naturalist's presence.

Natural Presence is about waking up, becoming alive once again to our world and our full humanness within it.

In traditional scientific practice *sensu stricto*, contemplative time has been a critical, if typically unrecognized, element of important scientific insight—along with hard work, of course. The mathematician Poincaré's experience is well known: "Disgusted with my failure [to complete a mathematical derivation], I went to spend a few days at the seaside and thought of something else. One morning, walking on the bluff, the idea came to me, with ... characteristics of brevity, suddenness, and immediate certainty" (Hadamard, 1945, pp.

13-14). Einstein's wife Elsa described his work habits: "Music helps him when he is thinking about his theories. He goes to his study, comes back, strikes a few chords on the piano, jots something down, returns to his study" (Pais, 1982, p. 301). Barbara McClintock, feeling discouraged, frustrated, and lost with the sense that she "wasn't getting anywhere," went to sit on a bench under eucalyptus trees on Stanford's campus. After half an hour, "[s]uddenly I jumped up, I couldn't wait to get back to the laboratory. I knew I was going to solve it" (Keller, 1983, p. 115). And in the next five days, she unraveled a long-term cytological problem. Poincaré's walk in nature, Einstein's music, and McClintock's sitting provided contemplative space essential for their creative work.

Re-entering Eden: Loving-Kindness Meditation, Compassion, and Natural History

The ongoing witnessing that naturalists bring in mind and body to our natural community builds a relationship of profound intimacy. Intimacy with and love for nature is the generative source for the naturalist's study. This sense of connection is often most easily found with living things, but a naturalist may also feel deeply connected to landscape, mountains, clouds, rivers, rocks.

Further, naturalists can feel intimate with a whole place, in addition to the intimacy they experience with its living or inorganic inhabitants. As children, most of us had special places in which we could wonder and ponder. How much more deeply might we experience this relationship with our adult's developed intellect, if we simply take the time to pay attention! Children's "ecological sense of continuity with nature ... aesthetic and infused with joy in the power to know and to be" (Cobb, 1977, p. 23) is often extinguished by the advent of adolescence. Natural Presence offers

us the opportunity to reenter this Eden with our adult's intellectual sophistication, depth of experience, and capacity for mature love.

When we are in love, we want to know the beloved Other. Mature love wants to know the Other as he, or she, or it actually is rather than as a projection

Photo: Glenn McCrea, www.dewdropworld.com

of ourselves, and so our love drives our curiosity and our learning rather than being divorced from it. "Expert tracing of contours is not unlike love-making—the earth becomes known—and the enterprise of the old-style topographers was in every sense an embrace of the planet" (Leveson, 1971, p. 71). Such love is primordial and visceral. E.O Wilson is eloquent on this subject: "Love the organisms for themselves first, then strain for general explanations, and, with good fortune, discoveries will follow. If they don't, the love and the pleasure will have been enough" (Wilson, 1994, p. 191).

A consequence of explicitly love-driven inquiry is that we strive to do no harm to those we investigate. Our observation is gentle, respectful, and noninvasive. We do not kill the creatures with whom we are in relationship in order to learn more about them. Child psychology has been characterized as "the science of the strange behavior of children in strange situations with strange adults for the briefest possible periods of time" (Bronfenbrenner, 1979, p. 19), and a parallel characterization could be made

of the conventional scientific study of nature. What wonderfully greater depth of insights about children, about nature, do we gain when we observe carefully *in situ* and over time? And without what profound costs to the Other and to ourselves?

Dissolution of Ego Boundaries

Many forms of contemplation are associated with a temporary loss of the sense of self, which many practitioners experience as a state of deep relaxation or even bliss. Contemplatives may speak of their sense of "oneness with the Universe" and a sense of enlargement of identity to encompass all living beings (Lutz, Dunne, & Davidson, 2007).

Both naturalists and other scientists describe similar experiences, forms of "flow." The concentration involved in looking through a microscope at a thin slice of mineral to determine its chemical characteristics can result in hours passing by in what seems like no time. Phenomenologically, we become the looking itself rather than the one doing the looking; we become a verb rather than a noun. We transcend ourselves. In Barbara McClintock's words, "As you look at these things, they become part of you. And you forget yourself. The main thing about it is you forget yourself" (Keller, 1983, p. 117). Jane Goodall writes, "It seemed to me ... that self was utterly absent: I and the chimpanzees, the earth and trees and air, seemed to merge, to become one with the spirit power of life itself" (Goodall, 1999, p. 173).

But the culture of science discourages its practitioners from expressing their spiritual reflections, whereas natural history supports expression of the full range of human experience, including the "naturalist's spirituality, the residue of awe which modern life has not (yet) erased ...." (Lopez, 2001, p. 40).

Natural Presence in College Science

Four key principles frame Natural Presence as an educational approach:

* *Whole person*: Bring our complete selves into presence with nature: intellect, emotion, aesthetic sensitivity, all physical senses, spiritual/transcendental dimensions.

* *Whole place*: Bring ourselves to nature where it lives, and be attentive to everything that goes on there, and caring for each creature who lives there.

* *Whole story*: Witness natural and personal dynamics as they unfold; follow the natural connections where they lead; encourage the student's interests to expand from the initial focus of interest.

* *Right pace*: Take time, recognizing that human and other natural processes each have their own rhythm; integrate active and contemplative elements. Instead of worrying about covering the material, what if we shifted our emphasis to dis-covering the subject instead? Focusing on discovery shifts a class's energy from passive to active, bringing science education closer to science as practiced, full of curiosity and surprises and insights.

Natural Presence exercises can be integrated into field exercises, student projects, and class sessions. These may be easily integrated with more conventional approaches to development of scientific skills in observation and interpretation, such as careful note-taking, measurement, data analysis. An advantage of consciously including contemplative or reflective time as a sanctioned part of in-class time, in addition to field or project time, is that students see its importance to you, the instructor. I use a variety of nature-focused contemplative practices in the classroom, adapted from various traditions or created for a particular course. Students are given an option to do a contemplative term project, in which they meditate on a natural image or theme for 90 minutes per week, then reflect on their experience. In the field, we may all sit quietly, sketch, walk slowly, or engage in guided meditations on the scientific topic of the exercise. The creative imagination of instructor and students can generate many additional rewarding Natural Presence experiences. Student comments confirm that their analytic learning and contemplative practice have complemented each other, with enhancement of both.

Desiderata

The human-nature relationship is in crisis. Natural Presence, a new integration of two ancient, interrelated approaches to knowledge and insight, can contribute to transforming this crisis into a future characterized by health and wholeness in the environment and its human members. It is readily adaptable to different places, people, and teaching and learning styles and goals. A Natural Presence student develops an attentive heart and mind, resulting in observational, analytical, and reflective skills that can be the basis for a renewed, vibrant, authentic, rewarding relationship with nature. Furthermore, students can use these skills in more advanced studies, as well as becoming citizens who are knowledgeable about and effective in caring for the natural-human world at home and at Home.

References

Abram, D. (1996). *The spell of the sensuous: Perception and language in a more-than-human world*. New York: Pantheon Books.

Ashby, F. G., Isen, A. M., & Turken, U. (1999). A neuropsychological theory of positive affect and its influence on cognition. *Psychological Review 106*(3), 529-550.

Bronfenbrenner, U. (1979). *The ecology of child development: Experiments by nature and design*. Cambridge, MA: Harvard University Press.

Carson, R. (1956). *The sense of wonder*. New York: Harper and Row.

Chambers, R., Chuen Yee Lo, B., & Allen, N. B. (2008). The impact of intensive mindfulness training on attentional control, cognitive style, and affect. *Cognitive Therapy and Research 32*, 303-322.

Cobb, E. (1977). *The ecology of imagination in childhood*. London and Henley: Routledge and Kegan Paul.

Davidson, R. J., Kabat-Zinn, J., Schumacher, J., Rosenkranz, M., Muller, D., Santorelli, S. F., Urbanowski, F., Harrington, A., Bonus, K., & Sheridan, J. F. (2003). Alterations in brain and immune function produced by mindfulness meditation. *Psychosomatic Medicine 65*, 564-570.

Goodall, J. (1999). *Reason for hope: A spiritual journey*. New York: Warner Books.

Hadamard, J. (1945). *An essay on the psychology of invention in the mathematical field*. Princeton: Princeton University Press.

Heidegger, M. (1966). *Discourse on thinking. A translation of* Gelassenheit. New York: Harper & Row.

Huxley, T. (1903). On the educational value of the natural history sciences. In *Lay sermons, addresses and reviews* (pp. 74-93). New York: D. Appleton and Company.

Jha, A. P., Krompinger, J., & Baime, M. J. (2007). Mindfulness training modifies subsystems of attention. *Cognitive, Affective, & Behavioral Neuroscience 7*(2), 109-119.

Jain, S., Shapiro, S. L., Swanick, S., Roesch, S. C., Mills, P. J., Bell, I., & Schwartz, G. E. (2008). A randomized controlled trial of mindfulness meditation versus relaxation training: Effects on distress, positive states of mind, rumination, and distraction. *Annals of Behavioral Medicine 33*(1), 11-21.

Keller, E. F. (1983). *A feeling for the organism: The life and work of Barbara McClintock*. New York: W.H. Freeman and Company.

Kohler, R. E. (2002). *Landscapes and labscapes: Exploring the field-lab border in biology*. Chicago and London: University of Chicago Press

Lazar, S. W., Kerr, C. E., Wasserman, R. H., Gray, J. R., Greve, D. N., Treadway, M. T., McGarvey, M., Quinn, B. T., Dusek, J. A., Benson, H., Rauch, S. L., Moore, C. I., & Fischl, B. (2005). Meditation experience is associated with increased cortical thickness. *Neuroreport 16*(17), 1893-1897.

Leveson, D. (1971). *A sense of the earth*. Garden City, New York: Doubleday.

Lopez, B. (2001). The Naturalist. *Orion 20*(4), 38-43.

Louv, R. (2006). *Last child in the woods*. Chapel Hill: Algonquin Books.

Lutz, A., Dunne, J. D., & Davidson, J. (2007). Meditation and the Neuroscience of Consciousness. In P. Zelazo, M. Moscovitch, & E. Thompson (Eds.), *Cambridge handbook of consciousness* (pp. 499-554). New York: Cambridge University Press.

Muir, J. (1890). The treasures of the Yosemite. *The Century Magazine XL*(4). http://www.sierraclub.org/john_muir_exhibit/writings/the_treasures_of_the_yosemite/ (accessed September 28, 2007)

Pais, A. (1982). *The science and life of Albert Einstein*. New York: Oxford University Press.

Palmer, P. J. (1998). *The courage to teach*. San Francisco: Jossey-Bass.

Pyle, R. M. (1993). *The thunder tree*. New York: Lyons Press.

Spirn, A. W. (1998). *The language of landscape*. New Haven: Yale University Press.

Tucker, T. (2004). Ecology and the spiritual exercises. *The Way 43*(1), 7-18.

Earthmind: Deschooling Education

The Imagination of the Earth for Us

Laura H. Mitchell

R eturning education to a focus on the Earth as the vast inexhaustible ground of all our purposes and meanings requires a revisioning of how we imagine ourselves and act within nature—a movement from the abstracted disembodied mind and objectified body to the lived body-mind in synergistic dynamic interweave with its place-worlds. The loss of connectivity to deep-seated primal structures, such as the lived body and the living presence of place, manifests as critical sites of individual and collective angst. The impoverishment of these relationships remains a very real crisis in human-planet viability. These primal structures are somatically embodied and constitute a first-hand experiential 'thinking' pro-

Laura H. Mitchell, PhD is a writer, artist, and psychotherapist with a private practice specializing in Depth Psychology and Ecopsychology. She directs the Place-base Expressive Arts Program at Sky Mountain Institute, California. As a Board Member of the Escondido Creek Conservancy, she designs watershed and habitat education and Art & Nature events. Her dissertation at Pacifica Graduate Institute focused on the ecological imagination and her article, Charting the Ecological Imagination appeared in Spring journal, Fall 2006. Her conference performances include: "Body's Landscapes as Earth Mappings." www.skymountain. org. Contact: 2842 Country Club Dr., Escondido, CA 92029, 760.745.9819, lali_mitchell@juno.com

cess germane to our radical participation in the imagination of Earth.

Earthmind is a term I am here using to indicate this first-hand immersion within earth processes and the ecological imagination (Mitchell, 2003) is the distinctive human mode of intersentience—the aspect of our ecological wiring, which attunes us to our kinship with all life forms and thus constitutes an ecopsychology. The earth-body and our experiencing lived bodies form a coextensive, interpenetrating unity. This foundational premise leads to a profound reversal in the organizational assumptions that drive present day thinking and behavior. It allows us to replace civilization-threatening myths of limitless growth and progress with the Gaian vision of an interwoven web of existence. The overlay of the experiencing body and the world (the bodyworld unity) is a view held by Merleau-Ponty (1945/1962) in his phenomenology of perception, by Edward Casey (1993) in his philosophy of place, and also by Paul Shepard (1996, 1998) in his view of the evolutionary mapping of the embodied mind and world wherein the whole of natural history remains encoded as an organizing structure within the modern human. As I shall emphasize, it is through direct experience, the lived body, the restoration of the imagination as coextensive with *anima mundi* (the animated living

intelligence of all beingness), and the re-grounding of identity within place-relations that we can recover educational approaches that bring the human back into an ecology of caring for our Earth-home.

Starting with this view that our place-worlds and our experiencing bodies are mutually mapped within each other and that they together form an inseparable unity has significant liberatory implications for education. I will explore this core understanding of our primal locatedness in the earth as a transformational vision for deschooling education both concretely as a grassroots movement and philosophically as a critical paradigm for education. When a new mythos, a new organizing idea takes form, the actual lived-trajectory of the vision will show up along cultural margins: in the concerns and modes of expression of our youth, in art, in interdisciplinary conversations, in the formation of grassroots responses in the local and global community, in collective pathologies, and in creative resistance to oppressive practices. Deschooling is one such trajectory.

Deschooling of Education

Deschooled sites are informal learning centers that exist largely outside the confines of the marketplace or institutional education (Holmgren, 2002). As way of illustration, sites may collect around and move out from specific leaders who have articulated approaches such as Brad Lancaster's work in Arizona with water harvesting (2006) or from an evolving shared knowledge base such as the permaculture movement or from nonprofit organizations such as The Quivira Coalition of ranchers and environmentalists or from the explosion in local organic food gardens and communities.

Such centers are oriented toward what Vandana Shiva calls living economies: ones that are localized, draw upon participants' creativity, and favor small-scale self-organization along with large networks of emerging interconnectedness often maintained through the Internet

The earth-body and our experiencing lived bodies form a coextensive, interpenetrating unity.

or itinerancy. The Internet, says Paul Hawkin (2007), is the perfect condition for the margins to unify by "creating a critical, fluid mass of information that evolves and grows as needed—very much like an immune response. "At the heart of all this is not technology but relationships" (p. 144). Shiva defines living economies as "based on the vibrant, resilient and renewable nature's economies and rich, divers, and sustainable people's economies" (Shiva 2005, p. 63). Because such economies are centered on an ethics of respecting renewable limits of natural resources and ensuring regard for biodiversity and social justice, they stand in contrast to the global market's economic goals of commodity production and capital accumulation.

The resurgence of earthmind out pictures in these deschooled sites as lived practices and experimentations with restoring a sus-

tainable embeddedness in our place-worlds. These trends will be examined by way of two prongs: 1) as a nomadic force breaking down cemented and destructive structures in the status quo and configuring and experimenting with new paradigms for creative thinking and action conducive to dealing with the escalating ecological crisis and 2) as exemplifying a new model (but also ancient) for revisioning education theory and praxis in an era of ecological consequence.

Nomadic Edges

Nomadic forces mobilize in response to rigid formations; they act like water, wearing away at the edges, bypassing and creating new courses along the main stream. Edges provide the ideal metaphor for this type of deschooling. Edges or, in earth language, ecotones are living interfaces as "between two bioregions where the distribution of species from both regions overlap creating greater biodiversity than in either of the respective regions" (Holmgren, 2002, p. 225). They can be quite narrow as those occurring in the microbial exchanges in the living soil or thousands of miles wide as those close to an ocean.

Photo: Glenn McCrea, www.dewdropworld.com

Edges are places where the most action happens and can analogously been seen

as the rich fertile ground of overlapping learning and ideas.

These deschooled forces, such as organic garden communities and inter-city food networks are the rich tidal pools at the edges of education, the incubation and hatching place of diverse ideas and experiential knowledge, crossing disciplines at will in an ecology of interaction, thinking, and innovation. The trend toward specialization in higher education has produced many breakthroughs but often has not been integrated with complex multidimensional realities. Formal education is largely based on written texts and secondary sources interpreted through existing fixed frameworks. "This reductionist approach, has contributed rather little toward actual solutions for the increasingly severe global realities of declining [species] populations, extinctions, or habitat loss" (Paul Dayton interview with Louv, 2002, p. 143).

Deleuze and Guattari's nomadic and sedentary positions inform understandings central to deschooling education and place-relations. A nomadic venture such as deschooling with its fluid nature and heterogeneous composition and experiential wanderings acts as counterpoint to state-sanctioned institutional forms of education. In many ways institutional education colludes with commercial-industrialist pursuits and policies crippling its ability to understand and work with the complexity of living systems with their emergent properties and unexpected creativity.

Deschooled groupings exhibit what Rosi Braidotti (1994) describes as a nomadic style of implacement. Nomadism, she say, is a critical and creative consciousness that resists socially coded modes of thought and behavior. It is an ability to flow from one set of experiences to another while maintaining quality interconnectedness but without appropriating what one has experienced in the form of identity, theory, or social artifact.

Braidotti describes identity as a passing through that cuts across many different levels without taking any kind of identity as permanent. Rather, it is a dissolution of the notion of center and identities that shifts away from hegemony. By decentering identity, the nomadic allows an acute sense of territory without possessiveness and functions within a net of multiple interconnections where the task is to recognize differences within an inclusive framework. It is "rather an emphatic proximity, intensive interconnectedness that allows one to think through and move across established categories and levels of experience" (p. 5). One's personal engagement with place insures ethical responsiveness based on a consciousness of gathering, reaping, and exchanging without exploiting.

These nomadic patternings can invigorate and infuse formal education as peripheral branches extending education out of the textbook and chair, back into the natural world.

Coalitions such as the Quivira Coalition, which began as collaboration between South West ranchers and environmentalists, speak to this cross-fertilization of thinking. Their projects illustrate the nomadic direction innovative solutions are taking. Unsuspected partnerships arise, as in the collaboration between United States ranchers, Maasai nomadic herders, and Southwest jaguar conservationists. Livestock and wildlife have coexisted for 3,000 years on the drought prone East African savannah. Because of current population pressures, the Maasai are searching for new ways of extending their pastoral practices: ranchers in the South West are looking for innovative approaches of utilizing the variability of local rainfall patterns. Besides this cross-global collaboration of herding-ranching traditions, there is also the possibility of protecting and increasing the handful of wild jaguars that still live along the Arizona-Mexican border by drawing upon the Maasai's deep knowledge about co-inhabitation with wildlife.

Building resilience in an age of consequence requires just such unsuspected polyglot collaborations. We need to have access to the amassed knowledge of all cultures and whenever possible to other periods of evolutionary and recent history that still live within our thinking structures. Nomadism is just this ability to flow from one set of experiences to another while maintaining quality ethical interconnectedness without appropriating what one has experienced in the

One's personal engagement with place insures ethical responsiveness based on a consciousness of gathering, reaping, and exchanging without exploiting.

form of identity or social exploitation. Deschooling is one of the sites where cultural workers are practicing these new types of identities and honing place-based practices that are now being gifted back into society and formal educational settings. These restorative actions are a testimony to an engaged compassionate response to caring for the earth.

While traveling between several organic gardening communities, I began to notice other place-based patterns and attitudes germane to deschooled sites of learning: the text at hand is the actual earth and hands-on experiential learning the mode of activity. Direct experience, engaged observation, and the dignity of labor are the prevailing modes of engagement. The learning environment is often out on the land or in the local community with a fluidity between work and play. Work arrangements are often through complementary currencies, work exchange, apprenticeships or seva (service). People of all ages and nationalities and social class intersect as they exchange and share knowledge learned elsewhere—a mode of wandering or itinerancy, and then move on to other deschooled communities. A language of place takes form

that does not prioritize the human at the expense of the earth; a specific type of decentered multiplicity emerges, a rhizomatic learning and sharing that can only "be explored by legwork" (Deleuze & Guattari, 1987, p. 371).

Sharing of knowledge gained is essential to the ongoing viability of the community because participants' know-how and experimentation lay down an accumulated history about what works and what does not in specific localized conditions: unique micro-climates, soil composition, rainwater run off, and absorption patterns. This communally held collaborative knowledge supports new cultural responses rather than encouraging accommodation to societal practices erected by dependencies on agro-business products and profit monopolies. A new kind of place-based thinking is unfolding forging alternative identities and human-earth relations.

The Imagination of the Earth for Us

It is clear that these kinds of deschooled sites have as inspiration and reference points a desire for co-creative collaborative relations with the natural world. This pull is magnetic reaching downward into the soil itself, toward restoring the fertility and viability of the earth's skin, toward being close to

A language of place takes form that does not prioritize the human at the expense of the earth

the food chain and the cycles of growth-fallowness-seed, and then, at the same time, reaching downward into the lived-body and the earth-maps dwelling within the human. The transformational vision for education that I am proposing emanates out of our entwinement with the living world wherein earth's mappings are body's landscapes and wherein this extensive collaboration with the earth as a living text forges implaced identities. What would a practice of education look like that decidedly begins with our most fundamental interinvolvement and consanguinity within earthmind and place?

We begin here with our original assumption of the body-world unity: the radical permeability and porosity between nature, our lived bodies, and our place-worlds. The earth-body and our experiencing bodies are mutually mapped within each other and together form an inseparable unity (Merleau-Ponty, 1962; Casey, 1993). It is clear to me that the starting place for understanding our relation to the natural order is not psychological in the sense of attachment to family but begins with the fact that we are already intimately and profoundly embedded within the earthbody and within the natural order. The beginning place is not the individual groundplan of the developing personality, but antecedent and anchored in each cell and organ is the earth-plan fully mapped within and without: a reversible skin. Starting with implacement in *oikos* — the earth house — is the definitive departure point for an implaced practice of education.

Place as Partner in Learning

We usually think of place as a background to our lives or a "sense of place" as only those locations that are filled with special meanings, beauty or significance. However, every experience happens somewhere, is always implaced whether that be physical, imaginal, or virtual places. Place is a living animated presence in its own right: it is part of us and the context of every experience—the ground that implaces everything we do. Without place we would be literally and figuratively nowhere. Thus place is the where of our activities, history, experiences, moods, and imaginings. It is also the where of the biotic and geographic environs in which we live and work. Because

place is part of us and we are part of it, together this commingling forms a concrete interweave (Casey, 1993).

In fact all our experiences, our thoughts, and our feelings are indivisibly geared into place. And it is through particular localized places that we are linked to the greater context of the world. Places are implaced by evermore inclusive places. The stone lying at my foot is implaced by its watershed, which is implaced by its bioregion, and so also by the planet and the cosmos. Self, stone, watershed, bioregion, planet, and cosmos are all telescopically nested within one another. Each is, as Bachelard (1958)— says, an "intimate immensity" the cosmos mirroring itself in each of its parts. Yet it is because we have a body that we can experience these remarkable qualities of place and stone.

Particular places have their own stories and suffering. Engaging these stories of a unique "locale includes how its empirical, ecological, cultural, personal, and even folkloric dimensions gather

Photo: Glenn McCrea, www.dewdropworld.com

into a meaningful narrative anchored in its unique geography" (Chalquist, 2007, p. 27). Place and person mutually co-inhabit these storied features of a specific locale. Furthermore, memory and identity are embedded in the textures of place "like the pegs in a vast storehouse on which our memories are hung. "They symbolize all the states of mind through which we have lived, with all their varied shades of feeling" (Tournier, 1968, p. 14): the tomato field where I felt so lonely as a child, the backroom with

the quietude of the winter sun streaming through the southern facing window. Place is an active participant mingling its colors, essence, and fullness—echoed and entangled within our felt tones and expanding upon our imaginings, fears, and anticipations. In this way one's own story also becomes part of the storied body of the tomato field, of the backroom: adding another layer of texture and dimensionality to the living presence of place.

Our complicity with the rich complexity of place is even all the more extraordinary when considering that we share this involvement with all the things and beings that make up the surrounding environs. Besides the human elements in my home place, there is the natural vegetation, the coyotes and rabbits, tunneling animals and varieties of flying birds, pollinating insects, the way the ecosystems operate in the valley, the climatic changes, winds funneling through the river valley—all this interlacing of life forms in symphonic interpenetration mutually constituting one another. We are always ecologically implaced.

Because our cultural constructs teach children to objectify and abstract the world, we gradually wrench the world and its places away from them, shatter the intimate bond that pours depth of meaning and intricacy of nuance into their experience and understanding; we abstract places so the egg stands alone as in a text book without its nest or even a dreary crowded wire cage. There is the wonderful feeling that a child has of "the transparency of places as direct, total, and natural communion," (Tournier, 1968, p. 18)— the sense of a fully lived place with its haunting invisible presences and compelling physical entanglement with the senses and the moving body. Re-sensitizing ourselves and regaining contact with the living presence of place is a way we can rediscover not a mechanistically articulated ecology, but one "diversely alive and polycentrically implaced" (Casey, 1993,

p. 266). If places co-create our identity, says O'Loughlin (2006) than the integrity and richness of these places and the multi-layered experiencing of these places are of paramount importance. If place is a placeholder for learning (all learning is implaced) then its centrality to educational praxis and theory is critical.

The renewed interest in a sense of place and place-based education is one of the most revolutionary resets intercepting the current tendency to abstract and mechanize learning as if it were taking place in a void. Thus stripped of the resonant field of complexity and overlapping contexts, learning becomes dissociated and looses its inherent relevancy and emotional fascination. Richard Louv (2005) chronicles the extraordinary movement of environmentally based, place-based, and garden-based learning that is beginning to put "place" back into the educational setting. The reinstatement of place-based learning is part of the larger need to re-localize our lives. Children may know about panda extinction in China, but may know nothing about the local insects and butterflies and plants that grow in the vacant meadows of their community. As Merleau-Ponty and Casey have convincingly shown, first-hand involvements with place and the intimate connection with a sense of place re-establishes the rich ground of existence and, I add, of learning. However it is not until we understand the full import of the body's relations to place that the full context of place-relations can be explored.

The Lived Body

Education, says Marjorie O'Loughlin (2004) must involve recognition of the primacy of implacement within a world of ecological bonds. Place is our link with the environment and it is by way of our somatic beingness—the lived body—that we are implaced within the seamless web of existence. It is to a deeper understanding of the lived body that we now turn. Place experience happens somewhere and that somewhere obviously is the body or more precisely, the body-world unity. Our body is the locus of perception and of our directly felt and lived experience.

We are somatically implaced: my body is the site where the place world reveals itself. Here we refer not to the objectified mechanical body or to cultural prescriptions of body image, but to the feeling, sensing body that extends within and also outwardly into its experiences, to the body that encompasses the total interactivity of the human organism as it actually experiences things in the world. If there is a savior in the postmodern saga — a way to return to sanity and re-ground in the natural world, it is the body and a new understanding of embodiment.

Our polycentrically located body is privy to another extensive mode of knowledge, more embedded and akin to the earthbody than to cultural contexts — a synesthesic direct knowing unedited by the mind or social lenses, a kind of fusion with the world wherein the world and my body are continuous with each other. Because the body is in the world, it has direct access — a preconscious embeddedness — in the continuous fabric of the world. Together body and world form an inseparable unity. This body-world unity sets the stage for intermundane experiencing and is, as I have proposed, the basic assumption central to a transformational revisioning of education.

Direct Experience

Education, says O'Loughlin, must involve recognition of the inherent order of human implacement and experience. Dwelling in the world is the location of the core self: loss of environment is loss of primal core. "This may mean that, initially, we need to become much less naive about how experience actual occurs" (O'Loughlin, 2004, p. 3). Shephard, Merleau-Ponty, and Casey show that the template for experiencing the natural order is already mapped into our thinking structures.

Early on during the romantic revolt against the severing of science from the imagination, Goethe held that the imagination is the cognitive mode that actually 'sees' the connections between things. He emphasized the radical significance of the two-fold unity of the sensory surface of a thing with its nonsensory (metaphoric/archetypal) meaning, which together move toward a new way of seeing in depth—a mode he calls the intuitive imaginal mode (Bortoft, 1996). A nest is not only a physical structure built by a bird, but also metaphorically a 'nest egg,' and also a cozy home, a love-nest, or so too emotional states such as the sorrow or elation of leaving the nest or of having an empty nest syndrome. Nature gives us myriads of thinking structures to understand processes, feelings, and aesthetic perceptions. Experience thus involves the entwining of the visible tangible thing with its invisible imaginal depth and thereby meaning. The profound importance of direct experience to educational theory and practice thickens.

Providing emotional and physical space for the child to stretch out into this expansive experiential terrain awakens core knowings and grounds the child in the living context of both his and her own experiences as profoundly commensurate with the natural world and the living images of an animate universe—*anima mundi*. These structurings and internalizations last a lifetime. We can now re-conceive of the imagination as an ecology of thought encompassing frames of reference that naturally contextualize and implace experience, making connections and mapping out relationships and thereby creating meaning. We have explored the educational significance of first-hand learning and a few suggestions of how regrounding in earthmind, experiential, place-based learning and place-relations can inspire relevant educative practices.

Educating with Earth in Mind

We have looked at deschooling as a nomadic venture coalescing at the fertile overlap of our cultural edges, bypassing outmoded assumptions and building new ways of relating to the earth and feeding these learnings back into the social system. If the journey into energy descent is to succeed, as David Holmgren and Paul Hawkin have suggested, it will require an enormous reinvigoration of observational and innovation skills, more efficient ways for people to learn through direct experience, and cross-disciplinary studies to create the necessary complexity and insight for an integrated understanding of living systems. The environmental crisis is also a crisis in thinking and identity that opens new realignments with nature requiring fluidity between modes of thinking, as between the imaginal and the analytic, between the mythic and the concrete, between the sensory surface and the imaginal depth, and between the global and the local.

Deschooling, along with its cultural workers, is one action form that re-engagement with the earth is taking. Because it is based in wandering, in multiplicities of perspectives, multisensory immediacy, a radical presence to place, and local sets of relationships, it cannot become encoded—it can only be enacted and modeled. Shared knowledge is drawn from transcultural sources such as the Maasai pastoral herding practice and old Europe permaculture traditions. As the green society increasingly becomes a societal focus and the global crisis continues to escalate, the edges between deschooled centers of learning become even more crucial for providing lived-solutions that can challenge and enliven the educational system.

Place is our link to becoming present to our environment and it is by way of our somatic beingness, the lived body, that we are implaced within the seamless web of existence. I have focused here on embodiment and place as a locus of learning and emphasized the role direct experience plays in connecting to the earth. As such, I have suggested a reorientation of educational theory to one informed by our embeddedness in earth processes. Only from this vantage point can we can develop educational practices, new ways of thinking and acting, and creative alternatives capable of making the systemic changes required for a viable planet and human presence. The Earth calls forth its dreams and requires us to listen attentively: our earthmind can respond and opt for living systems and living economies to create new possibilities for human-earth well being.

References

Abram, D. 1990. "The Perceptual Implications of Gaia." In A. H. Badiner (Ed.), *Dharma Gaia: A harvest of essays in Buddhism and ecology* (pp. 75-92). Berkeley: Parallax Press.

Abram, D. (1997). *The spell of the sensuous: Perception and language in the more- than-human world*. New York: Vintage Books.

Bachelard, G. (1958). *The poetics of space*. Boston: Beacon Press.

Bamford, C. (1994). "Introduction: Homage to Pythagoras." In C. Bamford (Ed.), *Homage to Pythagoras* (pp. 11-31). New York: Lindisfarne Books.

Berry, T. (1988). *The dream of the earth*. San Francisco: Sierra Club Books.

Bookchin, M. (1982). *The ecology of freedom*. Palo Alto, CA: Cheshire Books.

Bortoft, H. (1996). *The wholeness of nature: Goethe's way toward a science of conscious participation in nature*. New York: Lindisfarne Books.

Braidotti, R. (1994). *Nomadic subjects: Embodiment and sexual difference in contemporary feminist theory*. New York: Columbia University Press.

Casey, E. S. (1993). *Getting back into place: Toward a renewed understanding of the place-world*. Indianapolis: Indiana University Press.

Chalquist, C. (2007). *Terrapsychology: Re-engaging the soul of place*. New Orleans: Spring Journal Books.

Deleuze, G., & Guattari, F. (1987). *A thousand plateaus: Capitalism and schizophrenia*. Minneapolis: University of Minnesota Press.

Hawkin, P. (2007). *Blessed unrest*. New York: Viking Penguin.

Holmgren, D. (2002). *Permaculture: Principles and pathways beyond sustainability*. Hepburn, Australia: Holmgren Design Services.

Lancaster, B. (2006). *Rainwater harvesting for drylands and beyond*. Tucson: Rainsource Press.

Louv, R. (2006). *Last child in the woods: Saving our children from nature-deficit disorder*. Chapel Hill: Algonquin Books.

Merleau-Ponty, M. (1962). *Phenomenology of perception* (Trans. C. Smith). New York: Routledge Classics. (Original work published 1945)

Mitchell, L. M. (2005). *The eco-imaginal underpinnings of community identity in Harmony Grove Valley: Unbinding the ecological imagination*. (Unpublished doctoral dissertation). Pacifica Graduate Institute, Pacifica, CA.

O'Loughlin, M. (1995). Intelligent bodies and ecological subjectivities: Merleau-Ponty's corrective to postmodernism's "subjects" of education. University of Sydney. http://www.ed.uiuc.edu/EPS/PES_Yearbook95.docs/o'loughlin.html

O'Loughlin, M. (2006). *Embodiment and education: Exploring creatural existence*. The Netherlands: Springer.

Shepard, P. (1996). *A Paul Shepard reader: The only world we've got*. San Francisco: Sierra Club Books.

Shepard, P. (1998). *Coming home to the pleistocene* (Ed. F. Shepard). Washington, D.C.: Island Press/Shearwater Books.

Tournier, P. (1966). *A place for you*. New York: Harper & Row.

Watkins, M. (2003). Toward "splendid cities": The thirst for the imaginal in the life of community. Paper presented at the Seven on Dreams Conference, April 11-12, in Santa Barbara, California.

The Eros of Erosion

Revealing Archetypal Geology

Matthew Cochran

To the extent landscapes are mirrors to human psyche, these lost places can draw us in to wander unwittingly through the dynamic movements of Earth and Psyche, not only through a range of geography (such as Coastal California, the American Inner West, or the South American Alti-Plano) or along specific geomorphic pathways (river canyons, ice carved mountain valleys, wind driven sand dunes) but also deep into buried geological rhythms (fault blocks, spreading zones, mountain orogeny, metamorphism). From James Hillman's "imaginal geography", Ed Casey's remembered "sense of Place", and Craig Chalquist's "Terrapsychology", through an ability to experience locale as animated and acting upon us, we have reached a terrain that could be named archetypal geology. Deliberately leaving it undefined to hold its old wild-

Matthew Cochran's background degrees are in Geology, Surveying and Mapping and more recently a Masters in Depth Psychology from Pacifica Graduate Institute. Yet true wisdom and real life skills have been learned by wandering in the wild as well as through the painstaking work of simplifying his life from the complexity and inherent disconnection of western civilization. He now lives in southeast Utah finding vitality and contentment in alliance with a remarkable place adapting and changing in accord with nature as best he can. Contact: P.O. Box 1466, Boulder, UT 84716, matc787@gmail.com, (690) 435-9234.

ness, one could simply say geologic behavior has a running engagement with psyche's movements.

An approach to archetypal geology is best done through a tracking psyche: this ecological heritage we all carry, an innate remnant borne from the tens of thousand of years our species were hunter/gatherers. This ancestral skill is the fusion of all our senses into extensive and deeper full body awareness. By shifting our perspective into this domain,

concerns erosion itself, which will put us in touch with the deeper agility and force of psyche.

Through weathering, mass wasting, glaciations, flooding, rivering, waves and wind, erosion unmasks us, washes us down, sculpts us into the polished beasts and rough beauties we are, no matter if we are human, landscape or both. And it is a common suffering we all bear. To work down an archetypal vein is to expose the way of erosion, to

One could simply say geologic behavior has a running engagement with psyche's movements.

perhaps archetypal geology weds us back to the earth and embodies us in a more conscious authenticity and mythic movement; and this acts as an essential balance to a feral technology which has us exiling our subtle bodies and abandoning the planet itself, a lift off movement dangerously blind in flight. And so it is through *erosion* that we may begin to work our way back down through the surface cracks, fissures and joints to travel into the bone marrow of the earth. It is an attempt to work our way back into an ancestral wisdom that has been forgotten. Therefore the following essay

bring it to life so that we might recognize this natural event within our own psyches, ecologically, culturally, familially, and individually. By playing with the elements that constellate erosion, describing their many shape-shifting behaviors, looking into their transformative abilities, this love of beauty in-extremis, we can then place them in their larger context of earth dynamics and perhaps we can touch a blinded purpose, a specific facial expression of archetypal geology, one that hints at a deeper emotion of earth.

Elemental Erosion

Erosion is "the incorporation and transportation of material by a mobile agent, usually water, wind or ice" (Lutgens & Tarbuck, 1989, p. 75). It is in these elements of wind, water and ice, in their travels across the earth, that we see erosion created: "... *this movement of consciousness into psychological reality is experienced first as pathological; things fall apart as one becomes many.*

As the landscape is also the imaginal geography of our psyche, than erosion might be considered our own pathology.

Recognition of the multiple persons of the psyche is akin to the experience of multiple personality. Personifying means polycentricity, implicating us in a revolution of consciousness ... It will feel like breakdown and regression ... The rock crumbles; there is rebellion from within and below" (Hillman, 1975, p. 35). Erosion then, becomes a marriage of wind and water and fire with earth and its gravity; it happens in elemental caress, clash and confluence. Falling apart is visual evidence that we have been worked on from the outside in and the inside out. We are susceptible to tears, rage and shuddering breath.

If personification is bringing events into beings or persons, then erosion comes to life as "the mobile agent" (Hermes) or through each of the elementals involved. It would then be mercurial by nature, mediating between mountain and sea, alkali plain and sand dune, breaking down, dissolving, wind-driving, varnishing, scouring, uncovering, exposing somehow creating all at once. Most cultures have personified the elements from the Greeks, to the Japanese, to the Apache all dependent on how their cultural elementals behave in their particular landscapes. Yet erosion is still something beyond the four (or five) distinct elemental tribes, apparent more in their woven dances, their working in kinship, as if they live only in alliance where we touch and are touched.

Through incorporation (an alchemical process) and transportation (bearing), this animated and constant ecological work, a wholly differentiated landscape is continually being left ... which brings us to a glimpse of the erosive loss in such things as human grief (which I will discuss later in "glaciation").

Erosive Symptoms

One could say that the elemental convergence that erosion claims is a symptom of landscape, an ongoing symptom and therefore pathology itself. "I am introducing the term pathologizing to mean the psyche's autonomous ability to create illness, morbidity, disorder, abnormality, and suffering in my aspect of its behavior and to experience and imagine life through this deformed and afflicted perspective" (Hillman, 1975, p. 75). As the landscape is also the imaginal geography of our psyche, than erosion might be considered our own pathology, and in the following, poeticizing the scientific language of geology, we will sift through the different forces of erosion as if they were different aspects of pathology.

Weathering

Weathering the storm. The weathered old man. The Weather Channel. Weathering is affection by the elements and our bodies naturally sustain this attention, decorated by its fresh tracks and deepened by withstanding its imprinting. "We are a part of the nature around us, and the older we get the more we come to look like it. In the end we become part of the landscape with a face like the Badlands" (Lame Deer, 1972, p. 152). So we are marked by the age we carry unless this elemental playing upon is staved off through cosmetic surgery, as if we fear the natural authenticity

of our bodies and showing the history of our being. Landscaping is a bit like cosmetic surgery, a cautionary alteration of what we are, a taming of something wild. Yet erosion is hauntingly patient and enduring; feel a river washed stone and you begin to sense a certain delicate love infused in the process.

Weathering in geologic language is "the disintegration and decomposition of rock at or near the surface of the Earth" (Lutgens & Tarbuck, 1989, p. 75). There are many forms from frost wedging, where water enters cracks in rocks, freezes and expands then thaws, repeating this process through the fluctuation of temperatures until the rock splits (hence talus slopes at the base of cliffs, mountains wading in their own sediment), to exfoliation or sheeting, as if a rock were a snake shedding it's own skin, much like we do. Thermal expansion busts stone apart as if we were traps unspringing in slow motion, dawning through the ember of insight or, more drastically, through a fire of revelation. Along with this mechanical weathering there is also the chemical weathering of lichen, fungi, bacteria (even roots) and other organics that leach into the rock further breaking them down, like skin diseases and organisms we encounter on our own bodies. But psyche weathers as well, pelted by bitter insults, uprooted by inconsiderate actions and sometimes,

Photo: Glenn McCrea, www.dewdropworld.com

paradoxically, infiltrated by a testament of love that cracks us open irrevocably.

As a culture we have a certain obsession with weather, as if the more we are sheltered from it the more we must envision it (the Weather Channel junkies), this compulsive need to know what is coming, how to plan our day around it. It now controls our movement; the days are over when our indigenous bodies engaged it instead. John Muir would climb trees in a windstorm just to be closer to the force itself; ancient mariners sailing into the winds teeth, native culture's kinship with land. Sometimes we have no choice. These days, with hyperactive hurricanes, and world turning tsunamis, one wonders whether they are trying to get our attention, especially since we have shut out the daily weather and turned the heat up. Are they being audacious in order to engage us? Are they aware of the danger they impart? So there remains an undefined fear that is growing as we move away from the weathering process, but also the temptation of the heroic dare as seen in the proliferation of extreme sports that become an attempt to prove ascendancy over the elements.

Weathering necessarily weakens us, and allows the more direct erosive beings (see below) to have their way into us and begin to shape us into something else. Weathering is the initial foray, an attention to detail, whereas the larger erosive beings can alter entire landscapes, simultaneously scarring a place within and an entire outward life visibly. Weathering might just be trigger to a complex. The fact is we are born with these primary cracks, cleavages, our fault lines, our fractional crystalline structure, just like any stone, igneous, sedimentary or metamorphic, we are marked by strata, vesicles, textures (just look at our labyrinthine brains) and these portals and pathways lead into our deep cavernous interior, into our ancestral dreams, with unrecognized fossils, generations of petroglyphs, symbols of old, our clandestine chambers full of passionate

magma, our ancient water pockets, veins mineralized by silver, tungsten, copper, or flakes of gold ... these ways in allow erosion to carve and expose us causing our souls secrets to stand out like cinder cones, monuments, mesas and cliff faces, landmarks for others to encoun-

These ways in allow erosion to carve and expose us causing our souls secrets to stand out like cinder cones, monuments, mesas and cliff faces, landmarks for others to encounter.

ter. Somehow through weathering we become more visible. We are seen.

Mass Wasting

He's in a slump. A landslide election. Culture is full of mass wasting; this gravity induced sloughing of soil. This is another type of erosion that is indirectly produced by wind and water but caused mainly by gravity, that downward pulling descent, the entering into the underworld. Depression is a form of mass wasting, huge parts of us sometimes giving away in midlife or after enough weathering of youth and adoles-

Photo: Glenn McCrea, www.dewdropworld.com

cence. The matter of ourselves cannibalizes us, weighting us with feelings of earthy entombment, grounding us from puer flights of fancy. In politics a mass wasting occurs in the duality of our party system in every election, the stability

of the country dependent on the steeply-lying slope of party lines as opposed to a counciled slope rooted by imagination and weaved by many particular truths. The media gives us mass wastings in the form of televised catastrophes, where natural process is never innocent, simply guilty of murder with its mudslides and avalanches. Our culture's fascination with such events and the death and horror within them eclipses us from the frequency and normality of such events. The blame goes to the Other as if blame could bury the grief and too complex questions about ecological morality, ethics, or justice.

Except for teenage generations and the Dionysusian spring-break frenzies, or American cultures strange pride within addictions, mass wasting is not usually a thing glorified, but rather a thing to be feared, fierce omens, portending doom (legacies of Christianity). An unstable earth is an unstable psyche? We want firm ground to stand on. But mass wastings only give way to great changes after slowly creeping unconsciously to the verge and suddenly we snap and land in prison, or enter a twelveñstep program, we dramatically are forced to give up a whole way of being to survive, we have to let part of us just fall away. We must learn what we can sustainably build on, or more importantly ... for how long. Most of our mass wastings have lost their awareness so we feel an unnamed pain and go into therapy, or we consciously or unconsciously attempt to initiate through vision quest or suicide. The shedding of familiarity and safety is difficult to do but the truth is the earth shows us the movement of our souls; they are in a constant state of destabilization and a mass wasting has the scar of rite of passage, chosen or unchosen.

Glaciation

The glacial creatures (endangered) are by far the most awesome and immense erosive beings alive. They embody the element of water in the form of ice shape shifting in accordance with rock and gravity to wander away as melt waters. "The mountains flow and the flowing mountains" (Dogen, 1983, p. 98). Glaciers erode peaks into vales. They are the Great Mediators, mountain leviathans, the blue whales of the sea. A glacier moves by burrowing through rock, and with plucking, abrasion, and downward sliding they use the deitrus they pick up as sandpaper to further erode what lays before them. Very adaptive creatures incorporating whatever is at hand. They are akin to huge frozen rivers moving so slowly our imagination has trouble seeing them (in fact, you will notice, their language has not entered culture in the way of weathering or mass wasting). Yet today, with climate change, the receding of glaciers is occurring dangerously fast, within a human time scale, in generations.

that wanders across the continent. What is this behemoth glacial process in the psyche?

My own mimetic relationship with glacial margins has enabled me to understand something of denial and raw grief. The frozen feelings and emotions we carry as a modern technological race, this forgetfulness, selective memory and mass denial, the weight of this ice that grooves through the hardest of places, that thaws and can thaw (such as in my particular geographic region of the ancient glacial lake Missoula) in catastrophic floods draining huge areas, can change a landscape across vast distance and breadth; flooding that created the giant ripple marks of Camas Prairie, the Scablands of Eastern Washington, the fertile Palouse Hills, the deepened coulees of the Columbia Gorge. This release of waters is like a frozen grief expressed, changing the landscape of the

unwittingly mimic them in a delayed and stuttering way. And this reverie is fractional, doesn't match the imagination of ice sheets and glacial process. This is barely the tip of the iceberg. Underneath I think there are themes around locked grief and gushing praise, wide spread forgetting and focused remembering, cold denial and warm acceptance; something mirrored in the drama that parallels the edge society sits at, where frozen ice begins to melt, and overwhelming changes are about to spill over in a deluge of awakening force.

Rivers

Off the bow and wake of glaciers we have lithe and racing waters; we have dendritic river systems like the veins on leaves threading every continent. We have cash flow, liquid assets, rapid transit, clogged arteries, networks of dams to control waters movement and use, which cut flow creating classes and white water hierarchies. We have Blackwater. Rivers left free are clearly erosive beings but also contain a more hidden skill: deposition, one of erosions side effects or maybe its temporary purpose.

For humanity, rivers have been the old conquistador highways, navigational pathways into North America. This source of transportation, what rivers carry, is the erosive earth in motion, everything suspended by water. They bear the flickering gleam of gold and the weight of human greed. They bear earthen material and the blood of violence. They bear toxins and disease. But these melt waters and rain waters also have a furtive organizing principle: in studies of braided rivers we see how they act to disburse and distribute sediment, organizing them by size from boulders, gravels, pebbles, sand to fine silts. Very economical. If we look further downstream we see floods depositing wide sheets of rich soil, the fine sediment of what was once whole rock, the mountain itself. It should be no surprise that ancient civilizations sprung up like seeds along the wealth of river valleys. The Fertile Crescent. So, as rivers erode, simultaneously they also provide a ground for life. Rivers like the Mississippi, deposit and create land at their mouths (voice?), slowly building the continent out into

This release of waters is like a frozen grief expressed, changing the landscape of the soul, scouring out channels, depositing fertile soil in new places, rearranging the value and priority life holds.

Glaciers create intricate features below in which we have settled such as their outwash plains, moraines, braided rivers, glacial lakes powdered milk-blue with rock flour, eskers, drumlins, kettle holes, kames, even fjords; they deposit drift and till and glacial erratics. Up high as they retreat they leave the mountains with u-shaped valleys, hanging valleys, truncated spurs, arêtes, horns, cirques and strings of tiny tarn lakes: a high alpine wildness and sculpted beauty. The topography of ones soul after living through immense grief is detailed and patterned differently with an unearthly compassion. The work of glaciers is extensive; the most recent glacial age of the Pleistocene Epoch left its wake about 12,000 years ago where much of the present day North American Continent has been reshaped by the ice sheets. And there is a line left, which outlines the southward extent of those glaciers

soul, scouring out channels, depositing fertile soil in new places, rearranging the value and priority life holds. So here before us, written into the land, we have lessons, reflective events in time's cycle of the geologic spiral ... this grief being held static, thawed release, to change the face and body of an earth's psyche, our own mountains all the way down to our coasts. Tracks of tears from the continental divide to the Pacific Ocean.

This is a profound thing to have before us and not be able to see or sense, to walk upon without conscious knowing, to live underwater in an ancient glacial lake. How does this affect our psyche? How does our psyche reflect this, the particular locale of a place? I cannot underscore, as glaciers do, the incredible erosive beings around us and their tracks, all these geographies they have left for us to find and follow. They show us ourselves on a daily basis as we most

the Gulf of Mexico, all with the relics of interior lands.

The geography of a river has been compared to the stages of life ... the young and vivacious, tumbling mountain streams, beautifully noisy with their daring leaps as waterfalls all the way down

Instinct for a full wild intimacy is an instinct for the pandemic ecological psyche. We want to breach the civilized walls of ourselves, detonate the dams, scatter denial, and torch temerity.

to the slow, quiet, wide meander of the older river, wandering the path of least resistance, preparing to enter back into the mother of waters, the sea herself. So here erosion, this symptom and pathology of the land, leads to something else: as we are constantly being torn down by the play of grief, rage, guilt, loss, betrayal, doubt, loneliness, depression, despair, obsessions, addictions, fear, angst and anxiety (what is the particular place or process on earth for each of these?), something is being laid down, placed, sheeted across, spread out, left behind in the vales of soul and at the shores of our coasts, the edges of ourselves, this desire to wade out further into that archetypal ocean; all the hard places broken and blanketed by a new softness, an allowance, a place to grow? So as with glaciers, rivers are also a mediator, a mercurial creature connecting Olympus with the Underworld in many forms from fallen raindrops to springing currency, coins for the Ferryman in order to cross over. This liquid quality is a form that cuts through and down to the oldest of inner lands as in the Grand Canyon, exposing millions of years of evolution, constantly revealing a wisdom that has been forgotten.

Winds

Wind and water collaborate in a twin-

ship of erosion in the form of waves, cutting back coasts, dropping our edges, sweeping sediment up and down the shores of our being, but wind does more than just stir up water: it is an erosive being most apparent in desert environments where water is so seemingly scarce. It works with dust and finer grained sediments drifting them across alkali plains as dust devils whirling or gusting forth in blowouts and deflation. Desert pavement can be left behind, sandblasted rock floors stripped of its' layering, and ventifacts or wind varnished rocks that have their own sheen like ravens wings and are sibling to river washed stone in their smoothness.

Wind is somehow more transient then water, more carefree, more nomadic, not quite as predictable. In psyche's ecology then, wind is more of the hidden erosion. The winter wind in Wyoming High Plains has driven people mad yet it is this final reaching, this polishing touch,

Photo: Glenn McCrea, www.dewdropworld.com

these hands all over that leave us silent and still. Wind only makes sound as it touches another, bringing trees to life, shedding pine needles and winter buffalo coats. Wind in desert speeds in drying

out and in evaporative resurrection leaving behind salt as tears do.

It is difficult to look at wind from psyche's perspective: it has the qualities of water in its fluidity; it fluctuates according to the counter position of pressure systems. Wind is the daily erosion that wanders us, the dry humor, the laugh that is a letting go, the conscious sigh of giving up lightly that which serves us no more. Little things constantly. And wind moves us into action by its restlessness moving us much like the communal nomadism of barchan, transverse, parabolic or longitudinal sand dunes, shaping us in specific creeping movements that artfully migrate the desert floors of ourselves, the forsaken places, to surrender out like alluvial fans, to reveal one thing and cover another. The White Sands of the Tularosa Basin in New Mexico gleam from miles away, gypsum laden, cross bedding away from the Trinity Site towards the town of Alamogordo, exposing the bombed ranges of our souls to bury the militaristic bases of our own blind destructiveness. The irradiated soils, a blanketing loess, come to rest through the final touches, the delicate hand of erosion with its arid subtlety tracing our surfaces, whispering to those places that have all the signs of once being trickled through by gentle water.

The Pandemic Beholder

Seeing through erosion takes us into the sand blasted eye. Erosion comes from the French word erodére, having to do with the rodent, which explains its definition of "eating or wearing away; gnawing. Yet, hidden within and leading the word itself is Eros. Love, the eternal binder and great undoer. Biting love. Love bites. Yet this is erosion … it does have a love in it and through it a suffering and beauty both emerge. The reason we revere mountains are that they are beautiful. They've also been hellishly raged upon. There is a tremendous and horrific patience to them, an irrevocable scarring and immense power to what they have withstood, unable to shelter like we do. Defiantly not even needing shelter. A high alpine tree grows engaged with wind, bent backward, to sweep low and twisted, hovering the rocks, rooted out if its cracks. Beauty is not the perfection but the imperfection … the striving and daring to be exposed, to meet with the forces that shape us into what we are, to allow the erosion and strange haunting love to bleed into our deeper regions and territories of the place we are becoming. Landscape is not necessarily the romanticized pictures of beauty we frame, but on the ground may be a broken hearted, grief-stricken, falling apart, dissolving, dropping away being that has learned such compassion for loss, its love shames us: which may explain some of the unnamed guilt or excessive denial we shield ourselves with.

None of this accounts for our passionate volcanism, our continental drift, our plate tectonics that has us crashing together, uplifting us, and lazily shoring us up: we rise and fall all at once; one is not occurring without the other. So this love of psyche, this archetypal erosion is what reveals us to ourselves and other people. This shared passion contains a shared pain. People erode each other all the time. Look at marriage, such as between Zeus and Hera: conflict, deceit, jealousy, trickery, antics, lusts and love. Yet they would not be who they are without the other. Can we imagine the ugliness it takes to defend Aphrodite's beauty? Can we imagine Artemis trapped in the wild? We begin

to see eros is about erosion. It lives in connection, this erotic pulse that is unmanageable and has us going toward sweet decay against our will.

Instinct for a full wild intimacy is an instinct for the pandemic ecological psyche. We want to breach the civilized walls of ourselves, detonate the dams, scatter denial, and torch temerity. Erosion does not just act upon wild places as I've been focusing on; it is carefully and bluntly at work in cityscapes, swaying and rattling our skyscrapers, splitting our pavement, pot-holing our roads, defacing our architecture, dismantling our conservative patterns with its lethal and seduc-

To reach into an archetype of geology is like trying to understand something without words, it moves us first, affects our bodies deeply, blinks so slowly our lifetime might miss the expression.

tive unraveling, its honed curvatures and explosive upwellings of anger. Erosion is a very sophisticated pagan love. Its song is dark and hauntingly sensual.

Settling In

In attempting to expose erosion by attributing it to cultural complexes and components of soul, I've also tied it to human affect. Now, though, we return it back into the earth once again to point out that we have been discussing an incredibly complex phenomenon taken from its own context (extractive colonialism). I have bypassed it in its reflection to all other geologic process. I've unearthed it only so we can see the clearer tracks of our own process, in the hopes of scouting out the beginnings of ecological integrity.

Erosion has no end, no goal: water evaporates, transpires, sublimates, and forms back into air-born thunderstorms to fall as raindrops sinking back into the land. It is a circle as soul is. Archetypal

geology is incredibly weaved, braided, and incestuous, Medusa currents of snake inlaid hair, tresses of interlocking relations. A stratigraphy of emotions.

Nor have I discussed the seas prevailing abilities, the stealth of ground water or surprise of artesian springs, relentless lava flows, steaming eruptions, quiet ash fall, or wakeful earthquakes; or even approached the myriad and plentiful languages that are particular and specific erosive locales (thousands of rivers, each with their own style of erosive consciousness). I have only generalized from a pandemonium of natural entities and converged them into one being that we can perceive more easily.

To reach into an archetype of geology is like trying to understand something without words, it moves us first, affects our bodies deeply, blinks so slowly our lifetime might miss the expression. We might start in our own location, study the behavior of where we are, watch how natural forces speak through us, and how we enact the landscape. Erosive love is enduring love, endearing in its strange, unbearable beauty. The land upon which we live and have somehow decided we can live without, is holding us (for the moment), breathing against our feet.

References

Dogen, E. (1983). Mountains and water sutra. In Tanahashi, K. (Ed.): *Moon in a dewdrop* (pp. 97-107). New York: North Point Press. (Originally published 1240)

Hillman, J. (1975). *Re-visioning psychology*. New York: Harper Perennial.

Lame Deer, J., & Erdoes, Richard. 1972. *Lame Deer: Seeker of visions*. New York: Pocket Books.

Lutgens, F., & Tarbuck, E. (1989). *Essentials of geology*. Columbus, Ohio: Merrill Publishing.

Intimations About a 'Sense of Place'

Jorge Conesa-Sevilla

Humboldt County, California, was (and continues to be in my memories) a home-place once, perhaps the most enduring and personally enriching and transforming of all the places I have visited or lived. There, mountains and ocean are dialectically close to each other-- the integration of the introversion and extraversion (projections) qualities of a planet on its way to individuation (another projection).

Mountain alone is too secretive and taciturn; sea alone is too gossipy and noisy. If my own ecological unconscious (Roszak, 1992/2001, pp. 13-14) preserves a trace of a long ago sustained Pyrenees-Mediterranean dialectics (Catalan), then that would explain the attraction I had and the need I felt to begin a new life there. If some other more parsimonious explanation can account for this predilection, then it still has to clarify why the rocks and the water need to "speak" to each other in silence and

Jorge Conesa-Sevilla is an Associate Professor of Psychology at Northland (The Environmental) College. He approaches "ecopsychology" from diverse perspectives: Human Ecology, Evolutionary Science, Eco- & Biosemiotics, and Deep Ecology. Contact: Northland (The Environmental) College, Nature and Culture Program, 1411 Ellis Ave., Ashland, WI 54806, jconesa@northland.edu, Tel: (715) 682-1284, http://www.wix.com/jorgeconesasevilla/ecopsychology

noise simultaneously—why this contrast offers rich meaning to me.

A coincidence perhaps, in Humboldt County, more precisely at Humboldt State University, I listened to a series of lectures given by William Devall (Devall & Sessions, 1985) that centered on the question of "place." Rather than lectures, they were conversations, part of a Deep Ecology class. The mystifying thing was that, however hard we tried, what was meant by "place" changed

Some are great and good places that feed the soul, and others are benumbing and tiring. (Brewer, 2005, p. 85)

meanings and locations. For sure, an extensive knowledge of the local flora and fauna, their bioregional interconnections, how the ancient human dwellers of this land had shaped it, and how we were beginning to interact with it were important components of and a hopeful sign that were converging on a significant description of "place."

Many years later, it dawned on me that what we might have been talking about, generally speaking, was ecosemiosis (and biosemiosis), or how meaning about this elusive "sense of place" is experienced, transferred, communicated, interpreted, and internalized into a definite feeling, and certainty that our psyche had taken deep root somewhere in nature (Coletta, 1993; Nöth, 1998). But here is the tricky part--the psyche is also no-where. I mean, the psyche can represent any reality anywhere so, in principle, it can occupy any "place," surely any space. If so, the ambiguity that modern life exemplifies about owning a place, leaving it, discarding it, fouling it up, or being so attached to "it" that one would go to battle in its defense, suggests that "place" is inside rather than outside (Shepard, 1967/1991/2002, p. 29). And yet, as Daoist masters, ecopsychologists are called to explain and reconcile a lost sense of psychic space with a deep intimation of the natural-as-place. Again, as Daoist masters, language only gets in the way and we end up taking folks on kayak trips instead. Water has a way of directing thought in the service of clarity.

If "place" is really not 'out there,' that would explain why some humans, living and laboring under unsustainable conditions, do not have a clue about their impact on real, physical environments and "places." If I carry "place" in my head like a turtle carries its home on its back, where is "place" then? Or, an entirely different question, what happens if the bodily self of a turtle is its proprium?

What could happen, and often does, is that "paradise," as the perfect place, for example, is an ideal to which geography only approximates or an ideal entirely negated by earthly geography (Shepard, 1967/1991/2002; Tuan, 1974). "Paradise" also seems to gain in meaning and importance, surprisingly, if a simultaneous intimate and alienating relationship is established between our experience of the here and now and what came before me, this place, and now. Barry Lopez (1986, pp. 53-54) captures this ambiguity, connection, and final integration when he writes:

When I stand up and look out over the valley I can feel the tremendous depth of time: myself at this 100-year-old campsite, before a valley the scientists say was never touched by glacial ice, and which the modern Eskimo say is and has been a sacred precinct. The muskoxen graze out there as though I were of no more importance than a stone. The skulls of their ancestors lie in the sun at my feet, and cool winds come down the Kuptana slope and ride up over my bare head.

The "sacred precinct" to the Eskimo becomes Lopez's in an instant of ecopsychological insight and realization when he is able to transcend, like the Eskimo, his anthropocentric stance and relationship to the land. The muskoxen, their skulls, the cool winds rule Kuptana and accept Lopez's presence on their own terms. More importantly, he accepts himself on their terms.

In ecopsychologically authentic and ancestral contexts, a construction of the living "landscape," the "umwelt" from which early (and today also for natural humans) derived sustenance, required,

as in the Australian aboriginal concept of Dreamtime, a meaning equivalent that connected, for example, the actual behaviors of non-human animals to their tracks, and to the elemental ensemble of a geography of place. The activities and acts of killing and dying, or hunting

> **For the autistic mind, "place" is an internal acorn where the *Mitwelt* and the *Umwelt* cannot intrude, should not intrude. For John Muir it was the ever expanding horizon of peaks and valleys in almost interminable succession, his eco-psychical needs being both insatiable and boundless.**

and eating, were (are still) represented eco-semiotically, daily and inescapably, in mind and mud, in psyche and soil. In these inextricable existential doings, tracking and hunting become Logos, forms of language that existed for interpretation and lent themselves to communication (Conesa-Sevilla, in review). Thus, in the interactive complex context just described, Logos was (is) a naturally occurring emergent in situ.

This essay is an attempt to explore the elusive state-nature of what we try to mean when we say "place" and we think a clear answer has been given. From an ecopsychological perspective, our own "sense of place," whatever that means, has all to do with the many mansions and nuances of this phrase as we shift between inner and outer ecological realities, as we embrace or reject "wilderness," itself a word that suggests psychological projection rather than an intrinsic quality of place.

A Sense of Place

It is the smallest place that humans can occupy comfortably and safely, while making allowances for individual differ-

ences and climate and while dependably providing for basic necessities, which defines psychical needs and how societies are constructed—a significant place. The converse and more complex realization is that psychical needs and what society determines to be the "standard place" vary from time to time and from culture to culture. That is, for the most part, it seems that ten thousand years of agriculture and civilization has reshaped our psychical needs for "place" replacing it with a fleeing from Nature. A car, an elevator, a house, almost anything will do as a hide out.

For the autistic mind, "place" is an internal acorn where the *Mitwelt* and *Umwelt* cannot intrude, should not intrude. For John Muir it was the ever expanding horizon of peaks and valleys in almost interminable succession, his eco-psychical needs being both insatiable and boundless. In his unbound mind, and in the mind of others, "wilderness" is equally an uncontained need of their psychology as it is a real and an untamed vastness—both projections and reflections (Tuan, 1974). If so, the future of wilderness seems now to depend on whether a critical mass of unbound minds can preserve it or bring it back from the brink (Nash, 1982). For the Venezuelan mestizo vaqueros it is the expanding horizon of the Gran Sabana, mounted on horses that never

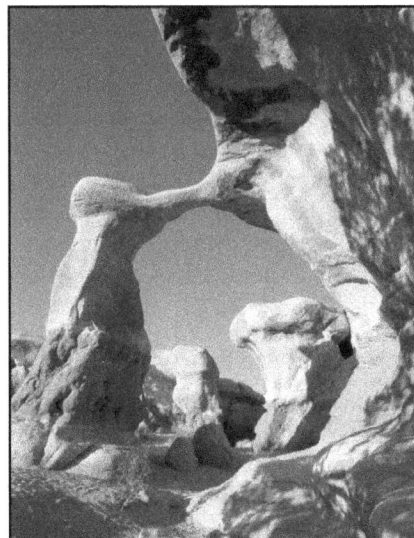

Photo: Glenn McCrea, www.dewdropworld.com

tire, watching over oceans of horned, hoofed animals.

A usual progression for personal space

and "place" begins first, before birth and for nine months, inside a warm colloidal sack of muffled sounds, subdued illumination, and feeding on demand. Afterwards, a solidly loving embrace, with temporary visits to crib or cradle board, delimits inner from outer realities. At this second stage, feeding too could be on demand provided healthy, caring, and devoted parents are present. Along the way, significant way-stations-as-places are encountered and occupied, fortifying or weakening our own development. Attachment studies assure us that without a secure base from which to explore the vastness of the world, mother as the first significant place, we grow up disturbed and insecure (Bowlby, 1988).

The transition from loving arms and cradle board to wigwam surrounded by vegetation or in suburbia, surrounded by nearby homes arranged neatly in rows and sporting green but otherwise unproductive yards, is where the difference between a sense of natural community and the fenced world stands in stark contrast. Instead of stands of fir and birch and a modestly located wigwam, each house competes to be extraordinarily ordinary in its insipidness while providing a false sense of security. Even the inner cityscape can be made up to look like the wigwam in the forest with enough money—an illusion paid for with the destruction of wilderness and the subjugation of some "foreigner." Ultimately, expensive look-alikes do not fool the Paleo-MIND.

Swiss Places and Spaces

A mural of extraordinary dimensions welcomes the visitor to the Swiss city of Neuchâtel's museum of art. The mural depicts on its left side, viewed from ascending spiraling stairs, a pastoral scene where Swiss-French farmers of *Val de Ruz*, swing their sickles gathering wheat while a forest spirit flies by antagonizing the righteous farmers wear-

ing white puffy cotton shirts. The forest spirit holds dead birds in his hand.

A journey to the citadel of *Gruyere* in the same country takes us to the principal chateau with the same name. Inside this castle, atop a rocky mesa which dominates a picture perfect 360-degree

If I carry "place" in my head like a turtle carries its home on its back, where is "place" then? Or, an entirely different question, what happens if the *bodily self* **of a turtle is its** *proprium***?**

pastoral view, the famous French painter Corot painted birds, fruits, and vegetation of all colors and shapes on wooden panels. Corot himself was in love with the tropics and spent years creating some of his best work in the Caribbean. In the very same cobbled street where nature is exalted by location and artistry, a mere two blocks from this very chateau, lays the H.R. Giger museum, a surreal and dark place, the very antagonist to the chateau's airy and open architecture. For those who do not remember, Giger was the Swiss artist who rendered the incredibly resilient beasts and spacecrafts for all the Alien movies: dark, frightening, metallic, and machinated spaces where only acid driven creatures dwell.

This single street of cobble stones in picturesque cheese-making Gruyere exemplifies the incongruence of our modern world and of our own conflicted sense of place, internal as well as external: we are equally at home with the unnaturally and fantastically grotesque as we are with the pastoral. Wilderness on the other hand is to be depicted and tamed simultaneously by the artist's hand. Only then does it cease to be threatening.

A contrast within a contrast, Switzerland proudly advertises, and it is entirely true, a vast network of trails where a hiker can walk from border to border, while attempting to decipher signs in four languages. Most of these trails can be accessed by train, tram, funicular,

and bicycle, reducing carbon costs in an impressive collection of labyrinthine pathways that can take you out into other countries, alpine heights, and tranquil lake shores. Switzerland is as picturesque as anything that word describes. However, there are no wild bears in Switzerland, and after undue exertion, and for a few francs, one can quench one's thirst with sparkling water or satisfy one's hunger with hearty meals in nearby villages or citadels like Gruyere--one can "switch gears" from rocky paths to exotic cheeses in minutes. The Swiss "sense of place" is also its tourism commodity, a pastoral and well-managed projection.

At its recondite depths, how does the Paleo-mind grasp the very actions and cognitive states associated with being able to walk unchallenged, unencumbered, and unimpeded for hundreds of kilometers? I mean, what changes take place in physiology and psychology when the next valley or hill offers similar vistas of tinkling cows and their devoted farmers with a semi-random spicing of mountain, rivulets, and rock? I mean to ask more precisely, is that all there is to Switzerland and MIND, or Nature, or "place?"

An Ecopsychological Journey: Placental Reconnection

Paul Shepard (Shepard, 1967/1991/ 2002, p. 85), in his book *Man in the Landscape*, describes yet another progression: the changing European environmental ethos from forests to pastures:

> Before the enclosures the old country house stood bleakly amid the medieval fields, isolated by dense woodlands; the formal garden, hedged in, was no longer imperiled by the disorder, menace, and avarice of the outer world. Reorganization of the estate embraced land units of hundreds of acres. The great forest that had immemorially surrounded the settlements had slowly shrunk to relic islands. Contacts were made between adjacent forest openings and groves were planted in isolated fields. In the language of physics, a phase reversal had occurred in which the countryside became one of patches of forest instead of clearings.

To the extent that our own western sense of psychical place has undergone similar shrinking and forest denuding, a "phase reversal," then the smallest place that humans can now occupy comfortably and safely, while making allowances for individual differences and climate, excludes not only the deforested landscape but also the means for surviving in any space, synthetic or natural. We are highly adaptable to a fault. We shape and transform at will. We clear-cut and build, or clear-cut and walk away.

To contrast the above degradation, and if we are to believe archeology, evolutionary psychology, and *ecopsychology*, in paleolithic terms at least, "place" was "out there" when nomadic life permitted the easier transportation of only a few essential items and when Paleolithic peoples the world over could make a living almost anywhere in "their" vast wilderness. Simply, "place" was where the hoof was, where it could be hunted; were the willow could be gathered to make baskets; where the acorns were abundant; or where the power-mushrooms could be collected. Thus the relationship between "place," blood sacrament, nest basket, and the "trip" that took you back to security-before-birth became indistinguishable from each other, like in a womb. This placental relationship

accounts for modern bad habits as well: a thermostatically adjusted and carpeted room, a well-stocked refrigerator near our favorite recliner and close to a plasma TV, and if the fridge can be incorporated into the recliner, much better.

On the other hand, could it be that some of our most persistent desires to climb every mountain, walk on every landscape, surf every wave, derive, precisely, from the fact that the novonomads aren't hunting, fishing, gathering, collecting magical herbs, or keeping a small garden? If true, fundamental existential components central to our Paleolithic mindset not only seem to be disconnected but may be very hard to replicate in cityscapes. Then, what is the *ecopsychological price* we all pay for this disconnection? If this is indeed some form of ontological memory urging us back to a placental state, then active "outdoorsy" life and "potato couch" existence are both alternatives to seeking *placental reconnection*. Conversely, a sense of *placental disconnection* could generate a myriad of behaviors, habitual or singular, a *womb drive*, toward recapturing some of these fundamental existential components that were once naturally integrated as they also appear in raw nature, "out there." We keep looking for the undiscovered cave that could lead us to The Center, a vaginal entrance to the original womb only to wander through iterated intestinal labyrinths.

This inter- and intra-psychic connection between landscape as "place" and the center of being is recognized by Leslie Marmon Silko (1986, p. 298) when she wrote:

Landscape thus has similarities with dreams. Both have the power to seize terrifying feelings and deep instincts and translate them into images—visual, aural, tactile—into the concrete where human beings may more readily confront and channel the terrifying instincts of powerful emotions into rituals and narratives which reassure the individual while reaffirming cherished values of the group. Whole is strengthened, and the terror of facing the world alone is extinguished.

Paul Shepard makes a similar observation (1967/1991/2002, p. 45) when he describes dreams as playing a role "in the morphogenesis of visionary landscapes". Joe Rose, Ojibwa elder from the Bad River band, speaks of the circular embrace of the white birch bark in holding a babe in a cradle, cooking and holding maple sugar, and finally serving as the sacred material for sending the soul into the spirit world. A womb drive was surely placated or astutely sublimated in this authentic LIFE circle.

Obviously, even the less "persistent" "potato couches," "weekend" or "summer warriors," still desire to be outdoors. Judging by their actions, it does seem that they expect to be "entertained," seek recreation, or some form of specific amusement in order to justify their presence in nature. That is not say that the infrequent snowmobiler who visits Yellowstone in the dead of winter, making unnatural noises, and allowing petrol derivatives to be soaked into virgin snow, is not "enjoying nature." That is not to say that the yearly visits and family tradition of visiting Yosemite and cooking packaged meat does not produce some sort of "connection." The point is that none of us from persistent trekker, to couch potato, to summer warrior, can completely appease the genome demands of paleolithic (and pre-paleo) adaptations. None of us, without a huge commitment and a drastic paradigm change can authentically replicate this ethos. But there are close facsimile of "place."

That is, intra-psychically at least, particularly during sensitive phases of human development, self-object differentiation undergoes an intense exploration of "inside" and "outside" realities, their intermingling, their contrast, when we define place as the nexus of our own being and bodily functions to be sure, but also as the theater where these realities and projections are played out. A human child, like the cartoon character Snoopy, may only need to sit atop a doghouse to imagine that she can fly. Moreover, naturally so, a child traverses the landscape in an unregulated way, violating adult-made restrictions and mores about how to properly move about in civilized space—their space is a gestalt (Werner, 1948; Tuan, 1974). Later in development, adulthood brings with it other burdens: a sense of ownership of specific locations, holding onto livable space, obligatory membership in a group that controls certain spaces, and/or the rejection of space as one hurries through it on the way to work—the workplace itself being decidedly noxious. Thus the fragmentation of PLACE into a mosaic of *places* suggests estrangement and alienation from a possible totality and gestalt—a paradise lost. New technology such as GPS pinpoints our locality and illustrates the erratic and equally exact nature of our confounded technology-driven wanderings—we seem lost while holding a map before us, or the semiotics situation Alfred Korzybski (1941) made into a slogan for General Semantics: "The map is not the territory." By analogy *without a "place" there is not Self.*

I Remember "Places"

I remember several places that were and still are "authentic." I remember a whole mountain that was "mine" outside Bellingham, Washington state. In three years of almost daily visits I saw only twenty people, equally secretive and protective of "their" mountain. I read bobcat and bear tracks. Deer eventually did not flee when I shared their food. I remember almost freezing to death one day when the weather turned and snowed, the temperature fell, when I had run too far and did not know the trail. I remember a stretch of beach south of Ferndale, Humboldt Co., California, where nobody except me seemed to be very interested in visiting, mostly

because it was too far out. This was a "place" for otters, sea lions, deer, and mink. I was naked, so were they. I had long hair, so did they. I ate clams and berries, so did some of them. I peed in the open air where a fox had marked a rock. I drank rain water that came from Alaska.

The transition from loving arms and cradle board to wigwam surrounded by vegetation or in suburbia, surrounded by nearby homes arranged neatly in rows and sporting green but otherwise unproductive yards, is where the difference between a sense of natural community and the fenced world stands in stark contrast.

There was a fort, a wigwam that I built with my siblings in a dark and cool forest. I remember South American lianas, how some broke when pulled by our weight and how one in ten was so strong that Tarzan was easy to play. I also remember going fishing with my dad for piranhas in the Orinoco River, how I bled from their tiny jaws.

I remember a huge cardboard box that held a wool blanket, an issue of National Geographic, and flowers. I remember crawling inside it with the blanket and the flowers and reading and imagining that I was in Canada instead of an apartment in Caracas. Canada, for a very long time, was my imagined Eden, the place I was going to visit and live sometime when I could learn to hunt moose. I practiced stabs and cuts with a small jackknife on the cardboard box in preparation for that journey and hunt. When the jackknife folded and I cut myself, I pretended I had killed the moose and it was bleeding.

I remember being very small; I was convalescing in a bed after peritonitis, my grandmother soaking French bread

in rich milk while singing me a song. The bed was huge, was not mine. The bed was a white raft in tranquil waters; strong women in its periphery. My right hip hurt but there was also comfort in the song from Andalusia.

I remember a blue corner in a tropical garden. I think I was about three. From the blue corner flew a gigantic moth. It had unblinking eyes on its purple wings and flew directly at me. It landed on my right hand and began "talking" with crackles and hisses. I remember everything it said until this day, especially the part about laying on the grass with my eyes closed, breathing calmly, and pretending to be a caterpillar inside a cocoon. It said:

Cierra los ojos, y como una polilla con alas verdes, todavía no te puedes mover: estás paralizado. Tu nombre no es Jorge, es Chitola—Zuñi por serpiente. Cuando tengas cincuenta años te recordarás de tu nombre de polilla. Ahora duerme chiquito en este capullo de seda. Aquí no hay tormentas ni mentiras[1]

In the modern language of sustainability as well as in the ancient connotation of "place," all of the above experiences demanded little from the environment but provided ample subterfuges to entice a more real aspect of SELF or MIND in connection to the natural world or an intimate and smaller human community.

To reiterate, at the heart of all our discussions about what a particular environment may mean for or elicit in each and every one of us (specifically, *an authentic sense of place*) is the psyche representing any reality anywhere and, in principle, occupying any "place," surely any space. Thus, the "smallest place" that authentic MIND can occupy is both an acorn and the universe, a dew

---

[1] Close your eyes, and like a moth with fragile wings, you cannot yet fly; you are paralyzed. Your name is not Jorge, is Chitola—ZuÒi for serpent. When you are fifty years old you will remember your moth's name. For the time being, sleep little one inside this silk cocoon. Here there are neither storms nor lies.

drop and an ocean, even a carcass and an entire herd.

That most of the industrialized modern world has experienced an *about face reversal*, from mind-in-nature to urban autism where even our neighbors are suspect, suggests *ecopsychological alienation* to be sure, but also the opportunity for healing. For ALL concerned, it is better that the "sacred precinct," as place and Self, are unequivocally authentic.

Epilog

As I write this essay I am still recuperating from a tick borne disease becoming increasingly common in our northern woods, Human granulocytic anaplasmosis (HGA), first reported in our own state of Wisconsin in 1991. Extreme fatigue, high fever, lack of appetite, and body aches are the symptoms of this disease. While recuperating, I had time to ponder about my illness as an indicator of "belonging to the woods." Rather than viewing it as a foreign affliction, I understood, ecosemiotically speaking, that the bacterium, ticks, white-footed mice (perhaps deer), myself, and the woods were

truly connected during the manifestation and progression of this "disease" *inside my body*. The symptoms, disagreeable and even painful as they were, only intensified my sense of self as being irrevocably connected (I am not staying away from **my** woods!) to this place. I am therefore suggesting that a sense of place is not solely recognized, described or signified as being benign and welcoming. All these complex connections, initially valued "good" or "bad," give rise to a *mature sense of place*.

References

Bowlby, J. (1988). *A secure base*. New York: Basic Books.

Brewer, S. (2005). *The poet of Tolstoy Park*. New York: Random House, Inc.

Coletta, W. J. (1993). The semiosis in nature: Towards an ecology of metaphor and a biology of mathematics. *American Journal of Semiotics, 10,* 223-246.

Conesa-Sevilla, J. (2010). Whispering the game forth: The semiotics of tracking and hunting. Sent to *Sign Systems Studies*—in revision.

Devall, W., & Sessions, G. (1985). *Deep ecology: Living as if nature mattered*. Salt Lake City: Peregrine Smith Books/Gibbs M. Smith.

Korzybski, A. (1941). *Science and sanity: An introduction to non-Aristotelian systems and general semantics*. Lancaster: Science Press.

Lopez, B. (1986). *Arctic dreams: Imagination and desire in a northern landscape*. NY: Macmillan.

Nash, R. (1982). *Wilderness in the American mind (3rd Ed.)*. New Haven, Connecticut: Yale University Press.

Nöth, W. (1998). Ecosemiotics. *Sign Systems Studies, 26,* 332-343.

Roszak, T. (1992/2001). *The voice of the earth*. New York: Simon & Schuster.

Shepard, P. (1967/1991/2002). *Man in the landscape: A historic view of the esthetics of nature*. London: The University of Georgia Press.

Silko, L. M. (1986). Landscape, history, and the pueblo imagination. In R. Jenseth & E. E. Lotto (Eds.), Constructing nature: Readings from the American Experience (pp. 289-299). Upper Saddle River, New Jersey: Blair Press/Prentice Hall. (Originally published in *Antaeus, 57.* Wylie, Aitken, & Stone)

Photo: Glenn McCrea, www.dewdropworld.com

Intimate Participation As Our Essence, Calling, and Path

Nonduality, Buddhist Psychology, and Our Ecological Imperative

Will W. Adams

How can our growing appreciation of participatory, interrelational, and nondual approaches actually transform our living relationships with the more-than-human community of nature? The present work offers one perspective for collaborative consideration, in hopes that this view will sponsor not only scholarly conversation but engaged, experiential inquiry and practice. Given the brevity of this article, my approach will be evocative and invitational rather than comprehensive.

Over the last several generations, scholars across various disciplines have developed powerful critiques of Carte-

Will W. Adams holds an M.A. in Psychology from West Georgia College and a Ph.D. in Clinical Psychology from Duquesne University. He previously served as a Clinical Fellow in Psychology at McLean Hospital/Harvard Medical School. He works as an Associate Professor of Psychology at Duquesne University and as a psychotherapist and ecopsychologist in private practice. Dr. Adams's interdisciplinary interests include ecological psychology, contemplative spirituality, art and literature, and psychotherapy. His work has appeared in *The Humanistic Psychologist, Journal of Humanistic Psychology, Journal of Transpersonal Psychology, Journal of Phenomenological Psychology, Existential Analysis,* and *Psychoanalysis and Contemporary Thought.* Contact Information Correspondence may be addressed to: Will W. Adams, Department of Psychology, 544 College Hall, Duquesne University, Pittsburgh, PA 15282 adamsw@duq.edu 412-396-4348

sian dualism and the associated worldviews of the modernism (e.g., Abram, 1996; Adams, 2006, 2010; Loy, 1998, 2002; Ferrer & Sherman, 2008; Heidegger, 1927/1996, 1951/1971; Merleau-Ponty, 1945/1962, 1964/1968; Wilber 2000). And long before, sages from the world's contemplative traditions warned of the dangers of being captivated by dualistic ways of knowing and being. While acknowledging the real contributions of the modern era, I trust that readers of *ReVison* are familiar with the socially constructed views and values we inherited from the cultures of Galileo, Bacon, Descartes, and Newton; and familiar as well with arguments regarding the limitations of these constructions. To oversimplify for conciseness, perhaps we can unite in concern over three key maladies of modernity: a predominantly egocentric, individualistic self-sense; dissociation of humankind from the rest of nature; and exclusively anthropocentric values and cultures. These may be considered the shadow side of modernity's emancipatory accomplishments.

Discussions regarding the hazards of dualistic (or separatist) ontologies, epistemologies, and psychologies are pervasive today. As evidenced by the

In an earlier version, some of this article was presented at the American Psychological Association Annual Convention, August 2007, San Francisco.

growing literature (including the present study), these critiques are definitely *informing* us cognitively. This is an important beginning. However, there is a danger that considerations of "duality" and "nonduality" may be taken up as esoteric philosophical issues or mere intellectual fancies. Yet, as a participant in these conversations, I know that we aspire to go further, allowing nondual realizations to actually *transform* our individual lives and larger culture(s). This move is crucial because the tangible consequences of dualistic dissociation from nature are unfathomably pernicious, impoverishing all those who share this one earth community.

Take the conventional presumption that I am a separate, skin-bounded, masterful, ego-centered subject. According to great spiritual teachers West and East, and increasingly in contemporary psychology and philosophy, this belief is the fundamental delusion of humankind and the pivotal source of unnecessary suffering. The conditions surrounding this conceptualization are uncanny, because what seems unquestionably true from our habitual perspective derives from illusion and confusion, from a gravely mistaken identity. And this confusion perpetuates immense suffering. For example, when identified *exclusively* with my *supposed separate* ego, all that is other than ego — all the rest of this wild-free world — appears as a potential threat or impediment to my gratification. When driven by this fear-based, self-centered dynamic, anything over which I gain some limited influence seems to be available for acquisition, exploitation, or consumption. It exists just to satisfy my wishes or bolster my security. Likewise, when humankind and the rest of nature are deemed separate and discontinuous, nature often appears merely as an alien danger, resource to exploit, or hindrance in human projects. Herein, humans and nature are desecrated together. Such a stance — dualistic, dissociated, alienated, frightened, greedy — breeds individ-

of discovering/creating/actualizing our essence and calling. Each of these is interwoven with the others. As we shall explore, our essence, calling, and path involve open, intimate, dynamic, participatory — and thus nondual/nonseparate — interrelating.[1]

In the previous paragraph I started to say that interresponsive participation is woven into the fabric of the world's being. But this does not go far enough. More radically, I want to suggest that intimate interrelating *is* the fabric, is the world's be-ing, is the world, is you and I. The phenomenological philosopher Martin Heidegger (1927/1996)

ence the phenomenon of) being as a verb: be-*ing*. Be-ing invokes the mutually creative interrelational arising into being of our self, world, and life. Thus be-ing is never a static presence but a dynamic "presenc*ing*," a revelatory term found in Heideggerian philosophy and in Buddhist psychology. To explore the primacy of this participatory be-ing/ presencing/interrelating we could create a generative dialogue involving Zen Buddhism and Heidegger's hermeneutical phenomenology (see also Adams, 2007). However, such an extensive study must be deferred. For now our inquiry will be guided by the phenomenology of

Three key maladies of modernity:

a predominantly egocentric, individualistic self-sense; dissociation of humankind from the rest of nature; and exclusively anthropocentric values and cultures.

ualistic narcissism and collective anthropocentrism, both immensely destructive ways of relating with others (and with oneself for that matter).

Thus the critique of dualism calls for practical, transformative alternatives. In this spirit I will propose a perspective for mutual consideration. Most importantly, this perspective must be coupled with lived encounters, direct experiences such as those that originally gave rise to this view and experiences that creatively inform our evolving perspective. Accordingly, at best, our present exploration may actually evoke the experience we are pondering together. Here then, stated most simply, is a proposal: Intimate participatory interrelating *is* our essence, our calling, and our path. For our purposes, "essence" signifies (one version of) the inherent nature of who we are and what the world is — that is, a key existential given or ontological condition of be-ing and be-ing human. "Calling" refers to a deep developmental aspiration and an ever-present ethical imperative (emerging not from extrinsic authoritative sources but from attunement to our direct experience). "Path" refers to the ongoing engaged practice

famously showed that an ordinary hammer can reveal the nature of be-ing. He was able to do this because our being is essentially nondual, nonseparate, interrelational, and participatory. To begin with, we can simply notice that the hammer is for hammering something, and thus it inherently manifests and carries forward our involvement in practical relational endeavors. Gradually we see that being is always being-in-the-world-with-others. Here "being" is not intended as noun denoting an entity or object — supposedly separate, independent, and merely present. Instead, regarding the being of humans and the world and the rest of nature, perhaps we can hear the word (and better, *experi-*

[1] Given our postmodern, constructionist sensibilities, let me comment on the term "essence" and phrases such as "the inherent nature of who we are and what the world is." Such language might suggest a positivist, essentialist epistemology and ontology that posit a single, objective, independent, pre-given reality. However, our present inquiry should make it clear that self and world are co-created and co-exist interresponsively, dynamically coming into being in, through, and as an infinite community of interrelationships. This nondual participatory co-involvement is radically post-positivist and non-essentialist. Thus we can appreciate intimate interrelating as a non-essentialist essence.

Buddhist psychology.

Nonduality; no self; emptiness; impermanence; interdependent co-arising (or dependent origination); enlightenment/ awakening: These Buddhist terms may sound strange upon first encounter, yet they express basic shared human experiences. To demystify things, let us contemplate the celebrated Jewel Net of Indra, familiar perhaps yet nonetheless illuminating if approached freshly (Cook 1977). Imagine a cosmic net flowing out infinitely in all directions. At every node there is a shimmering, multifaceted jewel. Among all these infinite jewels, every single one is absolutely unique, perhaps in the kind of stone, its coloring or size or shape, the way it has been cut or polished. Yet, while always shining forth distinctively, each jewel is simultaneously reflecting every other jewel in the net, which itself is reflecting all other jewels: infinite reflecting of infinite reflecting, endlessly.

Every jewel — every being, thing, presence, event — and the whole net are freshly, creatively co-arising and co-existing in, through, and as intimate, interdependent participation. Via infinite interresponsivity, each jewel and the whole net are co-creating the be-ing of every other jewel and the net as a whole. However, not realizing this, we tend to reify each supposedly separate jewel (including, especially, ourselves). And we are driven by confusion, fear, and greed (due to our misidentification as separate egoic subjects). Thus we suffer and bring suffering to others. Contemporary Zen master Thich Nhat Hanh (2001, p. 77) offers this example:

> In our ordinary discriminating world, we see a teapot as a single, independent object. But if we look deeply enough into the teapot, we will see that it contains many phenomena — earth, water, fire, air, space, and time — and we realize that in fact the entire universe has come together to make this teapot. That is the interdependent nature of the teapot ... That is interbeing ... everything is related to everything else ... All phenomena are like that.

All phenomena, including you and me and the community of nature. As Nhat Hanh (1988) attests, I and others and the world and nature "inter-are." All being is "interbeing." Thus our be-ing is characterized by "no-self" — which means, no separate self. There is no such thing as a *separate* self (nor even such a thing as a separate thing). Our self-representation as a separate autonomous ego is ultimately ungrounded and unreal: "empty" of independent existence. Corresponding arising of all phenomena are two different profiles of one unified interrelational experience — an experience that, when realized directly and vividly, constitutes (an) awakening. Thus the Buddha taught, "One who sees dependent

Photo: Glenn McCrea, www.dewdropworld.com

origination sees the Dhamma; one who sees the Dhamma sees dependent origination" (Bodhi, 1995, 283). The *Dhamma* (in Pali) or *Dharma* (in Sanskrit) means the way things are, the cosmic and that we, nature, and all phenomena are coming into be-ing, co-existing, and changing via responsive interrelating. Echoing countless Buddhist masters, the American Zen elder Robert Aitken Roshi (1996, p. 86) teaches that awakening involves "seeing into (essential) nature." Note that the key term in parentheses was not inserted by me, but was present in Aitken's original comment. Here we are highlighting awakening's simultaneously nondual and interrelational nature. Stated differently, in David Loy's (2002, p. 214) wise words: "awakening occurs when I realize that I am not other than the world: I am what the world is doing, right here, right now." And what the world is doing (everywhere and always, in local particulars and extending infinitely beyond) is being an open, wild, free, deep, subtle community of dependently co-arising, participatory interrelationships. In this light, consider that in *any* moment we may pause, become aware of our present experience, and affirm that "*This* is my life." Or even: "*This* is me" — since we can never be separate from our life. And what is "*this*?" Wherever we turn, it is our intimate interrelational participation with others and the world (whether we are aware of it or not). Or we could say it is interrelational participation of the

Transcending the ego leads us not *out* of this world but more deeply *into* incarnate, engaged, understanding, loving, even *erotic intimacy with and as this shared life-world.*

ingly, most essentially, we are engaged in an all pervading relational interchange with others, including the beings and presences of nature.

Emptiness and the interdependent co-law, the order of things, our essence or true nature. From this perspective, awakening involves the non-dual experiential realization that our (and all) existence is empty of a separate self; whole nondual world, springing forth precisely in and through and as this particular encounter. Thus the great Zen master Dogen demystifies enlightenment, conveying it as participatory intimacy with whatever is presencing right here and now: "To be enlightened is to be intimate with all things" (Dogen, quoted in Kornfield, 1993, p. 333).[2] Similarly, Aitken (1996, 89) attests that "'Intimacy' and 'realization' are synonyms in traditional Zen Buddhist texts." Crucially, therefore, when Buddhist psychology advocates "transcending one's ego," this kind of transcendence in no way takes us *out of the world* into some detached, disembodied abode or way of being. Rather, it leads us beyond our little, conventional, relatively superficial self and more deeply into incarnate, engaged, understanding, loving, even *erotic intimacy with and as this shared life-world* — an intimacy that is enacted on behalf of all our relations in this holy fellowship of being.

Zen teachers assert that while realizing "Buddha nature" is our supreme aspiration, we always already *are* that which we seek. Thus Hakuin (1685-1768) proclaims in his classic "Song of Zazen:" "All beings by nature are Buddha ... How sad that people ignore the near and search for truth afar, like someone in the midst of water crying out in thirst ... this very place is the Lotus Land [or Buddha realm], this very body the Buddha" (Hakuin, in Aitken 1993, pp. 179-180). In the words of my Zen teacher Bruce Harris (personal communication, October 2006): "Before we take even one step we have already arrived!" What then is this Buddha nature, this "essential" or "true" nature that can never be attained because it *is* who we are most deeply? To make any defini-

[2] This teaching is frequently quoted by respected experts on Buddhist psychology such as Jack Kornfield and Mark Epstein. However, I have not been able to locate this exact translation in Dogen's original (translated) writings. (I suspect it was derived from the "Genjokoan" fascicle in Dogen's *Shobogenzo*). Nonetheless, experiencing it as a profound and revelatory articulation of the heart of being human — awakening/enlightenment/realization as interrelational intimacy — I presented the quote to esteemed authorities such as the Buddhist scholar/teacher David Loy and the Zen teacher Bruce Harris. I asked if this particular translation/interpretation was appropriate and, more deeply, if the teaching (phrased in this way) conveyed the true spirit of Zen Buddhism. They each answered affirmatively to both queries (Loy, personal communication, November 2005; Harris, personal communication, October 2006).

tive positive assertion here is foolish and/or dangerous. Suggesting what it is *not* usually works better. And the very best is to go see for oneself, via direct practice and experience. But with some trepidation, and as a fleeting moment in an ongoing conversation, let me note a recurrent theme in the Buddhist tradition. From one perspective, according to the teachers and teachings presented above, Buddha nature manifests as the open, intimate, interrelational participation of the integral nondual world, the community of all beings and presences. Hui Neng, a great Chinese Ch'an (Zen) ancestor, puts it wonderfully: "our true nature is open communication and fluidity" (translated by Bruce

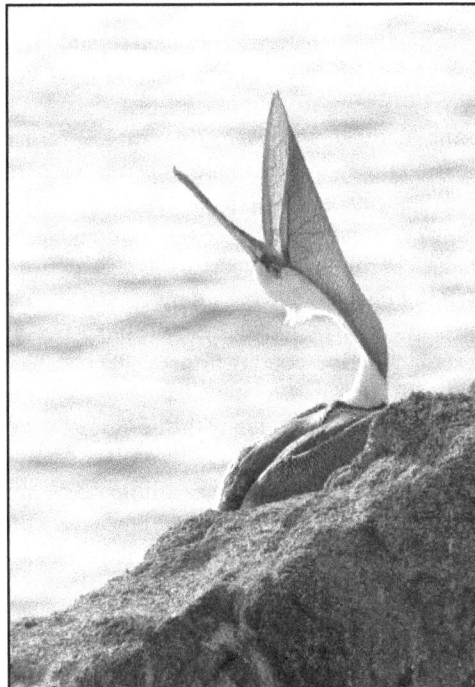

Photo: Glenn McCrea, www.dewdropworld.com

Harris, personal communication, May 2007). As all inclusive, this intimate participatory responsivity goes beyond the natural eco-systemic world, but (as nondual) may be experienced immanently in and as our local ecosphere and our situated relationships with particular others in the natural world.

A reflexive note might be helpful here. Upon reaching this point in writing the present article I wanted to ground these perspectives in a "real life" example, a lived experience akin to those which brought forth these views in the first

place. But I didn't know what to say at first. Then it occurred to me: If interrelational participation is our essence (which is *ever present and ever presencing*), then this suggests both a method of inquiry and a great psycho-spiritual invitation — that is, to be relationally attentive and responsive in every moment,

Nature is infinitely more deep, subtle, wild, and free than our ego and its desires.

even the most ordinary. So I decided to just walk into my back yard and notice what was happening:

Stepping out my door I see my garden and walk over to gather some raspberries. Beyond the garden a beckoning apple glistens with morning dew and sunlight. A couple of rabbits are grazing outside the garden fence. Now, the shining apple is not just dangling on the branch, but moving up and down. Oh ... it is moving together with a blue jay who is perched right above. The jay is pecking into another apple and sending reverberations through the nearby branches. Suddenly two red squirrels, youngsters I think, emerge from the background brush, playfully chasing each another. One scurries up the apple tree with the other in close pursuit. The blue jay flies away but circles back and alights in another part of the same tree, far enough to be safe but close enough to squawk loudly at the squirrels. Once up the tree, the squirrels realize they are in the midst of a feast. One squirrel takes an apple with both her hands and turns it as she eats. As I move in closer the squirrel almost tumbles when she hears me and jerks up, dropping her half-eaten apple (now a treat for the cottontails). Realizing I've startled the squirrel, I kneel down, turn sideways, and scratch in the grass as if I'm foraging for food (like the squirrel herself might do). She seems reassured that I'm not (much of) a threat, and finds another apple. The neighbor's dog starts barking, and the squirrels glance over warily. A goldfinch alights in the apple tree before floating over for some seeds from the sunflowers in our garden. Remembering now that raspberries had sounded good, I relish a moment of gratitude for being able to participate in this morning interplay: nothing special yet truly precious, sacred even. I nod spontaneously with a sort semi-bow of thanks. Then I find a few ripe berries and move into the rest of my day — wondering as well how the day will unfold for all the winged and four-legged and rooted and fruiting neighbors who graced this morning.

Coupled with Thich Nhat Hanh's illustration above, this story reveals the nondual, nonseparate, interrelational, participatory nature of our be-ing: We don't encounter a separate independent apple, but apple participating with sun with blue jay with squirrels with me and on and on... And still another dimension is explicit that was only implied earlier. That is, each being and presence is vibrantly relationally alive, freshly springing forth into be-ing moment by moment, encounter by encounter, ceaselessly emerging, presencing, sounding, shining forth in dynamic co-responsive, co-creative participation with all the others. In this interpermeating communion of beings and presences, the response of each resounds out to all the others, helping to bring the others' very be-ing into be-ing.

The great Buddhist sages directly state that *Buddha nature is always already our essential nature*. Yet in the same breath they urge us to *verify and clarify* this for ourselves, experientially, and live accordingly. Similarly, intimate interrelationality seems to be inherent in the very structure of be-ing and being human, but, afraid and confused, our relational capabilities tend to be left underdeveloped. I would like to suggest that open, wakeful, tender, wise, compassionate interresponding is one of the most useful criteria for what it is to be fully human. In other words, what if our lives were orientated by an appreciation that intimate participatory interrelating

is what well-being *is*, is what health, justice, truth, goodness, beauty, intelligence, consciousness, freedom *are* — all the deepest human aspirations and potentials?

Clearly, given our ecological crisis and the psycho-spiritual distress generated by our estrangement from the natural world, we are being *called* to transform our ways of participating with the

What if we realized that the shared earth community is appealing to us to bring forth awareness, understanding, and love?

community of nature. This call should resound with compelling familiarity: When we want to cultivate mutual well-being with another person — a lover or friend, say — we share experiences with our partner, learn his or her distinctive ways of be-ing, offer our care and understanding and support for the other to bring their unique bei-ng into its fullness, attend to and learn from the other's response, and respond in turn, on and on. Basically this interrelational path is (or could be) quite similar with the rest of the natural world.

Thus our essence and calling are simultaneously our path and practice. Let me briefly cite a few key orienting

What if we discovered that relating intimately, encounter by encounter, is itself the supreme path?

markers — evocative conceptual cairns, if you will — that might help us traverse this interrelational path. One is a growing appreciation that we are involved in an ongoing relationship with *real others* (right in the midst of nonduality). That is, each being and presence of nature expresses its own special kind of consciousness, intelligence, agency, and ways of be-ing. Similarly, the integral be-ing of nature manifests as a mysterious, open, wild, free, inconceivable,

undetermined, and unfathomable community of interrelating, a dynamic inter-responsive fellowship that is centered everywhere (or we could say centered nowhere *exclusively*) and that radiates infinitely from each of these infinite centers: centered in our inspiring breath this very moment, the city streets right outside, our home kitchen and back yard, our neighborhood woods and nearby wilderness.

Living egoically, we anxiously strive for mastery and control. But the natural world rarely responds in just the ways we want. Nature is infinitely more deep, subtle, wild, and free than our ego and its desires. (Notice that this is also true of our intimate human loved ones, yes?) Alluding to Thoreau, Gary Snyder (1990, p. 6) remarks that "Wildness is not just the 'preservation of the world,' it *is* the world." (And this is not limited to "wilderness." Nature is everywhere.) Thus inevitably, when we engage with nature its wild-free responding is uncontrollable, far beyond even our most wise and compassionate projects, much less our habitual, ego-centered ones. I set out birdseed and hummingbird feeders because I love to be in the presence of these marvelous beings, and migratory birds need all the help we can offer these days. Soon my beloved cat proudly brings me a gift, and my heart breaks open upon seeing a limp lifeless hummingbird, the glow fading from its ruby throat. Alas, offering an apology and a pledge, I put the feeders up higher and know my next cat will live and hunt indoors.

Herein lies one of the tragic givens of human existence. We *are* responsible for answering the call of our daily encounters, but *not responsible for nor able to control* the results of our reply. We are summoned to bring forth our best in the moment, but what happens next is beyond us. Sometimes even our best response turns out badly, generating suffering completely counter to our intentions. Thankfully, the interrelational conversation — *the participatory involvement which is our life* — is ongoing. I take this as an imperative to enter (with as much awareness as possible) into an authentic dialogue with (and within) the community of nature: to listen to the voice of nature, reply as best I can, stay attentive to what transpires, and reply time after time. As Dogen (1231/2002, p. 13) testifies: "The trees, grasses, and land ... emit a bright and shining light, preaching the profound and incomprehensible Dharma; and it is endless."

For now, rather than "saving the earth" perhaps we might embrace a more humble aspiration, that of fostering, more consciously and intentionally, an engaged conversational interaction and co-creative intimacy with the other participants in the natural community, especially those in our local ecoregion. In learning to listen and respond more deeply, we may keep the conversation going and maybe carry it a little further. As in the case of feeding the birds above, this is an ongoing call and response with other humans and with the rest of nature. For example, our garden is not growing well under the black walnut tree (because, we eventually discover, these trees emit a substance called juglone that is toxic to some plants); so we learn to grow squash and foxglove instead of tomatoes and columbine. Collectively we realize that spring is becoming dreadfully silent; so we choose to ban pesticides such as DDT; peregrine falcons and other birds begin to recover. We say (or let others say for us) that it is acceptable to spew millions of tons of carbon dioxide into the atmosphere each day; the earth becomes dangerously overheated; and so we choose to ... Well, who knows what we are going to choose? My point is that the quality of the interrelationship, and our devotion to participating openly and wakefully in an ongoing manner, are what really matters. This is no mere trial and error driven by the confusion, greed, and fear of our ego-centered self-sense and way of be-ing. Rather, it involves the courage and humility to suspend the priority of our narcissistic wishes, attend carefully, hearken nature's call as best we can (for the time being), send forth our best response, interpret what happens, and reengage in the ever-continuing interaction.

The present article is one moment, one offering in this ongoing collaboration. My hope is to plant a seed-perspective in these few pages. The seed is simple: Intimate participatory interrelating is our essence, our calling, and our path. This is so obvious that we tend to miss its significance. Yet, what if we experienced it vividly time and again, not just conceptually but in a heart-felt, fully thought, wholly enacted, and thoroughly lived way? What if we realized — as clearly as we would know our best friend walking into the room — that we are interrelational beings and the world is an interrelational world? What if we understood — at least from one view — that the essential structure and be-ing of self, world, nature, and reality involves ceaseless and infinite participatory interresponding? What if we knew that our interrelational engagement actually participates in co-creating self and world? Carrying these insights further, what if we realized that the shared earth community is appealing to us to bring forth awareness, understanding, and love in the service of others? What if we embraced this as our deepest calling and aspiration, knowing that be-ing fully human means responding well to this summons? And what if we discovered that relating intimately, encounter by encounter, is itself the supreme path — with limitless variations across individuals and cultures — for fulfilling this awesome aspiration?

Intimate participation is our essence, our calling, and our path, both in relation with other people and with the rest of the natural world. In this light nature can never exist separately, as a mere resource for or threat to humans. Nor is it restricted to some distant pristine place we might visit if we manage to get away from our busy lives. Following Buddhist psychology and the perspective of this article, the be-ing of the natural world, like our be-ing, is thoroughly interrelational. From this approach, nature reveals itself as an ever presencing, nondual, participatory community in which we belong as unique manifestations and co-creative participants, right in the midst of our busy life. With real intimacy ever again and again, for each of us in our own way, for all of us together: May we keep awakening to this nondual yet interrelational mystery, to this shared earth community, to this participatory fellowship of be-ing — awakening *to* it and *by* it and *in* it and *with* it and *as* it and (quintessentially) *for* it, *in its service*.

References

Abram, D. (1996). *The spell of the sensuous*. New York: Random House.

Adams, W.W. (2006). The ivory-billed woodpecker, ecopsychology, and the crisis of extinction: On annihilating and nurturing other beings, relationships, and ourselves. *The Humanistic Psychologist, 34*(2), 111-133.

Adams, W.W. (2007). The primacy of interrelating: Practicing ecological psychology with Buber, Levinas, and Merleau-Ponty. *Journal of Phenomenological Psychology, 38*(1), 24-61.

Adams, W.W. (2010). Nature's participatory psyche: A study of consciousness in the shared earth community. *The Humanistic Psychologist, 38*(1), 15-39.

Aitken, R. (1993). *Encouraging words*. New York: Pantheon.

Aitken, R. (1996). *Original dwelling place*. Washington, DC: Counterpoint.

Bodhi, B. (Ed. & Trans.). (1995). *The middle length discourses of the Buddha: A new translation of the Majjhima Nikaya*. (B. Nanamoli, Original Translator). Boston: Wisdom Publications.

Cook, F. H. (1977). *Hua-yen Buddhism: The jewel net of Indra*. University Park, PA: Pennsylvania State University Press.

Dogen. (2002). Bendowa (Negotiating the way). In *The Heart of Dogen's Shobogenzo* (N. Waddell and M. Abe, Trans.; pp. 161-184). Albany, NY: SUNY Press. Original work published 1231.

Ferrer, J. N. & Sherman, J. H. (2008). *The participatory turn*. Albany, NY: SUNY Press.

Heidegger, M. (1996). *Being and time*. (J. Stambaugh, Trans.). Albany, NY: SUNY Press. (Original work published 1951)

Heidegger, M. (1971). The thing. In *Poetry, Language, Thought*. (A. Hofstadter, Trans.; pp. 7-30). New York: Harper Colophon. Original work published 1951.

Kornfield, J. (1993). *A path with heart*. New York: Bantam.

Loy, D. (1998). *Nonduality*. Amherst, NY: Humanity Books.

Loy, D. (2002). *A Buddhist history of the West*. Albany, NY: SUNY Press.

Merleau-Ponty, M. (1962). *Phenomenology of perception* (C. Smith, Trans.). London: Routledge & Kegan Paul. (Original work published 1945)

Merleau-Ponty, M. (1968). *The visible and the invisible*. (A. Lingis, Trans.). Evanston, IL: Northwestern University Press. (Original work published 1964)

Nhat Hanh, T. (1988). *The heart of understanding: Commentaries on the Prajanaparamita Heart Sutra*. Berkeley: Parallax Press.

Nhat Hanh, T. (2001). *Transformation at the base*. Berkeley: Parallax Press.

Snyder, G. (1990). *The practice of the wild*. San Francisco: North Point Press.

The Nature of Transformation

Ecopsychology in Practice

Michal Fire

Ecopsychology, a term coined over 25 years ago by historian Theodore Roszak, one of the foremost contributors to the field, is grounded in sociobiologist Edward O. Wilson's (1993) notion of "biophilia," which posits that, as living beings, we possess an innate pull to interact with the living world within which we exist. In the words of psychotherapist and author Andy Fisher (2002), ecopsychology is the coming together of the logos, meaning the study, source, order, meaning, or speech, of the psyche or soul, in relation to its natural or earthly abode, eco, from the Greek *oikos*, referring to home. In essence, it is the acknowledgement that psyche cannot be separated from the natural environment within which it exists. And, that any study, discussion, or practice related to the psyche,

Michal Fire is currently completing a doctorate in clinical psychology at the California Institute of Integral Studies where her interests include examining the interconnectedness of psyche and nature. After receiving a B.A. in Psychology from McGill University in 1999 Michal worked for over six years as a professional wilderness guide and educator in the Himalayas and U.S. With an extensive background in wilderness expeditions and wilderness medicine, and a sensitivity for the powerful possibilities inherent in our connection to the natural world, Michal is thrilled to be a part of the emerging field of applied ecopsychology. Contact: missmichalfire@gmail.com, 415-508-7042, 425 Cascade Drive, Fairfax, CA 94930.

is fundamentally incomplete as long as it remains separate from our most basic home, the planet.

Much of ecopsychology draws upon some version of the Gaia hypothesis originally put forth by scientist James Lovelock and microbiologist Lynn Margulis in 1979, in which our planet is

You didn't come into this world. You came out of it, like a wave from the ocean. You are not a stranger here. (Watts 1996, p. 8)

seen as one gigantic living organism, constantly interacting so as to continually support life. Ecopsychology then posits that an emotional attachment to the living world exists within the genetic structure of humans as a result of our history of interaction with the natural environment; an environment which we mutually support and which serves to maintain our physical, psychological and evolutionary wellbeing (Hillman, 1995). As our society developed,

becoming more dependent on modern technology, so our world has become increasingly dehumanized and detached from the natural environment (Gorrell, 2001). Ecopsychologists believe, as Carl Gustav Jung alluded to, that, "man feels himself isolated in the cosmos, because he is no longer involved in nature" (1964, p. 95). This isolation is problematic for both man, woman, and the cosmos.

Applied ecopsychology, also referred to as "ecotherapy," "nature-based therapy," and "wilderness therapy," an emerging field since the 1960s, grew out of humanistic, transpersonal and existential therapies. Like other therapeutic modalities, applied ecopsychology utilizes our inherent connection to the natural world as a vehicle, or catalyst, for awakening to our deepest selves. Although variations of the terms ecopsychology and ecotherapy appear throughout the literature, often interchangeably, some subtle delineations can be made between the two.

Most ecotherapists focus on the inherent power of the individual's interconnectedness to the natural world in promoting psychological health in its many forms. Many ecopsychologists, in contrast, look to this field primarily as a calling to connect people to nature in an effort to heal and save the planet (Roszak, 1996; Davis, 1998). Whichever term is used, those applying the principles of ecopsychology argue that the individual must be considered against the backdrop of the natural environment. Much as psychologists point to the need for bringing the entire family into the picture in dealing with some forms of anxiety and neurotic behavior,

Ecopsychologists suspect that there are forms of neurosis, perhaps including the most emotionally corrosive kind, that trace back to our entrenched alienation from the natural environment. The crowded industrial city, with its killing pace and compulsive habits of consumption, may disseminate an 'urban madness' that takes a heavy toll upon both the person and the planet" (Roszak, 1993, *Sierra Magazine* website).

Through any number of practices, ecopsychology sees immense benefit in reconnecting individuals with nature.

Whether approached from the side of the person or the planet, one could argue that each will invariably lead to the other if we are to fully immerse ourselves in either approach. If ecopsychology is to live up to its highest task of true transformation whether individual or planetary, then we will have to move beyond the current dualities that exist in both perspectives which place either person

the many ideas, practices, and theories underlying this important field.

Our Integral Nature

An inherent challenge to a discussion of ecopsychology is that there is no singular paradigm which all practitioners agree upon. In many ways, ecopsychology is simply a means of giving language to communicate what *happens* to people in the wilderness. Ecotherapy itself acknowledges the integral use of nature, in some form, within the therapeutic context, or the therapeutic context within the field of nature, and most ecotherapists believe that reconnecting with nature requires a physical shift in order to facilitate a mental one (Gorrell, 2001). The actual form of ecotherapy may take any

gotten, nature. The process may happen as a solo experience, or within a group, and may incorporate practices such as mindfulness, rituals, pre- and post-experience work, and traditional therapeutic interventions, such as individual and group talk therapy (Davis, 1998). Whether or not other therapeutic techniques are interwoven into an ecotherapeutic model, contact with nature in some form is the crucial ingredient, and arguments regarding why this is deemed therapeutic, are varied.

Nature's Inherent Power

There may be little dispute that the natural environment has a soothing effect, leading to positive emotions and increased health. In one study, ninety-five percent of hospital patients, staff and visitors reported positive mood changes in relation to gardens and other outdoor spaces in hospitals (Cooper Marcus & Barnes, 1999). And, in his review of the effects of gardens on health, Roger Ulrich (1999) found that patients recovering from surgery who had a window through which they could see a natural setting from their room required less hospital days and less medication. Claire Cooper Marcus and Marni Barnes (1999) review a number of

Photo: Glenn McCrea, www.dewdropworld.com

Particularly in the Western societal drive towards individualism, conscious distancing from one another seems to further alienate us from an unconscious connection with something larger than ourselves.

or planet in the foreground. Although the discussion here is focused on the applied form of ecopsychology, which will also be referred to as ecotherary, it does not exhaust the possibilities for the shape that an ecotherapeutic model can take. Presented here are just a number of

number of shapes from gardening practices, nature explorations and dialogues with natural beings, to wilderness solos, vision quests, or wilderness experiences spanning over several days or weeks. Specific practices appear to be primarily important in their function as doorways for each individual to step through and access his or her own dormant, or for-

studies which have shown that gardening has a positive effect on people's well-being and that, in times of stress, people prefer outdoor settings.

There have also been studies looking at participants of wilderness adventure programs, with no overt therapeutic structure, such as Outward Bound (OB) and National Outdoor Leadership School (NOLS) programs. In their research studying wilderness-based programs of these kinds, University of Michigan researchers Stephen and Rachel Kaplan (1989) found that participants commonly indicated that experiences brought them a sense of peace, and an ability to think with more clarity. Although further empirical research is warranted, based on my own experiences as a professional guide and educator in the Himalayas and US, and as an instructor in a therapeutic wilderness program, participants in my work have reported being deeply affected by contact with nature, often resulting in a profound positive shift, during or following the experience.

On one level, there seems to be an agreement that nature in and of itself holds therapeutic value. But the question remains: Why? Just as nature embodies the innate wisdom to heal an injured landscape it may also be that it holds the power to heal our own physical, emotional, and psychic wounds (Cohen, 2002). Or, that our intrinsic intelligence as humans, having developed from over three billion years of evolutionary history, is put into perspective in a fundamental way when we are close to nature, experiencing, on an unconscious level, our inseparable nature from the minerals, air and water surrounding and literally defining us. A similar answer may be found in Roszak's eight principles of ecopsychology presented in his 1992 book *The Voice of the Earth*, following from which it is believed that an ecological unconscious is embedded at the core of the psyche, and when exposed to the natural environment, has the innate power to enliven and cultivate within us our capacity for health and overall wellbeing.

Roszak's idea of an ecological unconscious implies that the power of wilderness may be in our reconnecting, or rather remembering, something inherently in our psyche. Particularly in the Western societal drive towards individualism, conscious distancing from one another seems to further alienate us from

an unconscious connection with something larger than ourselves. But, as Jung (1970) believed, and Roszak (1992) builds off, such identity still remains latent in our consciousness, like so many other aspects, which have been turned away from, repressed, and seemingly forgotten. Coming into contact with it with this realm of the psyche, according to Jung, is a necessary aspect of restoring psychic health and, holds the potential for both transformation of the self, and the evolution of human consciousness as a whole (Yunt, 2001).

Inner and Outer Wilderness

In describing the estranged relationship between humans and the environment, Jung postulated that the "outer world," or nature, functions as an important psychological determinant, similar

When we immerse, or simply come into contact with nature, we are coming into contact with our internal darkness.

to that of the unconscious. Jung believed that much of what we turn away from, fear, and are also intrigued by in the wild is no more than our projections from unconscious parts of ourselves that we are not prepared to hold on our own. Jeremy Yunt (2001) in his own discussion of Jung's contribution to ecopsychology, claims that from the perspective of ecopsychology, environmental problems, "are rooted most fundamentally in the distorted understandings, repressed contents, conscious denials, and unconscious projections that exist in both the personal and societal dimensions of the human psyche" (p. 98). In this way, contact with nature may be likened to coming into contact with one's shadow, which might explain why entering wilderness is not always an easy transition.

When we immerse, or simply come into contact with nature, we are coming into contact with our internal darkness. Depth psychologist, ecotherapist,

and author Bill Plotkin, believes that this journey is of utmost importance, and that it will require us to journey into those parts of ourselves which we tend to avoid, and into a wilderness which may be equally difficult and unwelcoming to us (2003, 2007). This may explain why the first few days in the outdoors can be painful, lonely and even frightening.

Canadian professor of outdoor education, Robert Henderson, describes this transition as a shift from our dualistic experience of self versus other, to an embodiment of our interconnected nature to both inner and outer landscape. In our first moments in nature we might feel fear, experiencing ourselves as being taken over by, or in conflict with the elements. (Henderson, 2002). During this period of time we seek to overcome obstacles, bag peaks, and cover great distances of ground. As the self expands, something shifts; our curiosity is piqued and we find ourselves wanting *to know* our environment. Out of this emerges a feeling of sinking into the ground upon which we travel, and a seeking to be *with* the landscape, rock, and water which surrounds us (Henderson, 2002). Here, nature no longer frightens us in the same way, but instead offers a safety in allowing us to be ourselves. The overwhelming space around us becomes a spaciousness to come into contact with that which most frightens us; to expose ourselves. As I regularly witnessed as a wilderness guide, it is at this point that, with appropriate intervention, an individual can begin practicing new modes of being, supported by the spaciousness that a natural environment provides.

Our Inherent Oneness

One of the experiences often arising from this encounter is the blurring between the illusive boundaries of "I" and "Other." Immersed in nature, the borders of our personal identity become quite arbitrary (Yunt, 2001). This merging of inner and outer, self and other, or nonduality, is another oft mentioned experience which may be integral to the transformative potential of ecotherapeutic practices. Nonduality involves states of consciousness or being in which one's sense of separateness, individuality or autonomy dissolves in the unfolding flow of experience, in which personal identity and the world are not separate. Ecopsychology acknowledges this fundamental nonduality between ourselves and our environment, and attributes so many of the problems which we attempt to address as being born out of this basic split.

Ecopsychologist Robert Greenway

Photo: Glenn McCrea, www.dewdropworld.com

speaks explicitly to this type of psychological shift upon entering wilderness in that a clear transition is experienced, from a culturally reinforced tendency to experience ourselves as fundamentally separate to a way of processing reality in a nondualistic mode (Greenway, 1995). Consciousness remains, but the dominance of the need-hungry egoic process diminishes.

Wilderness guide and author Steven Harper (1995) asserts that our society is unique in the degree to which we have made efforts to distance ourselves from the natural world, something which is in stark contrast to the intimate relationship maintained by our ancestors. Harper believes that this splitting off contributes to a sense of duality that is pervasive in our culture. Our ancestors however knew that this split could be dissolved by coming into contact with nature, which had the power to make one "whole" again.

The moment we step across the threshold and outside our usual cultural environment, our boundaries, blinders, and bonds begin to loosen. It is called "culture shock" among travelers, although it is perhaps better termed "expanding-reality shock." This shift is made every time we enter an internal or external wilderness (Harper, 1995, p. 182).

Greenway (1995) sees a psychological gradient in the people with whom he works with, in which one can cross the wilderness boundary physically, but not psychologically. There may still be an effect, but it remains peripheral, and one's mode of information processing will likely continue to be culture-dominated, and dualistic in nature. The more attempts made to reproduce cultural comforts in the wilderness, the less likely one will be to cross this threshold according to Greenway (1995). Whether nonduality is experienced or not, powerful experiences are possible on many levels of this gradient, and it could certainly be argued that this alone contributes to a transformative process.

To Come to our Senses

One of the first things most people experience upon contact with nature is an enlivening of the five senses (Harper, 1995). "This awakening of the senses, or perhaps better stated, 'coming to our senses,' is a subtly powerful and underrated experience" (Harper, 1995, p. 189). In studies examining the effects of wilderness, people often describe feelings of expansion, reconnection, and a sense of remembering, as well as an experience of their own minds as "open" and "airy," a sensation which feels quite comfortable, as compared with the sense of mind being "tight," and "crowded" in urban environments (Greenway, 1995). Interestingly, women tend to find the experience of entering wilderness easier than men do, while men tend to find the transition back to the urban world easier than women do (Greenway, 1995).

The increased awareness of the senses, particularly if attention is brought to the experience, is thought to be one of the important aspects of ecotherapy. Just as awareness of our emotional states and patterned behaviors is a fundamental step in any other therapeutic milieu, the power of nature seems to be in its ability to accelerate this process. With the heightened awareness of the senses, people often recognize how deadened their senses have become.

In this sense, we could say that when humans can open their consciousness to natural processes, they find "nature reinforcing itself" (and of course when open to cultural processes, "culture reinforces itself") (Greenway, 1995, p. 132).

This may be one reason for the inherent difficulty in defining what constitutes an ecotherapeutic practice, because the focus is not on the practices themselves, but on their potential to enliven the senses in just this way.

Related to heightened sensory awareness, Harper (1995) describes a sustained continuum of mindfulness which

In the wilderness, everyday behaviors become magnified and those patterns which appear to make life harder for oneself come into focus in such a way that it feels intolerable to return home with them.

emerges in consciousness as a result of a wilderness excursion. This is not so much a single pointed mindfulness on a single object, but rather on the stream of awareness itself. "A journey through wilderness is in itself an awareness continuum. We are invited to observe with attentiveness what emerges around each bend of the trail, what unfolds before us over each hill" (Harper, 1995, pp. 189-190). In wilderness, the means becomes the end and the journey itself is of the highest importance.

Mountain as Metaphor

Psychotherapist and author Ralph Metzner (1998), in describing the parallels between place and story, sees a natural link and possibility for metaphor in the physical places we come into and the stories which encompass who we are. Metaphor often appears to be, on a basic level, a fundamental ingredient of some types of wilderness experiences. In the group context, the group becomes metaphor for the individual's family and extended social network. The

At its core, ecopsychology requires no less than a shift of perspective, of consciousness, of what we hold to be true.

unique challenges that living in the outdoors present are metaphor for how the participant functions in his or her life; the mountain peak becomes symbol for challenge, the river crossing is a milestone like any other, and the fire a symbol for what sustains, challenges, and changes us.

In the wilderness, people often come to recognize that how life plays out in the outdoors is merely a microcosm of how life is playing out in the urban world. The journey and correlating story that unfolds in the wilderness may tell us something about our lives as a whole. And, if we can change our story within this space, then maybe this can be taken back home as well. In the wilderness, everyday behaviors become magnified and those patterns which appear to make life harder for oneself come into focus in such a way that it feels intolerable to return home with them. The longer the experience, the more fully immersed one becomes, and the more common it is that at a certain point, there is an eagerness to

try to get over the same mountaintop in a new way, or to figure out how to bypass the mountain altogether.

On an even more basic level, the unique challenges presented by the wilderness milieu, and the process of working through these challenges, leads to increases in self-esteem, confidence and self-efficacy which are likely to promote changes back home as well. Some studies focusing on the use of wilderness therapy for sexual assault survivors have pointed to the increased sense of empowerment, confidence and self-esteem derived from experiences in the outdoors (Levine, 1994; Angell, 1994). These results seem to be related to the challenges presented in the wilderness context serving as metaphor for the experience of assault, and, in the wilderness context, the ability for participants to reformulate their traumatic story (Levine, 1994). Of course, there is also the powerful effect of simply taking someone out of their prescribed home environment, which may in and of itself be dysfunctional.

Upon Return

Whatever fundamental components of transformation might exist within the context of ecopsychology some would argue that, particularly in the case of full wilderness immersion, the most challenging task, and opportunity for more lasting transformation, begins when one returns.

> We emerge from wilderness changed. At some core level we feel deeply touched … We have felt the meaning of wholeness and holiness. We have experienced parts of ourselves and parts of the universe that have long been forgotten. Upon emergence from wilderness we are confronted with our inconsistencies and notice more than ever before how drastically out of balance we live (Harper, 1995, 197).

Even the most potent experiences can be lost in a few moments or days, "whether as therapy or as practice, the greatest challenge is bringing it all back home" (Harper, 1995, p. 197). Like other consciousness expanding experiences, when individuals come into contact with

nature in a profound way, the return is almost always a painful experience, and people often describe a variety of feelings including alienation, depression, and even violation (Shapiro, 2002). In returning, we are re-immersed in the forces that split consciousness from nature in the first place, and into our pattern reinforcing lives.

Although unpleasant, the return offers a unique opportunity to be mindful of the cultural elements within which we normally operate, but usually are outside our awareness (Greenway, 1995). Because of the shock that people often do encounter upon returning from wilderness, ecotherapeutic practices that focus on the incorporation of wilderness moments into people's lives, closer to home, holds immense value for many (Shapiro, 2002). Whether the experience is immersive or an intertwining of nature into one's own life, ecopsychologists often do extensive work before, in the midst and after the experience to assist in this transition.

In Closing

It may initially surprise us that modern psychology has given little credence to the inseparable nature of the individual and the natural environment. However, until recently, "psychology saw human interactions as taking place in a vacuum, with nature acting only as a lifeless backdrop to our unfolding relationships" (Yunt, 2001, p. 106). On one level, ecopsychology asks that the field of psychology broaden its principles and practices to account for this profound influence on the psyche, acknowledging that a deeply shared and reciprocal relationship between humans and nature exists, and that denial of this connection is a source of suffering for both (Davis, 1998). Although there is no singular template for what constitutes the practices of ecopsychology, tapping into this innate connection between humans and nature alone is thought to be healing.

Contact with nature has the ability to bring about profound experiences of nonduality, radical shifts in consciousness, a sense of meaning, an enlivening of the senses, and an increased clarity to one's own thoughts and behaviors. Whether these effects can be attributed to the meaning found within the natural context, the illumination of nature as metaphor, the enlivening of an ecological unconscious, or the structure which couches the ecotherapeutic experience, including the use of rituals, and traditional therapeutic techniques, is still a matter of deliberation. Despite the continued emergence of studies which look at the therapeutic impact of such experiences, it remains unclear whether it is the natural environment itself, other factors, or a combination of the two that promotes change. This is a direction for further research.

At its core, ecopsychology requires no less than a shift of perspective, of consciousness, of what we hold to be true. In the words of Andy Fisher (2002), it is about, "taking life-forwarding steps that emerge from making honest contact with presently felt reality" (p. xix). We are as subject to the laws of the natural world as any other beings, and we feel as isolated in our urban shelters as does the oak tree which stands outside the window amidst a sea of sidewalks. If we are to sink into, and awaken to the deepest parts of ourselves, just as the acorn becomes the oak, with no resistance to itself, we may find that our own reality is quite different than what we thought it to be. The deepest practice of this work might require even this; the willingness to step fully into the unknown and unborn, and move from this place. And, as we are awakened to the profound impact born out of connection to both our outer and inner nature, we begin, as Alan Watts (1991) so aptly suggests to "know nature from the inside." In doing so, we expand our ability to absorb nature's greatest gifts; awareness of our truest reality, a deep sense of wholeness, and profound transformative potential.

References

Angell, J. (1994). The wilderness solo: An empowering growth experience for women. *Women & Therapy 15*(3), 85-99.

Brookes, C. E. (1996). A Jungian view of transpersonal events in psychotherapy. In S. Boorstein (Ed.), *Transpersonal psychotherapy*, (pp. 75-99). Albany, NY: SUNY Press.

Brown, M. H. (1989). Transpersonal psychology: Facilitating transformation in outdoor experiential education. *Journal of Experiential Education 12*,14-21.

Cohen, M. J. (2002). Wilderness revisited: The twilight's last gleaming. In C. Adams (Ed.), *The soul unearthed: Celebrating wildness and spiritual renewal through nature* (2nd ed.) (pp. 146-150). Boulder: Sentient Publications.

Cooper M. C., & Barnes, M. (1999). *Healing gardens: Therapeutic benefits and design recommendations*. Canada: John Wiley and Sons.

Davis, J. (1998). The transpersonal dimensions of ecopsychology: Nature, nonduality, and spiritual practice. *The Humanistic Psychologist 26*(1), 69-100.

Fabry, J. (1996). Use of the transpersonal in logotherapy. In S. Boorstein (Ed.), *Transpersonal psychotherapy* (pp. 101-115). New York: SUNY.

Fisher, A. (2002). *Radical ecopsychology: Psychology in the service of life*. Albany, NY: SUNY Press.

Gorrell, C. (2001). Nature's path to inner peace. *Psychology Today 34*(4), 62-66.

Henderson, R. (2002). Thoughts on the idea of adventure. In C. Adams (Ed.), *The soul unearthed: Celebrating wildness and spiritual renewal through nature* (2nd ed.) (pp. 134-138). Boulder: Sentient Publications.

Jung, C. G. (1964). *Man and his symbols*. New York: Random House.

Greenway, R. (1995). The wilderness effect and ecopsychology. In T. Roszak, M. E. Gomes, & A. D. Kanner (Eds.), *Ecopsychology: Restoring the earth, healing the mind*, (pp. 122-135). San Francisco: Sierra Club Books.

Harper, S. (1995). The way of wilderness. In T. Roszak, M. E. Gomes, & A. D. Kanner (Eds.), *Ecopsychology: Restoring the earth, healing the mind*, (pp. 183-200). San Francisco: Sierra Club Books.

Kaplan, R., & Kaplan, S. (1989). *The experience of nature: A psychological perspective*. New York: Cambridge University Press.

Levine, D. (1994). Breaking through barriers: Wilderness therapy for sexual assault survivors. *Women & Therapy 15*(4), 175-184.

Lovelock, J. (1979). *Gaia: A new look at life on earth*. New York: Oxford University Press.

Metzner, R. (1998). The place and the story: Ecopsychology and bioregionalism. *The Humanistic Psychologist 26*(1), 35-49.

Olsen, A., & Schell, S. (2005). Sense of place: An interview with Andrea Olsen. *A Moving Journal 12*(3), 3-8.

Plotkin, B. (2007). *Nature and the human soul: Cultivating wholeness and community in a fragmented world*. Novato: New World Library.

Plotkin, B. (2003). *Soulcraft*. Novato: New World Library.

Roszak, T. (1993). Beyond the reality principle: Ecological conception of sanity. *Sierra*, March-April 1993, http://findarticles.com/p/articles/mi_m1525/is_n2_v78/ai_13475749

Roszak, T. (1992). *The voice of the earth*. New York: Simon and Schuster.

Shapiro, E. (2002). Back-home pilgrimage. In C. Adams (Ed.), *The soul unearthed: Celebrating wildness and spiritual renewal through nature* (2nd ed.) (pp. 203-207). Boulder: Sentient Publications.

Thoms, L. (2003). Back to our roots for serenity? *Psychologist 16*(7), 356-359.

Ulrich, R. S. (1999). Effects of gardens on health outcomes: Theory and research. In C. C. Marcus & Marni Barnes, *Healing gardens: Therapeutic benefits and design recommendations* (pp. 27-86). Canada: John Wiley and Sons.

Watts, A. W. (1991). *Nature, man and woman*. New York: Vintage Books.

Watts, A. W. (1966). *The book on the taboo against knowing who you are*. New York: Pantheon Books.

Eating the Shadow

Polluted Nature in *A Thousand Acres*

Rinda West

Rinda West received a Ph.D in English from the University of Leeds, and began her career at the University of Chicago but an intense engagement with the anti-war movement led her to decide, in 1971 to move to a community college where she could help make the revolution. She taught at Oakton Community College until 2002. Her first book, Myself among Others was published by Scott, Foresman in 1990. Her second book, Out of the Shadow: Ecopsychology, Story, and Encounters with the Land was published in 2007 by the University of Virginia Press. Currently designs landscapes in Chicago. Contact: 4313 N. Bell Ave., Chicago, IL 60618, 773-575-1205, rinda.west@gmail.com

Ecopsychological concepts that help us to figure out how to promote a green consciousness, or a greater sense of moral responsibility for the planet, come from many sources. This paper draws on C. G. Jung's concept of the Shadow to argue that the geography of psyche mirrors the relationship between humans and the natural world: the ego stands in relation to the whole of psyche in much the same way the human stands in relation to nature. Cultures that consider nature hostile and seek to conquer, subdue, and exploit it also frequently consider psychic energies and contents threatening and either ignore, contain, pathologize, 'harness,' or project them. The psyche generated by such cultures — and Western culture is the paradigm — permits and even encourages damage to body, soul, and world. (I use soul and psyche more or less interchangeably to indicate the larger mind of which ego is just one element. Readers who have trouble with the term 'soul' may want to think of 'soul music' or 'soul food.') What we do to the earth, we also do to our own bodies, our families, our souls.

Fictions contribute to understanding the relationship of psyche and nature because they offer an arc of change in a condensed form; in fiction, the process of psychological development can be comprehended in a few hours' reading, whereas in life, it usually takes years if not decades. Fiction can suggest pathways to a changed way of being in nature that mirrors a new psychological orientation. One such is Jane Smiley's *A Thousand Acres*, which retells the story of *King Lear* from the point of view of Ginny (Goneril), who lives on an Iowa farm in 1979. This puts *A Thousand Acres* in the company of other recent revisions of canonical works that are retold by the outsider, the marginalized, sometimes the colonized. It's a device that allows writers to explore the shadows of the dominant culture.

King Lear is all about ego, will, power, and suffering. With his armies, Lear has so much power that he does not need to — and indeed cannot — distinguish between his desires and the world on which he inflicts them. What effect does the unbridled will of Lear have on others? Shakespeare wasn't telling, but writing the story from Ginny's point of view, Smiley explores the effects of power on its objects: what on earth would cause children to treat their fathers so badly? how does it feel to be betrayed by your sister? what is the condition of the land? how is the abuse of power in families reflected in nature? *A Thousand Acres* deconstructs *King Lear*, flows into its crevices and eats away at its bedrock. The novel form allows Smiley also to explore subtle changes in Ginny's consciousness that shape the story.

Smiley keeps the skeleton of *Lear*. Larry Cook has built his farm to 1000 acres, a kingdom in Iowa, and the other farmers look to him for the last word on anything. But Larry decides to form a corporation, in which each of his daughters will have an equal share; he will retire and they will run the farm. Rose and Ginny, used to placating their father, agree to go along, but Caroline, speaking "as a lawyer when she should have spoken as a daughter," (Smiley, 1991, p. 21) says, 'I don't know,' and this is enough for Larry to disown her.

Gloucester, Edgar and Edmund are played by Harold, Loren and Jess Clark, neighbors, longtime friends and rivals. Jess (Edmund) went to Canada rather than fight in Vietnam; he has just returned after thirteen years. Smiley has transformed Shakespeare's bastard into a natural: a vegetarian, a jogger, a would-be organic farmer. Ginny falls for him-- and so does Rose. Through the summer and autumn that take up most of the action, Ginny feels herself absorbed with two stories, the story of her father and the story of Jess Clark.

Hard work and thrift paid off for Larry Cook, but years of pesticides and fertilizers, fall plowing and tiled fields had altered nature; even human nature could no longer be counted on. Remembering her family's history, Ginny meditates on the effort to drain the land: "There was no way to tell by looking that the land beneath my childish feet wasn't the primeval mold I read about at school, but it was new, created by magic lines of tile my father would talk about with pleasure and reverence … It took … a generation, twenty-five years, to lay the tile lines and dig the drainage wells and cisterns …. However much these acres looked like a gift of nature, or of God, they were not. We went to church to pay our respects, not to give thanks" (Smiley, 1991, p. 15). The last lines of this passage present the farmer's hubris; he, not God or nature, made the land, domesticated its wildness, changed it into property. It may look like nature, but it's not. This is the consciousness Ginny later identifies as her father's: "He says, "I say what goes around here." He says, "I don't care if--I'm telling you--I mean it." He shouts, "I - I - I -" roaring and glorying in his self-definition. I did this and I did that and don't think you can tell me this and you haven't the foggiest idea about that, and then he impresses us by blows with the weight of his "I" and the feathery nonexistence of ourselves, our questions, our doubts, our differences of opinion. That was Daddy" (p. 306).

Larry drove out obstacles and hindrances and subdued nature by force of will. He sees no boundary between his will and external reality, whether that reality be physical, financial, natural or human. What he can't embrace is the idea that others might have rights, that they might have their own ways of experiencing; He doesn't seem to get it that others have selves that are different from his own.

This is the world Ginny inherits, these the lessons she has absorbed into her bones. But with them she has also absorbed the consequences, the runoff from the pesticides and fertilizer that have drained into the aquifer and come back to her as well water. It takes Jess Clark to make Ginny see the connection between the water and her five miscarriages. Rose has breast cancer, which also killed Jess's and quite possibly Ginny and Rose's mother and grandmother as well. In recounting the history of her father's acquisition of a thousand acres, Ginny notes that every time a woman died, the men acquired more land. In many ways throughout the novel, Smiley links the land and the female. Her answer to the central puzzle--how could these daughters be so ungrateful - lies in the incestuous sex their father forced on them as girls. Just as he accumulated and controlled the land, Larry owned his daughters and poisoned Ginny's will, her memory, and her body.

Moreover, the poison is invisible, underground, slow. You can watch the crops grow, feed the hogs, plow the land. You can repeat and repeat the lessons of a good farmer, deny or ignore what you don't want to hear, cloak in secrecy what the neighbors shouldn't know. This to me is key for developing an ecopsychology: the damage takes place out of view of daily life. We don't see carbon dioxide as it rises and traps heat, we don't see the landfills, the nuclear waste, we don't see absence, extinction, the loss of fresh water, dwindling forests. We think it's normal to come to want more and more things, to need new gadgets, new fashions. We don't think one person matters, or if we do, too often we think all that's required is reducing, reusing, and recycling. It takes a Katrina, a tsunami — a breach in the normal order — to wake us from our getting and spending, and even then, we're so easily distracted. What has to happen for the earth to come into focus? What weight, what power has the land — rivers, creatures, soil — when custom and logic deny their claim?

Habit and consciousness work in opposition in the novel. Larry - and the tradition, the values and opinions that support him — has shaped Ginny's thought, denied her memory, and damaged her ego. But her association with

Photo: Glenn McCrea, www.dewdropworld.com

Jess Clark exposes her more and more to a new way of seeing and understanding that allows her to claim her own life. The crisis allows a variety of points of view to come to light, making it possible to imagine other ways of knowing and being. Throughout the novel, Smiley uses the water underground. as an image of the power of new ways of being: Ginny thinks:

I was always aware, I think, of the water

in the soil, the way it travels from particle to particle, molecules adhering, clustering, evaporating, heating, cooling, freezing, rising upward to the surface and fogging the cool air or sinking downward, dissolving this nutrient and that, quick in everything it does, endlessly working and flowing, a river sometimes, a lake sometimes. When I was very young, I imagined it ready at any time to rise and cover the earth again, except for the tile lines. Prairie settlers always saw a sea or an ocean of grass, could never think of any other metaphor, since most of them had lately seen the Atlantic. (Smiley, 1991, p. 16)

This underground water does the work we need it to — but it does so of its own accord, by nature. Like psyche, it is mysterious. We manipulate it, we poison it, we drain it, but it persists, a force of its own, which we can imagine rising again. In Iowa in 1979, the native people have been dislocated, the native vegetation consigned to the dump and the old quarry. Only the water remains. And water is a fitting image for the natural flow of soul: it inhabits the physical and makes it capable of supporting life. In this novel as, I believe, in life, the way back to sanity requires a reconnection with the earth, a realignment of psyche and nature that acknowledges a continuum, a common pulse, and not a great chain of being, with humans on the top.

Ginny's consciousness is the battleground for the action. For most of her story Ginny is frightened: she tells us her earliest memories of her father are of "being afraid to look him in the eye, to look at him at all" (Smiley, 1991, p. 19.) She feels anxiety, shame, guilt and fear. "I was," she says, "after all, my father's daughter, and I automatically did believe in the unbroken surface of the unsaid" (p. 94) But the freedom she gains after Larry divides the farm slowly makes other opinions possible, and so we have a story.

As in *King Lear*, the breach in the old order releases dark forces - lust, appetite, foolishness, betrayal. Here, Jung's concept of the Shadow proves helpful. According to Jung, the process of developing an ego involves also the construction of the shadow, which contains parts of the self that are unacceptable in the family and culture of origin. Threatening instincts like incest, rage, and greed must be contained in shadow, but in the process some life-giving qualities get amputated as well. In powerless people, such as children, resistance may be seen as threatening and be cast in shadow. A strong sense of self will be excised. As a result, all these qualities commingle, steeped in shame and anxiety, and denied as part of the self. Frequently they are also projected onto Others, as a way of preserving ego and rationalizing behavior that is personally unacceptable.

In *Lear*, shadow forces are concentrated in the conspiracies of Goneril, Regan, Edmund and Cornwall; Lear and Gloucester are willful and gullible, but not actively evil. In inverting the point of view, Smiley reflects on these patriarchs. Here, most of the evil snakes back to Larry. This is a world where fathers beat and fuck their daughters, convincing them that "it was okay, that it must be okay if he said it was, since he was the rule maker" (Smiley, 1991, p. 190).

Photo: Glenn McCrea, www.dewdropworld.com

Smiley's use of the obscenity underlines how casual and brutal was the act itself. As Rose says, "We were just his, to do with as he pleased, like the pond or the houses or the hogs or the crops." (p. 191) Both women's bodies and the land are property, disposable at the wish of the owner. And this, Larry let her know, is the law. So Larry acts out the shadow and then legalizes his behavior; he takes not just his daughters' bodies, but their minds as well.

At the beginning of the novel, Ginny still assumes what Larry assumes. She has virtually no sense of herself as separate from her father. Gradually, however, she begins to understand that other points of view exist. Seeing her sisters as separate persons helps Ginny begin to differentiate herself. To Caroline's cool distance, Smiley opposes Rose's anger, the force that carries her and shapes all her decisions. Faced with conflict, Ginny begins to ask questions about how she has lived. Although she cannot change Larry, at least Ginny begins to move beyond magical thinking, impossible when Larry was running things.

This is part of the process of bringing shadow to consciousness, which, according to Jung, is the essential first step in the process of individuation, or reintegration of the psyche. For those with little power, the first step is often the recognition of alternative points of view about oneself. The subjective experience of people in the Other position in any culture has been distorted by the projections cast onto them by the powerful, who blame the victims. The victims, in turn, internalize their condition as a function of their own failures, as Smiley suggests in Ginny's willingness to blame herself for her miscarriages. When another perspective can be entertained, the person may look more critically at his or her own experience, step out of the fog and consider that perhaps not everything wrong is his or her fault.

Jess Clark supplies Ginny experience and insights she needs. He draws Ginny's notice away from the conventional; he shows her how things looked from the other side of the easy "we all thought." He also gives her some language for thinking about her own experience.

As her attraction to Jess grows, her imagination fastens onto him, and although she only has sex with him once — at the old dump, where he knows all the native plants - that one betrayal, that one indulgence, expands to fill her thoughts. Sex with Jess allows the shadow into Ginny's consciousness. She knows the part of victim well, but this first real disobedience of Ginny's life plants in her a seed of the knowledge of good and evil that constitutes the only child she bears to term.

We see a first fruit of this new outlook

in the next chapter, when Ginny reflects on her own thinking:

> I seemed, on the surface, to be continually talking to myself, ... busily working my rational faculties over every aspect of Jess and my feelings for him ... Beneath this voice, flowing more sweetly, was the story: what he did and what I did and what he then did and what I did after that, seductive, dreamy, mostly wordless, renewing itself ceaselessly ... And beneath this was an animal, a dog living in me, shaking itself, jumping, barking, attacking, gobbling at things the way a dog gulps its food. (Smiley, 1991, p. 172)

Beneath reason is the story; beneath the story is the instinct, like water beneath the fields. Instinct occupies shadow; it is rarely conscious, the animal whose promptings drive the story of desire. All three cohabit, all the time; Ginny sees she is more than simply Larry's daughter. Suddenly Jess is "all mysterious," (Smiley, 1991, p. 172), an Other whose inwardness she can only imagine, but one she constructs and reconstructs endlessly.

Bathed with these thoughts of Jess, Ginny tries to reason with Larry, get him to exercise, to stop driving, but he waves her off. For the first time in the narrative, she opposes him, mildly of course, but that was enough. Ginny had showed herself separate; she had opposed his will. For her, this mild self-assertion represents a growth in consciousness. For Larry it represents an intolerable insubordination. That night, Larry rages at Rose and Ginny in the gathering storm.

As in *King Lear*, the storm widens the tear in the social fabric beyond repair. It also precipitates the beginnings of memory, first Ginny's memory of being strapped as a child for losing her shoe, then Rose's revelation of how Larry seduced her and she let him continue coming to her bed at night in order to protect Caroline. At first, Ginny can't believe Rose; she must hear Rose's voice again and again. Rose tells her: "'I know that his face is a black ocean and there's always always always the temptation to drown in that ocean, to just give yourself up and sink. You've got to stare back. You've got to remind yourself what he is, what he does, what he did'" (Smiley, 1991, p. 216). Without memory, Ginny will fall back into Larry's "black ocean" of unconsciousness. Memory, however,

her own story, allows Ginny to construct a different version of their common experience. To do this, though, Ginny must walk through the shadow, through shame.

Sex with Jess Clark makes Ginny more than a victim, and it opens her to knowledge. This guilty sex merges in her mind with the memories Rose is awakening. Adultery, which carries a powerful burden of shame, stimulates her memory of her father's coming to her childhood room at night: "Lying here, I knew that he had been in there to me, that my father had lain with me on that bed, that I had looked at the top of his head, at his balding spot in the brown grizzled hair, while feeling him suck my breasts." (Smiley, 1991, p. 228) She feels "dissolved into a strong solution of shame" (p. 195) Such shame indicates an opening to the knowledge that malevolence is not only in others. But shame is also connected to self-transformation.

The new consciousness, as we see it enacted through Ginny in *A Thousand Acres*, is a matter of imagination, memory, confession, and incorporation

The self-audible wish experienced in moments of acute shame — 'I wish the ground would open up and swallow me' — Marie-Louise von Frantz calls "the desire to return to the womb." The mortifying quality of shame — the wish to die, or the feeling that one has been made rigid and invisible — "signals the death of an ego-ideal. This ego consciousness has to die — be swallowed — in order for a new awareness of oneself to expand and include the shadow or the dark side of the Self" (von Franz, 1964, p. 175).

I said earlier that stepping out of the shadow of the powerful first requires the effort of rejecting the limiting identity that has been projected onto one. But to grow ethically, it's important not to invert victimization and become like

Rose. But Rose is her father's daughter: she tells Ginny everything about her affair with Jess, knowing Ginny too loves him. Rose, who insists that Larry should show remorse, cannot own that she has hurt her sister. What Rose does to Ginny is almost as vicious as the blinding of Gloucester. Calmly she dismisses the suffering of others, including her sister. Just here, the narrative poises on a fulcrum. Rose is both victim — she's right about Larry and the smooth public face that allows him and men like him to dispose of their daughters as they will — and a villain. Memory does not heal her, it goads her and feeds her anger. Ginny and Rose typify different ways of responding to shadow. Rose enters it and lives it, wallows in it; shadow fires her anger and gives her tremendous stamina and persistence. Ginny respects its power, owns it, even acts on it in preparing poison for her sister. But she manages to contain it, ultimately to come to terms with it. The distinction is important, because connecting with shadow does not mean succumbing to it; wildness does not mean savagery, and instinct does not mean brutality.

Although it hurts her deeply, knowing about Rose and Jess opens Ginny's eyes. The state of mind she enters is "a feeling of being drenched with insight, swollen with it like a wet sponge. Rather than feeling 'not myself,' I felt intensely, newly, more myself than ever before" (Smiley, 1991, p. 305). Again, Smiley uses watery images to suggest a quality of soul. Most of all, Ginny knows Rose, and her knowledge "transformed... the past, not the future" (p. 308). Knowledge reframes what she has lived; Rose "had answered my foolish love with jealousy and grasping selfishness" (p. 308). Ginny researches common poison plants and prepares a hemlock sausage with which to poison Rose. She delights in the preparation, the secrecy, the exactness of her choice; Jess would not eat meat, the girls would not eat sausage. "Rose's own appetite would select her death" (p. 313).

In *A Thousand Acres*, the shadow has two faces: it is dangerous, truly dan-

The subjective experience of people in the Other position in any culture has been distorted by the projections cast onto them by the powerful, who blame the victims.

gerous, but it locks up great energy. When we confront it, we awaken from the numbness of innocence, the prison of self-righteousness. I believe that the encounter with shadow is crucial to the development of an environmental consciousness. Only when we have understood and felt deeply how our actions, and the economic and political system that governs us, have endangered all life on earth, can we begin to act out of compassion for other forms of life.

The goal of shadow work is to develop an ethical capacity to own and contain impulse — to accept our animal human 'nature.' For ecopsychologists interested in thinking about greening consciousness, this means that as important as it is to raise awareness of environmental degradation, it's also essential to acknowledge one's own complicity and to strategize ethically and politically, not simply to vent. It also means that appeals to guilt will be limited in their effectiveness: environmentalists need to foster a love for the earth and an ethical commitment to it as to a lover. I believe that new stories about the earth and our relationship with it can help people to change.

The new consciousness, as we see it enacted through Ginny in *A Thousand Acres*, is a matter of imagination, memory, confession, and incorporation. In the Epilogue, Ginny brings her story into the 1980's, when events in the larger economy beached many family farms, but for Ginny, her past, and the land's history, are fully in her body:

> My inheritance is with me, sitting in my chair. Lodged in my every cell, along with the DNA, are molecules of topsoil and atrazine and paraquat and anhydrous ammonia and diesel fuel and plant dust, and also molecules of memory: the bracing summer chill of floating on my back in Mel's pond, staring at the sky; the exotic redolence of the dresses in my mother's closet; the sharp odor of wet tomato vines; the stripes of pain my father's belt laid across my skin; the deep chill of waiting for the school bus in the blue of a winter's

dawn. All of it is present now, here, each particle weighs some fraction of the hundred and thirty-six pounds that attaches me to the earth, perhaps as much as the print weighs in other sorts of histories. (Smiley, 1991, p. 369)

What we put in the soil, we put in our bodies. What we deny poisons us. Ginny takes something from each of the people she loved: from Jess, eyes to see the poison we drank from; from Rose, anger; from Ty a memory of an ordered world. From "my dead young self" she takes "a canning jar of poisoned sausage and the ability it confers of remembering what you can't imagine. I can't say that I forgive my father, but now I can imagine what he probably chose never to remember--the goad of an unthinkable urge, pricking him, pressing him, wrapping him in an impenetrable fog of self that must have seemed...like the very darkness"(Smiley, 1991, pp. 370-71) This final potent confession is made to the reader, made so she can remember as real what she cannot imagine herself capable of. Her confession becomes a kind of communion; a way to eat the shadow.

This ending is very satisfying indeed if what we are concerned with is consciousness. It does not, however, take care of Ginny or the land, and Smiley is too much a realist to end her novel with an unjustifiable optimism. Ginny, after all, is a waitress in a roadside Perkins. Her farm belongs to the Heartland Corporation, and we can be reasonably sure that they will use bigger machines, more fertilizers, specialized pesticides. Smiley leaves us, then, in the real world. Jess Clark has gone back to the west coast.

Perhaps, what we know of psyche may offer us ways to think about the earth. Psyche, or soul, is in inner reality, life force, memory, the particularity that defines each individual's experience of the world; ego mediates between this and the outer world. One way this happens is through imagination; when an impulse

is thwarted, we develop images of its satisfaction. When our ethics require that we own and control our instincts and consider the needs and wishes of others, conscious imagination allows us to construct acceptable images for our impulses. We come to be able to bring our instincts--our animal heritage--into an ethical relation with others.

When we bring our own instinctual nature into consciousness, we recognize our potential to do harm, but we also open the flow of our life energies. This does not mean that we must then act on our instincts; instead, we transform them in our imaginations so that we don't act them out or project them unknowingly. We make art, we play, we daydream. Imagination gives us greater sympathy with the complicated inwardness of others, and greater ability to achieve connection with them. In the process, we enlarge consciousness; the ego stores and processes information about our darker, more "natural" selves. While we will never — by definition — incorporate the shadow into consciousness, we can increase our ability to move around between ego and soul.

Restoring imagination may lead us to the woods, the water, the prairie, and the desert. It may even lead us to reimagine farming, along with mining and manufacture. It may lead us to ask more from community. Imagination may even show us ways to reconcile with both inner and outer nature.

References

Smiley, J. (1991). *A thousand acres*. New York: Ballantine Books.

von Franz, M.-L. (1964). The process of individuation. In C. G. Jung, *Man and his symbols* (pp. 157-254). New York: Dell.

A Jungian Perspective on Ecopsychology

Dennis L. Merritt

I discovered Jung as a Ph.D. entomologist and was impressed that his intimate relationship with nature was reflected in the holistic concepts and ecological principals in his theories and practice. Jung's concept of the Self as reframed by complexity theory adds an important dimension to ecopsychology, and his critique of Christianity can transform our relationship with the animal world. I see Hermes as the god of ecopsychology and complexity theory and a guide for using dreams to connect us to nature.

I think of Jung as being the prototypical ecopsychologist as revealed in his autobiography, *Memories, Dreams, Reflections* and Margaret Sabini's *The Earth has a Soul—the Nature Writings of C. G. Jung*. Nature was a world of incomparable beauty for Jung, with a mysterious dark side that reflected his

Dennis Merritt is a Jungian analyst and ecopsychologist in private practice in Madison and Milwaukee, Wisconsin. He formed a deep connection to the land by growing up on a small dairy farm in Wisconsin where he roamed the woods and marshes with his dog. He received a doctorate from Berkeley in entomology, a masters in Humanistic Psychology from Sonoma State, and graduated from the Jung Institute in Zurich. He recently finished a manuscript, *The Dairy Farmer's Guide to the Universe—Jung, Hermes and Ecopsychology*. Contact: 2963 North Prospect Ave., Milwaukee, WI 53211, (414) 906-1507, dennismerritt4@hotmail.com.

deep insecurities. A nightmare at age four of a huge, frightening phallus on an underground throne initiated Jung into "the realm of darkness" and "the secrets of the earth" (Jung, 1965, p. 13). It became the foundation of his sense of the Spirit in nature, of God in matter, and his psycho-spiritual interest in alchemy. Jung began to develop a second personality in his twelfth year of a God "close to nature, the earth, the sun, the moon, the weather, all living creatures" (pp. 44-45). Nature, it seemed, was a better expression of God than His human creation. To enter God's realm was like entering a temple where one was "transformed and suddenly overpowered by a vision of the whole cosmos, so that he could only marvel and admire, forgetful of himself" (p. 45)

As an adult, Jung would identify personality number two with the archetypal realm and the collective unconscious. He realized it was inflationary and unbalancing to identify with that realm as he did in his youth. It is the source of dreams, myths and the underpinnings of consciousness, best related to in a humble I-Thou manner. This is expressed by the Chinese ideogram for the sage described as "the ear listening to the Inner King," that can be seen as the goal and the process of Jungian psychology.

Several ecopsychological tenants

are implicit in the sage model. There is no dominance of ego consciousness over the more holistic and all-encompassing unconscious that compensates consciousness. Jung saw the collective unconscious as being part of nature. The ego's relationship to the unconscious mimics the human relationship to the environment. We are to continually attune ourselves to the unconscious as we are to attune to nature, seeking a meaningful and humble place in the inner and outer cosmos.

The Inner King also implies a spiritual dimension. Carl Sagan believed that unless we can re-establish a sense of the sacred about the environment, we cannot overcome the powerful forces in ourselves and our systems that are destroying it (Sagan, 1972). Sagan challenged religions to re-orient themselves vis à vis nature and for non-religious people to develop a sense of sacredness about nature.

Jung discovered a new myth for himself and Western culture after engaging in a perilous 3-1/2 year journey into the depth of the unconscious after his troublesome split from Freud in 1913. He did this through dreamwork and letting the unconscious express itself through sandplay, art work, spontaneous body movements, and active dialogue and interaction with the images that arose from the unconscious. His greatest discovery was the archetype of the Self, an ecopsychological concept illustrated by his Liverpool dream in 1927. In the center of Liverpool was a flowering magnolia tree, bathed in its own light, on an island in the center of a circle. The circle was in the center of a city square from which roads radiated out to the four quarters of the city each containing a replica of the city center (Jung, 1965, pp. 197-199). The circle is an ideal image for the whole and the relationship between all differences and opposites because all elements on the periphery of a circle are related to all other elements through the central point of the circle.

Jung discovered many images of the Self including the hermaphrodite, animals like the bear and whale, crystals and the number four. An experience of the Self gives life a sense of meaning and orientation because one sees one's place in the big picture and one's relationship to other entities. To be in touch with the Self allows one to follow a path with heart as one journeys through life with hints from the Inner King.

The archetype of the Self is an organic concept seen at all levels of the living and the inorganic world. Complexity theory reveals self-organization beginning with energy fields and extending through natural systems and the galaxies. Smaller self-organizing units are nested within larger and larger units and time frames, all interacting with each other. This describes an organism, an archetypal image of the Self (Merritt, 1983, pp. 78-79; Ho, 1998). The nesting of self-organizing entities in the human psychological experience encompasses the ego in relation to the unconscious (containing, as Jung said, "the little people within"), an individual in relation to another, interactions in and between groups and societies, and humans in relation to the broadest organic and inorganic environment out of which we emerge and into which we return at death.

Jung's Liverpool dream revealed the relationship of individual centers to a larger center and a beautiful relationship between the human-created and the natural world. The very center was a tree, a Self symbol appearing in many cultures across time frames — an archetype, in other words. The tree becomes a Self symbol by virtue of its size and age; its functioning in the three realms of earth, the human level, and the sky; and its mystery as a plant of capturing light energy from the sun and converting it into chemical bonds that serve as the energy source for all other life forms. Humans built a city (Liverpool) and civilization around this center and centering element in nature (attributes of the Self). Jung's tree had its own light, what medieval writers called "the light of nature"—God's nature and ways as revealed through nature itself. It was also a light in the dark; the dream was of a dark and rainy night in Liverpool. Jung's phallic childhood Self-symbol also had its own light in the darkness of the underworld.

The spontaneous emergence of the archetype of the Self within an individual psyche is like receiving a personal image of God, a numinous experience that provides the foundation for the development of a new, more complete ego structure. The Self manifests in various forms in different cultures at different periods of their cultural history, such as Yahweh, Jesus, Buddha and *Wakantanka* (Lakota Sioux). It becomes the basis for a culture's religion, ethics, morals, worldviews, and attitudes towards women, sex, and the environment.

Jung offered a basic analysis of our culture in his interpretation of a Christ-Satan split in the dominant Self-image in the West (Jung, 1968, 1969a). The split runs like a f,ractal through every individual in our culture and through its social, economic and political systems. Jung noted something seriously wrong with the 'final solution' to the problem of Evil as presented in the Book of Revelation—the dark side was never integrated, and Good was achieved over the mutilated carcasses of all those who had participated in the joys of sex, sensuality, and the body. This was exemplified by the destruction of the Whore of Babylon, a central archetypal figure of the old goddess cults of the ancient Middle East. The Sacred Prostitutes embodied the goddess via instruction in lovemaking and the use of beer, erotic dances, ceremonies, and sacred intercourse as vehicles to ecstatic states and spiritual development (Qualls-Corbett, 1988).

Jung described the darkening at the end of the Age of Pisces, the Christian era, as a manifestation of God's split-off dark side. He saw this in Nazi Germany, *the destruction of nature* and indigenous cultures, the atom bomb and *overpopulation*. He believed a new consciousness would begin to emerge that would usher

I think of Jung as being the prototypical ecopsychologist.

in a New Age with the coming of the astrological Age of Aquarius, two terms he coined.

The *myth* Jung articulated over decades of writing is that God wants to enter space-time through the human psyche and thereby raise Its consciousness (Jung, 1965, pp. 338-339). Humans are the conscious part of God's creation and co-creators with God, serving the vital role of incarnating God and giving It and creation objective existence. God must be fully and emotionally engaged in order to become real and incarnate through the emotions and thoughts stirred up in the human psyche. This inevitably makes us aware of God's dark side within us associated with the dark side of nature (ibid. p. 334). Not being conscious of the evil in our psyches means we blindly act it out. Buddha and Jesus intended for humans to become fully conscious at some point in the future, but the challenge is so great that substitutes arose like a *belief* in endless incarnations to reach the goal or enlightenment achieved only in the afterlife (Jung, 1970, p. 526).

Jung discovered in alchemy a symbolic map of the process of unifying all opposites, including God and the Devil (Jung, 1965, pp. 334-336, p. 341). Alchemy provided a historical base and description for his personal experiences during his "confrontation with the unconscious" and became the main symbolic system of Jungian psychology. The alchemists took up the question of evil that Christianity was unable to address by projecting the post-Christian unconscious into their vessels and retorts. They

Photo: Glenn McCrea, www.dewdropworld.com

looked into matter and not to the heavens for a solution to the distorted God image, engaging matter with careful observations, dreams, visions, and reflections. One of the many metaphors for their process, that of transmuting lead into gold, can be interpreted as finding wholeness and greatest value (gold) by engaging the dark rejected elements in our own psyches and in our culture (the lead). The alchemists sought to redeem the macrocosm, the material universe, just as Christ had redeemed the microcosm, humankind, by placing high value on the feminine, the earth, the body, and sexuality.

The Greek god Hermes became the god of alchemy where he represented *the spirit in nature and matter*. Most Greeks knew the gods weren't real, but powerful forces within and outside the body were very real. The gods were simply the personifications of these forces, enabling the Greeks to become more conscious of the forces and how they played out in the human psyche and in the world (Paris, 1990, p. 138). It put humans in an I-Thou relationship to the gods, thereby averting the danger of inflation by believing one personally possessed such powers. The reality is that we are then unconsciously possessed by gods.

Hermes in one form was worshipped as a phallus, offering the Western male a much-needed sacred image of the archetypal masculine source. Hermes was very close to the feminine and displays many shadowy elements because he holds the archetypal position between consciousness and the unconscious. He represents a consciousness that can penetrate close to the origin of consciousness, the deep physiological realm connected with the vegetative nervous system, and the somatic (body) unconscious associated with synchronicity (Schwartz-Salant, 1982, p. 119 & 120). He was intimate with the animal realm and was the source of myths and genealogies of the gods. Being so close to the source made him the god of transitions and liminal spaces, like birth, death, adolescence, initiations, hinges, and journeying.

The Homeric Hymn about newborn Hermes stealing Apollo's cattle can be a guiding ecopsychological myth for our time. Apollo, the god of science and the bright, far-sighted, pure, and favorite son of Zeus, had a vulnerable cow side. Zeus commanded the two brothers to love each other. This can be seen as a challenge to the West to achieve a fruitful union between science and religion, consciousness and the unconscious, the rational and the irrational, the body and spirit.

The essence of Hermes and the guiding image for the relation to opposites is symbolized by his wand—a figure eight ("8") with a gap at the top. The two upper arms represent the full development of differences and opposites and a lively dance between them. Projecting one's shadow onto another and labeling them as an evil to be exterminated destroys the Hermetic spirit. Hermes is the god of diplomats, ad men, and psychologists, where persuasiveness, half-truths, or whatever moves the psyche rules the day. I see Hermes as the god of ecopsychology because he symbolizes a consciousness of the spirit in nature and the imaginative diplomatic skills needed to co-exist with each other and other nations, to address complex environmental issues, and to make the difficult adjustments to live sustainability.

Hermes symbolizes a type of psychology Jung called for. "We need more psychology," Jung said, "because the only real danger is man himself; we are the origin of all coming evil" (Carol, 1980, p. 390). We need more than a study of rats and monkeys, with mazes and statistics. We need a psychology that addresses the dark side of humans and offers an archetypal basis for becoming whole beings in intimate relationship with the environment. Jung said academia will never fully address the human psyche until it recognizes the

We are to continually attune ourselves to the unconscious as we are to attune to nature, seeking a meaningful and humble place in the inner and outer cosmos.

numinous—human's greatest experience (Jung, 1969a, pp. 451-452). The best we can do in describing the human condition is a story, with myths[1] as the major sym-

---

[1] Jung emphasized that consciousness needs a mythic dimension to achieve a sense of meaning in life and psychologically and religiously approach "the Word of God": "The need for mythic statements is satisfied when we frame a view of the world which adequately explains the meaning of human existence in the cosmos, a view which springs from our psychic wholeness, from the co-operation between conscious and unconscious. Meaninglessness inhibits fullness of life and is therefore equivalent to illness" (Jung, 1965, pp. 340-341).

bolic stories of a culture, but there is a lack of appreciation, even disrespect, for the mythic and symbolic realms, even in psychology and psychiatry departments.

Jung's challenge for those interested in ecopsychology is to become as conscious as possible, especially of the cultural influences behind our dysfunctional relationship with the environment. One must know what archetypal forces are active within oneself and without facilitated by knowing what gods or goddesses are operative. This increases consciousness and freedom in relation to these powerful forces plus knowing the

of the human psyche, another domain of Hermes. To individuate and become a whole person necessitates a journey to the depths of the psyche that Jung associated with the animal soul. He perceived this to be the realm of the instincts with archetypes being images of the instincts. Jung believed our identity with Christ had deeply wounded our animal nature, causing us to lose a sense of the animal form of God presenting as the shadow of God (Jung, 1965, pp. 215-217). He saw most neurotic problems as a consequence of the repression of the animal drives, especially sexuality (Jung 1966,

spirit animals, as personal guides and messengers from another dimension of psychic experience. When around your spirit animal remind yourself, "This is what my soul looks like when it appears in an animal form." Use the animal as an entré to connect deeply with the ecosystem it lives in.

Hermes is the god of dreams, what Jung considered to be natural, unadulterated products of nature and the unconscious. Dreams are broader and deeper than ego consciousness, illustrated by the ego being but one element in a dream. The dream maker turns our life events into a developing story, and big dreams turn our lives into a mythic adventure and an affiliation with all of humanity.

Jung believed our identity with Christ had deeply wounded our animal nature, causing us to lose a sense of the animal form of God presenting as the shadow of God.

parameters one is operating within. "One does not become enlightened by imagining figures of light, but by making the darkness conscious," said Jung, noting this process is not popular (Jung, 1967, pp. 265-266). It is a movement towards wholeness by integrating the contents of the unconscious. This leads simultaneously to development of one's unique individual nature (individuation) and a connection with the rest of humanity. If properly framed it can lead to deeper relationship to the natural world. Ultimately it is a spiritual journey and the only journey worth taking—the best antidote to the promise of happiness through shopping.

Another guiding thought for ecopsychology arises from Jung's challenge to unite our cultured sides with "the 2 million-year-old-man within." Jung studied indigenous people, children and dreams for examples of the human psyche undistorted by the plague of rationality. Indigenous consciousness is sustained by a mythic, symbolic relationship with nature. Jung advocated garden plots for city apartment dwellers so the primate within them could come to life (Carol, 1980, pp. 201-203).

The indigenous person is close to what Jung called the "animal soul" level

pp. 260-261). Repressed energy turns against us and bursts out in a savage forms such as war (Jung, 1970, p. 21).

Jung suggested an extension of the Christian love of our neighbor to *the animal in us* (Jung, 1970, p. 22). People would value life more highly if they were

Dreams can be used to connect us to every aspect of nature and develop a sense of place. An example is how I worked with a single-image dream I had about a year before finishing my training at the Jung Institute in Zurich. The scene was of a typical upper Midwest meadow on a bright summer day. Every atom glowed with a numinous inner light to make this simple landscape the most beautiful and sacred landscape I had ever seen.

The dream has led and inspired me over the last 25 years to try to achieve

We need a psychology that addresses the dark side of humans and offers an archetypal basis for becoming whole beings in intimate relationship with the environment.

in better relationship to the animal within, and "react instinctively against any institution or organization that had the power to destroy life on a large scale" (p. 2). Because animals are closely adapted to living in particular environments filling distinct niches, Jung believed a sense of rootedness and place was part of our instinctual animal nature. It is conservative and maintained by traditions (Jung, 1954, pp. 98-99).

Animals can speak and nature can have a spiritual dimension in our dreams. Animals appearing in dreams in a sacred and numinous manner can be treated as

when awake what I experienced with the environment in my dream. I have taken a typical Jungian approach to doing this by looking at individual natural elements in the upper Midwest and the personalities of its many ecosystems (Lewis, 1996). When in my favorite places in the Midwest I remind myself, "This is what my soul looks like when it takes the form of a landscape." With an imaginative heart (Hillman, 1992, p. 108) I have tried to respond to the sensuality of every element in the environment. I explored their metaphoric and symbolic dimensions in addition to scientific information and stories about them and the systems they are contained in. I did this with the weather and seasons, flora and fauna, geology and topography, water formations (lakes, bogs, ponds and rivers), etc.[2] My wife and I conducted weeklong seminars, "Spirit in the Land, Spirit in Animals, Spirit in People," using science, Jungian psychology, and Native American spirituality in a didactic and experiential manner to deeply immerse participants into our local ecosystems.[3]

Jung's autobiography is replete with examples illustrating how his dreams, visions, symbolic acts, synchronistic experiences, and his immersion in nature wedded him to his beloved Swiss soil and profoundly affected his psychological system. Jung described many synchronistic experiences that he honored. Synchronicity is another domain ruled by Hermes concerning the uncanny, acausal, meaningful experiences linking across levels of reality and recognized by all indigenous cultures. With reference to the psyche, synchronicity suggests there are other avenues of connection between things—avenues that are outside of space-time and causality (Sheldrake, 1999, pp. 54-63). Jung proposed that synchronicity be added to the principles of causality, the conservation of matter and energy, and space-time to have a complete picture of the universe (Jung, 1969b, pp. 512-515).[4]

Going from the archaic to the modern, I propose that Hermes is the god of complexity and dynamic systems theories. This mathematics, on a par with relativity theory and quantum mechanics in terms of its revolutionary nature, describes the emergence and evolution of complex systems. Jungian analyst George Hogenson has been a champion in applying dynamic systems theory to Jungian psychology, presenting a cogent argument for archetypes as emergent phenomena and not inherited neural programs (Hogenson, 2001, 2004; Merritt 2008). He describes Jung's system of word association, complex, archetype, the Self, and synchronicity as a continuum of levels within *the symbolic universe that humans inhabit* (Hogenson, 2005). When the "symbolic density" at any level reaches a maximum, one enters a transition stage where the system self-organizes into the next and more complex level. When one's *personal* complex reaches an extreme, for example, one may transit into the archetypal domain, the mythic dimension of

Dreams can be used to connect us to every aspect of nature and develop a sense of place.

human experience that links us to all other humans. The great myths of a culture are those that undergo a sort of Darwinian selection to best suit brain structure and functioning, the developmental stage of an individual or culture, and the environment the species must adapt to (Hogenson, 2001, pp. 604-608; 2004, pp. 74-75).

Hermes is the god that best personifies these phenomena. He is the god of the journey and not the goal, related to the non-linear phenomena covered by complexity and dynamic systems theories. Hermes is about accidents and unpredictable changes of fate: sensitive dependence on initial conditions. He is the god of transitional and liminal states as the emergence of archetypal positions and a consciousness of their worldviews (basic phase states and strange attractors). As the messenger of the gods and god of synchronicity he is involved with the interaction of powerful complex systems. He is cognizant of deep underlying forces (archetypes as strange attractors) and their relationship between levels (fractals). Hermes personifies the unique

human ability to consciously, emotionally, and symbolically experience the basic dynamics of the organic and inorganic worlds described by complexity and dynamic systems theories.

The symbolic domain ruled by Hermes is *the most fundamental* ecopsycyhological level as described by Hogenson: "The symbolic can be understood as a part of nature, sharing the characteristics of other great processes in nature, from the ion transfers in the brain to the destructive force of a great volcano" (Hogenson, 2005, p. 283).

Hermes as the god of Jungian ecopsychology offers an archetypal framework embracing the intrapsychic and inorganic phenomena, relating the personal and individual to the collective, and emphasizing interaction and journeying with "all my relatives." He highlights the symbolic and numinous, offering a means of connecting the individual and a society to its environment in a mythic and sacred manner. Hermes facilitates a relationship with indigenous peoples and their wisdom of the earth, helping connect our cultured side with our animal soul and the 2 million-year-old-man within. Hail Hermes!

References

Carol, H. (1980). *Man and his environment. C. G. Jung speaking: interviews and encounters* (Ed. W. McGuire & R. Hull). London: Picador. Originally published in Hans Carol, Neue Zuricher Zeitung, June 2, 1963.

Hillman, J. (1992). *The thought of the heart and the soul of the world*. Woodstock, Connecticut: Spring Publications.

Ho, M.-W. (1998). Organism and psyche in a participatory universe. In D. Loy, *The evolutionary outrider: the impact of the human agent on evolution* (pp. 49 - 65). Santa Barbara, CA: Praeger.

Hogenson, G. (2001). The Baldwin effect: a neglected influence on C. G. Jung's evolutionary thinking. *Journal of Analytical Psychology, 46*, 591-611.

Hogenson, G. (2004). What are symbols made of?: Situated action, mythological bootstrapping and the emergence of the self. *Journal of Analytical Psychology, 49*, 67-81.

Hogenson, G. (2005). The Self, the symbolic and synchronicity: Virtual realities and the emergence of the psyche. *Journal of Analytical Psychology, 50*, 271-284.

Jung, C. G. (1954). *The practice of psychotherapy*. In *The collected works of C. G. Jung, Vol. 16* (H. Read, M. Fordham, G. Adler, & W. McGuire (Eds.); R. F. C. Hull (Trans.)). Princeton: Princeton University Press.

Jung, C. G. (1965). *Memories, dreams, reflections*

---

[2] For an example of how I worked with the glacial influence in the Midwest see Merritt (1993), also available on my website at http://www.ecojung.com. *The Dairy Farmer's Guide to the Universe—Jung, Hermes and Ecopsychology* (in preparation) explores the many dimensions of the Midwest environment to illustrate basic Jungian ecopsychological principles. Also see Merritt (2008)

[3] See a description of the Spirit in the Land seminars on my website listed in note 2.

[4] I explored the relationship between synchronicity and the theory of evolution in my thesis at the Jung Institute (Merritt 1983).

(A. Jaffe (Ed.) & R. & C. Winston (Trans.)). New York: Vintage Books.

Jung, C. G. (1966). *Two essays in analytical psychology*. In *The collected works of C. G. Jung, Vol. 7*, 2nd ed. (H. Read, M. Fordham, G. Adler, & W. McGuire (Eds.); R. F. C. Hull (Trans.)). Princeton: Princeton University Press.

Jung, C. G. (1967). *Alchemical studies*. In *The collected works of C. G. Jung, Vol. 13*, 1st ed. (H. Read, M. Fordham, G. Adler, & W. McGuire (Eds.); R. F. C. Hull (Trans.)). Princeton: Princeton University Press.

Jung, C. G. (1968). *Aion*. In *The collected works of C. G. Jung, Vol. 9, II*, 2nd ed. (H. Read, M. Fordham, G. Adler, & W. McGuire (Eds.); R. F. C. Hull (Trans.)). Princeton: Princeton University Press.

Jung, C. G. (1969a). *Answer to Job*. In *The collected works of C. G. Jung, Vol. 11*, 2nd (pp. 57-470). (H. Read, M. Fordham, G. Adler, & W. McGuire (Eds.); R. F. C. Hull (Trans.)). Princeton: Princeton University Press. Originally published as C. G. Jung, *Antwort auf Hiob* (Zürich, 1952).

Jung, C. G. (1969b). *Synchronicity: An acausal connecting principle*. In H. Read, M. Fordham, G. Adler & W. McGuire (Eds.), *The collected works of C. G. Jung, Vol. 8* (pp. 419-519) (H. Read, M. Fordham, G. Adler, & W. McGuire (Eds.); R. F. C. Hull (Trans.)). Princeton: Princeton University Press. Originally published in C. G. Jung & W. Pauli, *Naturerklärung und Psyche (Studien aus dem C. G. Jung Institut, IV)* (Zürich, 1952).

Jung, C. G. (1970). *Civilization in transition*. In *The collected works of C. G. Jung, Vol. 10*, 2nd ed. (H. Read, M. Fordham, G. Adler, & W. McGuire (Eds.); R. F. C. Hull (Trans.)). Princeton: Princeton University Press.

Lewis, P. 1996. *Tomorrow by design*. New York: John Wiley & Sons.

Merritt, D. (1983). *Synchronicity experiments with the I Ching and their relevance to the theory of evolution* (Unpublished doctoral dissertation). C. G. Jung Institute, Zürich.

Merritt, D. (1993). The soul of glacier country. *Mythos Journal I*(2), 33-37. Also available at <www.ecojung.com>

Merritt, D. (2008). Sacred landscapes, sacred seasons: A Jungian ecopsychological perspective. In G. Nash & G. Children (Eds), *The archaeology of semiotics and the social order of things* (pp. 153-170). Oxford: Archaeopress.

Paris, G. (1990). *Pagan grace* (Trans. J. Mott). Dallas: Spring Publications.

Qualls-Corbett, N. (1988). *The sacred prostitute*. Toronto: Inner City Books.

Sabini, M. (Ed.). (2002). *The earth has a soul: The nature writings of C. G. Jung*. Berkeley: North Atlantic Books.

Sagan, C. (1992). To avert a common danger. Parade Magazine, March 1. PAGE NUMBERS MISSING

Schwartz-Salant, N. (1982). *Narcissism and character transformation*. Toronto: Inner City Books.

Sheldrake, R. (1999). *Dogs that know when their owners are coming home*. New York: Three Rivers Press.

Photo: Glenn McCrea, www.dewdropworld.com

Artist's Statement

Glenn McCrae

As a kid who had the run of 26 acres in the Ohio countryside, I developed an early fascination with nature. By the third grade, when I learned I was near-sighted and was fitted with glasses, I had become most intrigued with those creatures that I could hold in my hands and examine closely. I have been interested

in the details of the natural world since that time. My tactile orientation is probably also related to this desire to pick up and study the world around me. Many of the images presented here, then, are of creatures and objects that I can study close at hand. As a beautyholic, though, I point my camera at anything that catches my eye. So you will find a lot more here than close-up images of nature.

If I have a signature body of work, it would

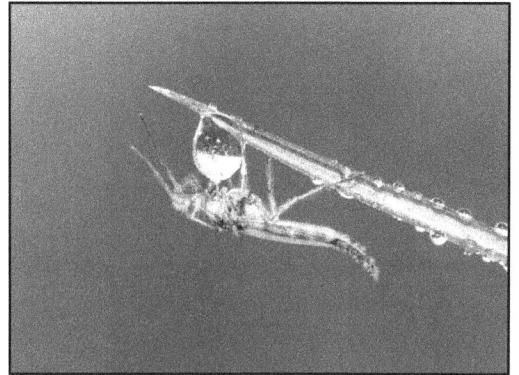

have to be my dewdrop images. Obtaining good close-up photographs of dewdrops presents special challenges to the macro photographer. Trying to capture a beautiful refracted scene within a dewdrop is a bit like writing haiku or a sonnet. A single blade of grass with dew, for instance, presents predictable and challenging obstacles to the photographer. Successfully working within those constraints can be incredibly satisfying, and the possible variations on this simple theme are infinite.

Over the past several years, my photographs have appeared several times in both *Bay Nature* and California Coast & Ocean magazines. Contacts through my website (www. positively-phototropic.com or www. dewdropworld.com) after its inception

in 2001 have resulted in photographic projects ranging from inclusion in a video of still images that was part of the American Museum of Natural History's 2004 exhibit, *Frogs: A Chorus of Colors*, to an article illustrated with 15 of my photos on finding and photographing the rattlesnakes of the "sky islands" of southeastern Arizona I wrote for a Czech magazine, *Akva Tera Forum*, that was published in the fall of 2006. Numerous scientific websites use my photos, many of which found my photos through Cal-Photos (http://calphotos.berkeley.edu). More recently, one of my frog images graced the backs of buses in San Jose, California, as part of a water conservation campaign. A recent issue of Bay Nature contains two of my images taken at Salt Point State Park.

Phototropism means growth or movement in response to light, which is why I chose to call my website *Positively Phototropic*. Almost all of the photographs therein were taken with natural light, and because light is of paramount importance to photography and to me, *Positively Phototropic* is in many ways an outgrowth of my own appreciation of and aspiration toward light in its many guises.

Cosmic Symbolic Transformations

Religious Architecture & the Epic of Evolution

Stephen Dunn

Thomas Berry and Brian Swimme made a public launch of their book *The Universe Story* (Swimme & Berry, 1992) surrounded by a hundred or so people gathered at Holy Cross Retreat Center on the Canadian north shore of Lake Erie. Interestingly, two years before, in conversation with Berry, the staff of that center had already created a contemplative pilgrimage honoring the Universe Story. It was a series of modest outdoor meditation sites, or "stations". In Berry's terminology, these were profound readings of the cosmic "scriptures of the earth". They highlighted eight irreversible transformations within that Evolutionary Epic: four of the macro universe, four of earth's evolution once the human emerged.[1] Additionally, a series of eight stained glass windows in the retreat center's chapel visually portrayed the Epic. (The image on this page shows a picture of the chapel's Fourth Station, titled *The Human Emerges*,

Stephen Dunn was the founding director of the Elliott Allen Institute for Theology and Ecology at St. Michael's Faculty of Theology in the University of Toronto (1991). A fellow Passionist with Thomas Berry, he enjoyed several decades of active collaboration with him. Stationed in Toronto, he was privileged to act as "Client" in the evolution of North America's first LEED "Gold" certified ecological church (2006). Contact: stephen.dunn@utoronto.ca.

providing a visual sense of the Stations in their original setting.)

Practical situations eventually required selling the center property, but an equally practical event offered an exceptional opportunity to advance this

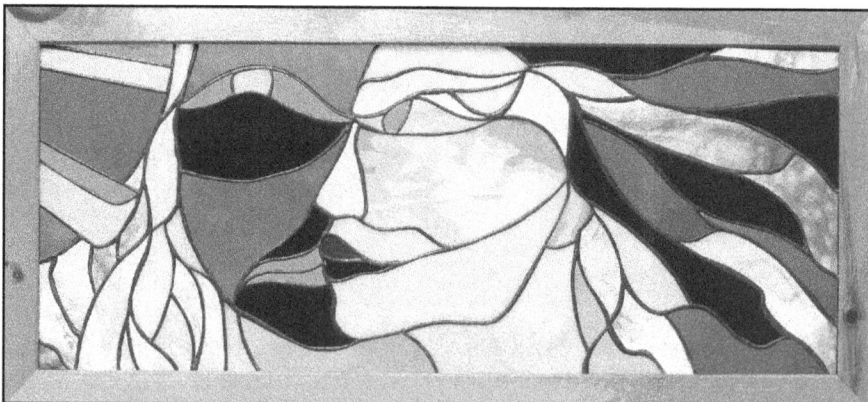

The Human Emerges, the fourth chapel station at the Holy Cross Retreat Center on the Canadian north shore of Lake Erie. Artist: Carolyn Delaney. Photo: A. Peacock

spiritual quest. The Passionist Community is the "monastic community" to which Thomas Berry dedicated *Evening Thoughts* (Tucker, 2006). Having embraced his vision on the shore of Lake Erie, the Canadian Passionists saw the chance of a lifetime when a new subway line was to be built right in

front of St. Gabriel Passionist Parish in Toronto. It was now financially possible to build a new ecologically sound church as well as address the spiritual challenge Berry calls being "between two stories".[2] The Passionists feel it also addressed the deep religious question raised by Thomas Berry in a creative way.

Charles Taylor's impressive recent work framed the question of being between stories in a common sense way. He asked: "why was it virtually impossible not to believe in God in, say 1500 in

[1] Two volumes published by the Center had set the stage for this strong commitment to explore the Epic of Evolution: Lonergan & Richards (1987) and Dunn & Lonergan (1991).

[2] In 2007 the church achieved Gold Certification for Leadership in Energy and Environmental Design (LEED), reflecting its ecological integrity.

our Western society, while in 2000 many of us find this not only easy, but even inescapable?" (Taylor, 2007, p. 25). This article will probe some central aspects of that spiritual gulf. The insights of Louis Dupré, a philosopher of religion at Yale, and David Tracy, a theologian and member of the Committee on Social Thought of the University of Chicago, will give us perspective. The aim is to offer a few indications of how the church's architecture is helping to articulate a way ahead in a religiously fragile culture.

Symbols: Secular and Religious

So many of our everyday symbols arose within historic worldviews that now we can only appreciate through critical study. But the demands of the twenty-first century require us to do that reflection. Sometimes that leads to relinquishing them, sometimes to freshly engaging them. The "smokestack," when the industrial world was forming, was a powerful indicator of employment, productivity, and hopefulness for the future The crisis over climate change has transformed it into an anti-symbol, powerfully suggesting pollution, the devouring of non-renewable resources, and in many cases signalling inhumane working conditions. Or, think of the much earlier bucolic image of the "Family Farm." It spoke of productivity as well as the fostering of community and was esteemed as the core element of society. Although a dominant symbol within the early agricultural economy, it is now all but forgotten, sometimes scorned, except of course in its seductive neo-commercial use to suggest organic authenticity — a use unmasked in the film *Food Inc.* (2009).

Religious symbols have not fared any better. Philosophically speaking, just as family agriculture lost its former meaning and smokestack industrialism rapidly fell from favor, religion has lost significant relevance. That loss has a very long history, as Taylor's study gives evidence. The new St. Gabriel church, beyond its leadership significance (symbolic and real) regarding energy conservation and the restraint of its environmental footprint, is the embodiment of an attempt to address *spiritual relevance* by artistically engaging religious symbolism.

Louis Dupré

The magisterial historical work of Louis Dupré (1993) is helpful in the task of understanding the source of religion's altered status, particularly in reference to the cosmos. His candid and clarifying approach takes aim at a strategic historical crossroad, the early stages of modernity in the 15th,16th and 17th centuries. The value of this research is the fundamental context it sets for understanding the spiritual challenge of the architecture for the new church. Dupré characterizes this early turn towards modernity in Western culture as a gradual *emancipation*, and therefore autonomy, of its three strategic elements:

> Modernity is an *event* that has transformed the relation between the cosmos, its transcendent source, and its human interpreter. To explain this as the outcome of historical precedents is to ignore its most significant quality — namely, its success in rendering all rival views of the real obsolete. (Dupré, 1993, p. 249).

He further describes the historic transformation of each of these three core elements of Western culture. In the modern worldview, the *cosmic* is understood as "the sufficiency of a self supporting cosmos," the human subject moves inexorably to "absolute dominance," the transcendent is "omitted in the meaning-giving process" (Dupré, 1993, p. 251). As he traces this last development, particularly in these its initial stages, he notes "when early humanists placed a new and strong emphasis on human creativity, they added a secondary center to the one traditionally reserved to the transcendent source of power. The philosophy of the subject converted this center into a primary one" (Dupré, 1993, p. 250).

Curiously, in modernism's early phase a poet like Dante could at one and the same time exemplify the new humanism of the movement and yet sustain the traditional religious synthesis. The human and the divine as well as nature and the divine were still together for him. Yet, "he became first and foremost the great poet of the individual" (Dupré, 1993, p. 45). David Tracy suggests that Dante's artistic device was to ground poetic "understandings of human creativity in the divine Word creating ex nihilo" (1998, p. 17). By the time of high

modernity, however, his synthesis would be appreciated as purely (and merely) artistic, not "confessional." The symbols no longer spoke directly. Faith was losing its place in Western culture.

David Tracy

But the fortunes of modernism itself, over the intervening centuries, have also been turbulent. On the one hand, in its high period, it achieved near absolute dominance while on the other, astoundingly, it has become debilitated from withering postmodern critique. Tracy, describing the contemporary situation, characterizes the radical dimension of this postmodern situation. For its adherents, "the death of the subject is now upon us as the last receding wave of the death of God." (1994, p. 3) He spells out how it is that "we live in an age that cannot name itself". (p. 3)

> For modernity, the present is more of the same — the same evolutionary history of the triumph and taken for granted superiority of Western scientific, technological, pluralistic and democratic Enlightenment. For *anti-modernity* … all traditions are being destroyed by the inexorable force of that same modernity.… For *postmodernity*, modernity and tradition alike are now exposed as self-deceiving exercises attempting to ground what cannot be grounded: a secure foundation for all knowledge and life. (1994, p. 3)

While the human subject has been the focus of flourishing intellectual conflicts, any deep sense of the cosmos seems to have been lost to battles between science and religion. Neither science, holding fast to modernist positivism, nor religion, ignoring the relevance of scientific discoveries, has been gaining from those conflicts. This point arises in a study of Dupré's contribution to spirituality. James Wiseman observes that "[w]hile a realization of the vastness and complexity of the universe is by no means inimical to a sense of religious awe … in *fact* it has proven religiously alienating for man [sic]" (1998, p. 178, emphasis mine). Here we could also recall the already famous concluding thought of Steven Weinburg's scientific work, *The First Three Minutes* (1998, p. 154): "The more the universe seems comprehensible, the more it also seems pointless". By way of corrective, Wiseman quotes theologian Gordon Kauff-

Architectural Elements Transforming Sacred Symbols: Ecological/Cosmic "Connectors"

Sacred Space

The Curtain Wall

The basic design of the church is intended to link the traditionally sacred space of the assembled congregation with the traditionally neglected sacred space of the Garden. Rochon (2006, R4) comments: "Rather than creating an introverted experience of worship inspired by stained glass windows, the emphasis has been placed on the mystery of the natural world"

Community

The Narthex and the Living Wall

The Narthex, or meeting space, is spacious and welcoming. Brightly lit by floor to ceiling clear glass, it opens out on an extensive piazza. The parishioners traditionally have been renowned for building relationships and fostering an inclusive spirit. The presence of a very large "living wall," symbol of the rainforest, expands the sense of community to include living nature. The living wall is the first feature of the church that parishioners encounter as they walk up the stairs from the underground parking. Bright and living, it not only purifies the air in the building, but makes this further statement about inclusiveness with the natural world.

man: "Most contemporary theological reflection has almost completely ignored this task (connecting with cosmology, evolution and ecology) and this has contributed substantially to the increasing implausibility of the symbol 'God' in the modern intellectual world" (1998, pp. 178-179). Tracy, however, points to "the urgency of a theological return to cosmological interests. There can be little doubt that the events symbolized by the names Copernicus, Galileo, Newton, and Darwin changed forever the landscape of theological thought" (1994, pp. 73-74).

The Way Ahead

Paradoxically, while Continental philosophy has given us searing deconstructive studies, it has also yielded (at least for some), much more than iconoclasm. Authors such as Heidegger, Kierkegaard, Husserl, Derrida, Marion, Gadamer, and Ricoeur (among many others) have contributed rich resources for more constructive tasks. For instance, a recent volume explores "The Religious Turn in Continental Philosophy" in the work of Richard Kearney, himself a Continental philosopher of religion and student of Ricoeur. The very title of the book is witness to the paradoxes of the present situation. The volume goes under the title *After God* (Manoussakis, 2007). Here the human subject is delivered from the vortex modernism seemed to establish as its fate. Far from nihilism, there is a deep search for ethical expressiveness. Following the lead of Emmanuel Levinas, the subject's authenticity is sought and discovered in encountering the Other. Catherine Keller, in yet another volume exploring the fate of transcendence in contemporary intellectual life, quotes Tamara Cohn Eskenazi regarding the feminist significance of Levinas' turn to the other.

> Levinas dethrones logocentrism in philosophical discourse and replaces it with relation. He constitutes a subject — a self — on the model of connectivity, rather than the dominant patriarchal, separatist object/subject self. He opposes the fusing self of normative Western tradition with one that does not merge/assimilate the other into oneself, but remains, instead, in relation of responsibility. (Keller, 2007, p. 147, ftn. 10)

This development establishes a new context for discussions of transcendence. The Other could also be the Divine Other. This would seem to authenticate indications found in Dupré's work that ultimately, the salvation of the Self would not mean relinquishing the achievement of subjectivity. Rather it would come from deepening and enriching it with a more informed and profound spirituality. On reaching that point, one would be able to shed the rationalistic dimensions of modernity (especially in reference to the transcendent and "ontotheology") in favour of what had been previously thought of (restrictively) as mystical.

St. Gabriel's: A Way Ahead?

Theologian George Schner reflects this imperative when commenting on Dupré's critical study of religious symbols. He points to the artistic (in our case architectural) challenge:

> We encounter a dilemma. The sacred is no longer available from outer sources of piety. Modern women and men cannot take seriously the traditional expressions of the transcendent, do not hold as true or efficacious the narratives and actions of historical religions. Thus, the rediscovery of the transcendent rests interiorly, in the inner self. Yet where and how is that inner self to mediate the transcendent? The problem for contemporary religious art is a good index of this dilemma. Recognition is no longer spontaneous or effective" (Schner, 1998, p. 262).

Despite these obstacles, the design created for St. Gabriel's Church by architect Roberto Chiotti seems to have moved us somewhat closer to meeting the criterion of spontaneity. In the estimation of Lisa Rochon, architecture critic for the *Globe and Mail*,

> St. Gabriel's Church … is an exemplar of high, minimal design supported not by flying buttresses but by its serious grounding in environmental design and placemaking. Step onto the property and it's possible, even if temporarily, to set aside your preconceptions about the Catholic Church. (Rochon, 2006, R4)

Cosmic Allurement: Transformative

Rochon recalls Thomas Berry's spiritual guidance, "To wantonly destroy a living species is to silence forever a Divine voice." Her own critical conclusion about the new structure is that

Architectural Elements Transforming Sacred Symbols: Religious "Connectors" to Ecology/Cosmos

Community

The Worship Space: Nave Earth Community Axis

The worship space, voluminous and bright, also features a seating arrangement that is seldom seen elsewhere. It is "antiphonal": people face each other, with the main ceremonial features — the baptism font, the preaching lectern, and the main altar all in the middle arranged in a north-south axis leading directly to the Garden. Significantly, the Presider's chair is also "among the people" and at the same level. A distinction of functions does not expand into a built hierarchical form.

Religion as "Connector"

Baptism Font Ecologically Sacred Water

Within the Nave

A distinctive element of the Baptism Font is a design that allows water to flow from the basin of the font to a small bed of stones on the nave floor. The water flows constantly. Although traditionally water is intimately tied to the rite of Baptism, an additional emphasis is present here. As ecological consciousness alerts us to the various ways we contaminate our water, this privileged use obviously urges a concern for the water's purity.

In the "Riverbed" Pool

On the south external wall of the Narthex, a modest sized pool with rocks and plants to simulate a riverbed is quite prominent. It is designed to collect the water flowing from a spout high on the wall. This fountain only functions during a rain fall, fed by water on the roof. It has a practical function of tempering storm water flooding as well as providing water for the garden. It is also another "consciousness raising" symbol of our ecological dependency on water.

Architectural Elements Transforming Sacred Symbols: Sacred Space, Community, and Religion as "Connectors"

To Light

Stained Glass Skylights

Perhaps the most striking aspect of the church design is the way it showcases a unique installation of stained glass. Each piece is a strong solid color, without ornament. These skylights line the periphery of the three walls other than the south wall. The changing patterns of color that bathe the bare concrete walls are very arresting and aesthetically beautiful. (This can be seen in a three minute time-lapse video: http://www.thestar.com/videozone/454732 .) The symbolism, however, is linked to the fact that this worship space is "fine tuned" to the sun. The rainbow of color is constantly changing with Earth's positioning towards the sun. Thus the context of every liturgy is actually cosmological. No longer is the religious event detached from either the natural world or cosmos.

To the Earth

The Cosmic Pilgrimage Garden

There are several aspects of the Garden that easily rise to the symbolic. Most of our car parking is underground. The result is that the garage roof becomes a green roof. In addition to being a place of beauty, it is making a statement about reclaiming natural space. The flowers and grasses are chosen for their beauty, but also for their ability to establish a "light footprint" on the land in terms of water consumption. The space is set out in such a way as to provide interesting walking areas and a large circle for resting or meditating. The emergency exit from the underground parking has been enhanced by a mosaic that recreates the final stained glass window of the "Cosmic Stations" in another artistic form. Those Stations, as panels, are distributed along the pathway, to establish a meditative pilgrimage while walking toward the entrance of the church. Very noticeably, the natural Cross, "a honey locust tree, reclaimed from the original church property, with a stump resembling a bowed head and branches splayed outward like suffering arms," (Rochon 2006, R4) is placed in the Garden rather than on the building.

"[r]emembering [Berry's guidance], and attempting to move us one step forward, is what makes St. Gabriel's a miracle" (2006, R4). Christopher Hume, the architecture critic for Toronto's other major newspaper, the *Toronto Star* wrote:

> This extraordinary building ... embodies an approach to the environment that isn't simply religious, it's spiritual.... [It] illustrates and teaches a new cosmology based on respect for the planet.... Essentially, Chiotti has reinvented that most ancient of architectural forms, the church. (Hume, 2007, p. 1)

This reception in the secular press leads me to conclude that the contact between the sacred symbols and the Story of the Universe has been a fruitful one. It seems to be providing an "open" space (especially to the Cosmos) that is firmly stimulating a contemplation of Divine Transcendence in the contemporary setting of the Epic of the Universe. Such reflections are not encumbered by anti-modern elements. (Some heritage items from the former church, including stained glass, find a place in the new structure, but obviously transformed to suit the new space). Nor is the atmosphere rationalistic. Although architecturally it is a "resolutely-Modernist" structure (Phillips, 2007, p. 16), it seems to have taken steps to achieve that sensitivity to the modern so evident in Dupré. It invites an interiority capable of moving ahead with the gains of modernism, yet leaving hope that once again, but in dramatically different terms, "fragments" at least of a cosmos- anthropostheos synthesis can once again sustain a vibrant culture.

Architecturally, this is a church that permits the splendor of the cosmos to speak to us in religious terms while existentially inviting us to engage in the wonders we are constantly discovering in the Epic of Evolution. Brian Swimme and Thomas Berry express that scientific wonder in a very ample way:

> *All the energy that would ever exist in the entire course of time erupted as a single quantum—a singular gift—existence. If in the future, stars would blaze and lizards would blink in their light, these actions would be powered by the same numinous energy that flared forth at the dawn of time.* (Swimme & Berry, 1992, p. 17, italics added)

References

Caputo, J. D., & Scanlon, M. J. (Eds.). (2007). *Transcendence and beyond: A postmodern inquiry*. Bloomington: Indiana University Press.

Casarella, P. J., & Schner, G. P. (Eds.). (1998). *Christian spirituality & the culture of modernity*. Grand Rapids Michigan: William B. Eerdmans Publishing Co.

Dunn, S. & Lonergan, A. (Eds.). (1991). *Befriending the earth*. Mystic: Twenty Third Publications.

Dupré, L. (1987). *Passage to modernity*. New Haven: Yale University Press.

Hume, C. (2007). It's easier being green. *Toronto Star*, Supplement: Doors Open, 5/17/07, p. 1.

Keller, C. (2007). Rumours of transcendence: The movement, state and sex of "beyond". In J. D. Caputo & M. J. Scanlon (Eds.), *Transcendence and beyond: A postmodern inquiry* (pp. 129-150). Bloomington: Indiana University Press.

Kenner, R. (Producer/Director). (2009). *Food, Inc.* [Motion Picture]. New York: Magnolia Home Entertainment.

Lonergan, A. & Richards, C. (Eds.). (1987). *Thomas Berry and the new cosmology*. Mystic: Twenty Third Publications.

Manoussakis, J. P. (Ed.). (2007). *After God*. New York: Fordham Univ. Press

Phillips, R. (2007, June /July). The spirit of Green. *Building*, pp. 15-17.

Rochon, L. (2006). Seeing the light on Sheppard. *Toronto Globe and Mail*, 10/5/06, p. R4.

Schner, G. (1998). Louis Dupré's philosophy of religion: An indispensable discourse on fragments of meaning. In P. J. Casarella & G. P. Schner (Eds.), *Christian spirituality & the culture of modernity* (pp. 225-274). Grand Rapids, MI: Eerdmans Pub.

Swimme, B., & Berry, T. (1992). *The universe story*. San Francisco: Harper.

Taylor, C. (2007). *A secular age*. Cambridge, Massachussetts: Harvard University Press.

Tracy, D. (1994). *On naming the present*. Maryknoll, NY: Orbis Press.

Tracy, D. (1998). Fragments of synthesis? The hopeful paradox of Dupré's modernity. In P. J. Casarella & G. P. Schner (Eds.), *Christian spirituality & the culture of modernity* (pp. 9-24). Grand Rapids, MI: Eerdmans Pub.

Tucker, M. E. (Ed.). (2006). *Evening thoughts: Reflecting on earth as sacred community*. San Francisco: Sierra Club Books.

Weinberg, S. (1998). *The first three minutes: A modern view of the origin of the universe*. New York: Basic Books.

Wiseman, J. (1998). Mystical literature and modern unbelief. In P. J. Casarella & G. P. Schner (Eds.), *Christian spirituality & the culture of modernity* (pp. 176-188). Grand Rapids, MI: Eerdmans Pub.

Additional Photo Credits

Stephen Dunn and commercial renderings (pp. 76 & 77)

Connecting with Nature, Caring for Others

An Ecopsychological Perspective on Positive Youth Development

Julie S. Johnson-Pynn, Laura R. Johnson, & Thomas M. Pynn

Economic expansion, technological advancements, and increases in population rates and mobility have changed the contexts of youth development. Youth's schooling, work, and travel experiences have become increasingly multicultural and global. To understand the ways young people navigate developmental challenges and position themselves in society, we must adopt an ecological systems view of the environmental factors that impact their lives. In this paper, we describe a youth development program rooted in Bronfenbrenner's (2004, pp. 4-17) ecological theory, and draw

from phenomenology to examine the development of youth's connections and caring for nature. A phenomenologically based ecological-psychology proposes that connectivity and an ethic of care arise from reciprocal engagement between the self, others, and the natural world. This viewpoint recognizes youth's capabilities, creative freedom, and mutuality as positive developmental influences on their compassion towards persons and environments. The person-in-environment perspective proposes that the socializing influences of caregivers, teachers, classmates, and neighborhood residents are primary to

development and embedded in cultural values. Attention to socio-cultural factors in different ethnic communities is often emphasized as key to positive youth developmental outcomes (Christiansen, Utas, & Vigh, 2006, pp. 9-28). A convergence of thinking about youth development as agentive and polylithic has been recognized by researchers and practitioners (National Clearinghouse on Families and Youth, 2007, pp. 1-47).

With this perspective in mind, we describe a program rooted in ecopsychological principles and present results on measures of youth development, connection to nature, and program experiences for youth in different cultural contexts.

Julie S. Johnson-Pynn, Ph.D. is an associate professor of psychology at Berry College, a liberal arts college, where she teaches child and adolescent psychology, foundations of education and psychology, and cultural immersion courses in Italy and Tanzania. Her primary research interests are youth civic engagement, environmental education programming, and the influence of cultural contexts on youth development. Julie's research, which has been funded by the Fulbright Foundation and The National Geographic Society, benefits national and international non-governmental organizations with missions to promote conservation, animal welfare, and enrichment of children and youth. She has published articles in the areas of youth development, education, and comparative psychology. Contact: Dept. of Psychology, Berry College, Mt. Berry, GA 30140, Phone: 706.368.5651, Fax: 706.368.6971, jpynn@berry.edu.

Laura R. Johnson, Ph.D., is an associate professor of psychology at the University of Mississippi, where she teaches psychotherapy theories, multicultural psychology, intercultural communication, psychology study abroad, and statistics. Her clinical and research interests reflect a convergence of international, cultural, and conservation psychology perspectives on positive development and civic engagement in youth and emerging adults across diverse contexts. Laura's research is international and interdisciplinary in scope, with a focus on traditionally underserved populations. Laura has published several articles and book chapters related to cultural diversity. She is a former Fulbright Scholar, Peace Corps volunteer and Refugee Mental Health intern, and she currently serves on the American Psychological Association's Committee on International Relations in Psychology. Contact: Dept. of Psychology, University of Mississippi, University, MS 38677, Phone: 662-915-5185, Fax: 662-915-5398, ljohnson@olemiss.edu.

Thomas M. Pynn, M.A. is an assistant professor of philosophy at Kennesaw State University and coordinator of the Peace Studies Program. His research interests include existentialism, phenomenology, comparative philosophy (Buddhism, Daoism, and Yoga), contemporary American poetry, and environmental ethics. His poetry has appeared in VOX, Interdisciplinary Studies in Literature and the Environment, Earth First! Journal, Potlatch: A Creative Arts Journal, and The Chattahoochee Review. His essays have appeared in Buddha Nature and Animality, Asian Texts, Asian Contexts (forthcoming), The Beats and Philosophy, The Southeast Review of Asian Studies, The Virginia Review of Asian Studies. Contact: Dept. of History and Philosophy, Kennesaw State University, Kennesaw GA 30144, Phone: 678-797-2049, Fax: 770-423-6432, tpynn@kennesaw.edu

Positive Youth Development

Adhering to a strengths-based rather than a deficits-based approach to youth development aids in intergenerational understanding because it recognizes the successful practices and strategies that youth invoke on their journey to adulthood. The co-construction of the adult-youth relationship, with all its tensions,

A phenomenological ecopsychology considers the conception of self as central to connectivity to nature.

negotiations, and possibilities, becomes a platform for innovation, creativity, and growth, as we have seen in programs that promote positive youth development (hereafter PYD, Lerner et al., 2005, pp. 10-16). PYD programs nurture youths' capacity to understand their environment and become agents of change. Thus, they are viewed as problem solvers rather than problems to be solved (National Clearinghouse on Children and Youth, 2007, pp. 1-47). PYD emphasizes young people's assets as they build skills, participate in communities, and exercise leadership. When community institutions value youth as resources by offering a supportive framework for exploration and success, the ability of young people to handle stress and overcome adversity is optimized (Flanagan and Faison, 2001, pp. 3-15). Furthermore, PYD programs develop protective factors in youth, enhancing youth identity and resilience by cultivating academic, vocational, and socio-emotional competencies as well as feelings of self worth and a sense of community mindedness and belonging (Catalano et al., 2002, pp. 1-111; Flanagan & Van Horn, 2001, pp. 1-11).

Over the last 30 years, PYD programs have grown dramatically (Lerner et al., 2002, pp. 11-34; Lerner, Fisher and Wein-

berg, 2000a, pp. 11-20). The outcomes of PYD have been framed in terms of the "Six Cs" (Competence, Connection, Confidence, Character, Compassion and Civic Engagement), denoting clusters of individual attributes. These include intellectual and cognitive abilities, social competencies, positive bonds with people and institutions, integrity and moral centeredness, positive self regard and self-efficacy, empathy, social justice values and finally, civic engagement or contribution to society (Lerner, Fisher and Weinberg, 2000b, pp. 24-29). Effective PYD programs provide supportive adult relationships; close relationships with peers; developmentally appropriate activities; opportunities for skill building and mastery; links between families, school and broader community resources; and opportunities to develop confidence through community contributions. While attention towards the socio-cultural factors is key to positive youth development

Roots & Shoots is a positive youth development program rooted in Dr. Jane Goodall's ecopsychological philosophy that promotes connectivity with and caring for the self, the natural world, and the human community.

and the formation of effective youth programs, an ecological systems model also requires attention to the person as immersed in a natural environing system (Kahn & Kellert, 2002, pp. vii-xix; Kahn, 2001, pp. 9-23).

Nature's role in positive youth development, however, has been largely absent. This is surprising given threats to the natural environments that youth will inherit. Children and adolescents account for 39% of the world's population of nearly 6 billion, and most of the approximately one billion children who will be born in the next decade will reside

in developing nations with substantial poverty (Population Resource Center, 2005, pp. 1-32). Though population rates are on the rise, natural resources are dwindling. Hence, providing youth with a sustainable means of living in contexts with novel environmental pressures is a major concern. Integrating ecopsychological perspectives into PYD efforts is appropriate and timely given the concerns facing youth and the natural world.

Many youth are disconnected from nature, which may result in poor physical health; and, as ecopsychologists assert, psychological distress, such as feelings of alienation from nature, denial of environmental problems, fear and anxiety, and existential angst (Louv, 2008, pp. 71-85). Regaining a sense of connectivity to nature, often through direct contact with nature, is healing for youth and the environment (Kahn, 1997, pp. 1-61; Myers Jr. & Saunders, 2002, pp. 153-178). From a behavioral perspective, the natural world presents an important and, we argue, an increasingly essential learning context for youth to grow developmental assets. Nature, with its diverse, aesthetic, and responsive/interactive qualities, provides a unique and ideal platform for youth to learn

life lessons that build compassion, self efficacy, and sense of purpose (Chawla 2008; Kellert, 2002, pp. 117-152). Our previous research findings demonstrated that youth's positive attitudes towards nature and their care and concern for each other were stimulated by direct contact with nature, particularly visits to national parks and wildlife sanctuaries (Johnson-Pynn & Johnson, 2005a, pp. 25-40).

Ecopsychology represents a converging of interests from philosophy, psychology and ecology that focus on the human-nature relationship and the implications

The authors gratefully acknowledge the U.S. Fulbright Foundation and the National Geographic Society for grants that supported this work. We would also like to thank, Rebecca Hamblin, Herieth Balagaye, Claire Bangirani and Robert Martin for their assistance in data collection and analysis, and Jeanne McCarty, Shawn Sweeney, Elan Wang and Betsy McWhirt, of the Jane Goodall Institute, for their cooperation with this research.

of this relationship for the psychological and physical health of humans and the environment. Ecopsychology is rooted in the philosophy of human-nature interrelatedness. Similar to an ecological-systems perspective of human development (see Bronfenbrenner, 2004, pp. 4-20), a phenomenologically informed ecopsychology describes how humans are inextricably connected to their natural environment in a synergistic relationship, fragile tension with the totality of their respective environments. This conception of self is a shift from an ego-logical self to an eco-logical self. Ecopsychology calls for a paradigm shift in the way we motivate pro-environmental action--from reactive responses based on fear, denial, coercion, shame, and blame, to thoughtful actions of conservation and restoration motivated by devotion and care. The promotion of positive attitudes nities or the natural world, bolster ethical reasoning capacities, and foster empathic understanding (Bowdon, Billig & Holland, 2008, pp. ix-xix; Eyler & Giles, 1999, pp. 5-10; Giles & Eyler, 1994, pp. 77-85). Studies on service learning have demonstrated that young people perceive themselves as agents of socialization, seeking to establish just societies, their civic participation being motivated by a sense of idealism and belief in a just world (Guessous & Watts, 2005).

Roots & Shoots: A Global Youth Program Based on Jane Goodall's Ecopsychological Vision and Service-Learning Pedagogy

Roots & Shoots (hereafter R&S) is a positive youth development program rooted in Dr. Jane Goodall's ecopsychological philosophy that promotes connectivity with and caring for the self, the natural world, and the human community. R&S grew out of Dr. Jane Goodall's efforts to improve conditions for wild chimpanzees at her study site in East Africa. Dr. Goodall began R&S by teaching a group of high school students from Tanzania about conservation issues that were affecting their community (Johnson-Pynn & Pynn 2003, p. 142). For Goodall, the scientific and the spiritual are not mutually exclusive. Rather, they are different windows from which to view the world. She writes, "For those who have experienced the joy of being alone with nature, there is really little need for me to say much more; for those who have not, no words of mine can ever describe the powerful, almost mystical knowledge of beauty and eternity that come, suddenly, and unexpected" (Goodall, 1999, p. 170). Goodall asserts that an understanding of the interconnectedness of the natural world comes when one observes with mind and heart.

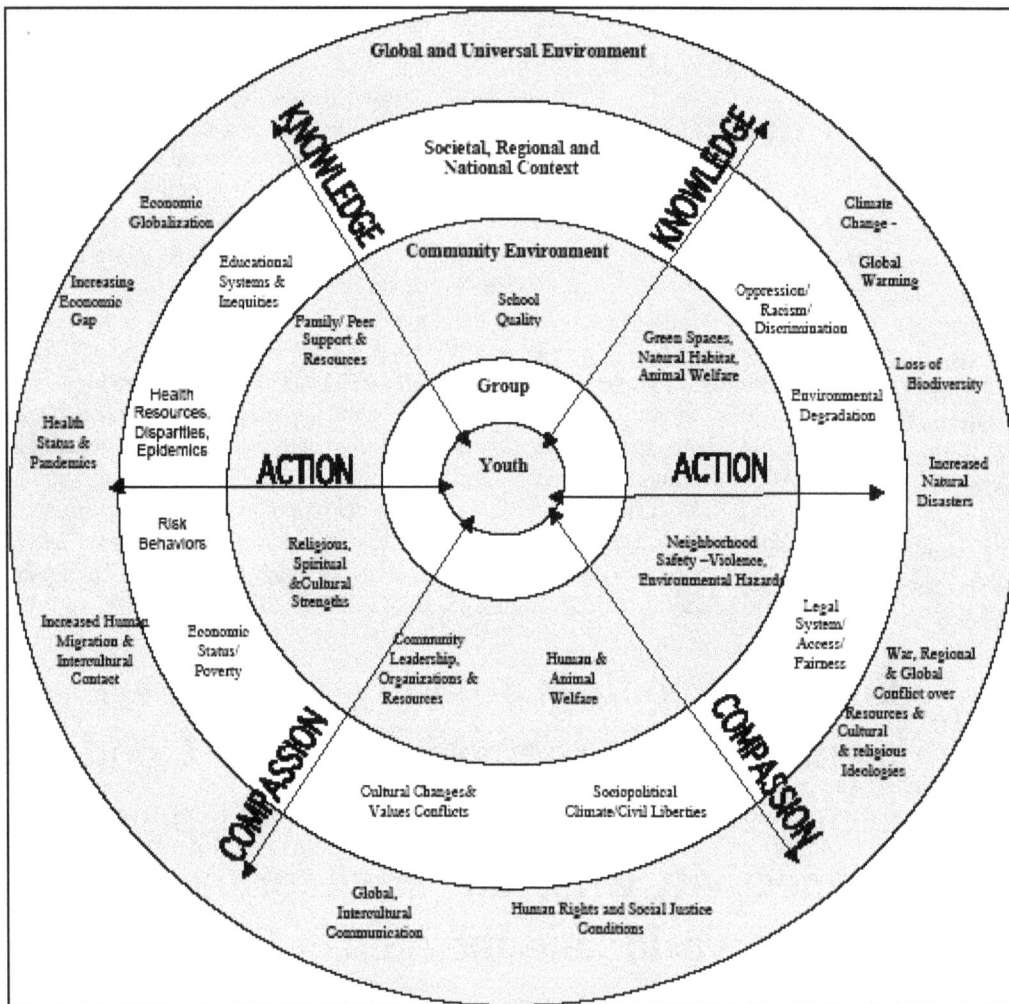

Figure 1. Roots & Shoots encourages knowledge, compassion, and action across multiple ecological contexts of youth development.

such that the health of one impacts the health of the other. Contrary to the dominant Western scientific and religious hierarchical view of humans over nature, humans can no longer conceptualize themselves as divorced from nature. A phenomenological ecopsychology considers the conception of self as central to connectivity to nature. An ecological self envisions the biosphere as an ensemble of relations operating as a whole living system in which organisms are held in a and self-determination are motivating factors in the formulation of solutions to environmental problems (Pelletier, 2002, pp. 205-232).

In the environmental education domain, individuals are likely to form positive attitudes towards the environment in service learning based pedagogy. Broadly stated, service learning takes place through students' active participation in culturally meaningful activities that are designed to connect to commu-

Likewise, when individuals from diverse cultures and religious backgrounds are accepted on their own terms, common bonds rather than superficial differences, are recognized. Consideration of others' perspectives and working to achieve compromise are characteristics of Goodall's cultural orientation-- one that conceives of the world as an intricate web of relationships.

The R&S program mission is to foster by community needs. The R&S pedagogical model fosters knowledge, compassion, and action in projects across multiple ecological contexts (see Figure 1). While youth are encouraged to address local concerns through community needs assessments in neighborhoods and schools, R&S is increasingly providing support for youth partnering at national and global levels. Global networking sites promote collective activeries in Tanzania and to plant trees in the U.S. The Peace Dove Campaign, which coincides with the annual United Nations International Day of Peace, is a celebration in which R&S members from diverse cultural backgrounds fly peace dove puppets constructed from recycled materials (see Figure 2). The Tchimpounga Sanctuary Campaign, initiated by the U.S. R&S youth leadership council, highlights care and concern for animals across borders by aiming to rebuild an animal orphanage that houses chimpanzees in the Democratic Republic of Congo.

Researching PYD From an Ecological Perspective

Since 2000, we have conducted research on R&S school-based programs by interviewing and surveying R&S members, sponsoring teachers, and program coordinators, with a primary focus on Africa, where R&S began, and China, one of the latest sites for R&S programs. An important ecological factor that distinguished R&S members from Africa and China was the perceived impact of R&S participation on academic performance. In China, youth voiced their view that pressure to succeed on national exams (intensified by national entrance exams for university and family pressure to succeed arising from the One Child Policy) was a major concern. Participation in R&S activities was often hampered by study time (Johnson, Johnson-Pynn & Pynn, 2007, pp. 355-386). In contrast, R&S participation was seen as adding to academic success by both students and teachers in Africa, probably because R&S offered opportunities for gaining knowledge and acquiring skills that were more immediately useful. (Johnson & Johnson-Pynn, 2007, pp. 1-14).

Recently, 100 youth leaders from 28 countries were brought together for Jane Goodall's Global Youth Summit, in which youth developed action plans on environmental issues of shared concern, including water, poverty, social conflict, and wildlife conservation. We explored the R&S learning model through participant observation, key informant interviews, and analysis of youth's journals. Table 1 depicts some of the themes derived from content analysis of these

Response domain of the learning model	Content from qualitative data sources	Themes derived from content
Knowledge	Interconnectedness of environment/humans/animals Community/local environmental issues National environmental issues Global environmental concerns Social costs of consumerism and development to natural environment, species diversity, and human community	Youth learned of issues facing the environment and humans both at local and global levels. Youth mentioned learning about interconnection between the environment, humans, and animals, such as a loss of species diversity that comes from development's effects on the loss of habitat. "Roots & Shoots has made me more aware of various local or world issues that have an effect on many groups. I know now the severity of these problems."
Action	Be more active in community Make a difference in the future Help with future project planning Be more environmentally conscious Set and achieve goals Inspire/teach/lead Conserve resources Collaborate with others	Youth reported taking action by helping others through projects or helping the environment by conserving resources. They set goals for the future, planned to be more active in the community, and participate in project planning. Many desired to be more environmentally conscious. Youth inspired, taught, and led others. "It makes me want to take a stand to make a change. I want also to tell my peers about it {R&S} so together we can make this change happen."
Compassion	Care for environment Care for world/other cultures Care for other R&S groups Feeling interconnected with others Changed attitude Sense of purpose and hope	Youth came to care for environment, for others, and for their communities. They felt a sense of interconnectedness with others and with other R&S groups. They experienced a sense of compassion for other cultures and in general, reported a changed attitude toward diverse groups of people. "In a small community, it is easy to feel like we are the only group working for environmental protection. Roots & Shoots truly opened my eyes to the overwhelming number of people and groups like us around the country and world. It showed us that there is hope!"

Table 1. Content analysis from youth's interviews and journals indicates effectiveness of the Roots & Shoots program's service learning model.

respect and compassion for the natural world, living beings and cultures by bringing dedicated young people together to design and participate in service projects. Youth engagement is maximized because projects are driven by youth's interests and abilities as well as ism that spans communities such as three global campaigns that are focused on R&S's three project areas: the environment, animal, and human communities. ReBirth the Earth began after US youth visited Tanzanian youth and were inspired to raise funds to build tree nurs-

data sources along with representative quotations from members that pertained to the R&S knowledge-action-compassion pedagogy model. Self efficacy, or the belief in one's ability to effect change and devise and meet goals, emerged as a

on the R&S page of The Jane Goodall Institute's website. R&S members came from: Tanzania, the United States, Canada, Qatar, Australia, China, Singapore, Germany, South Korea, Taiwan, Denmark, Japan, New Zealand, and the

petency in this area improved in Tanzanian members with more schooling and hours of weekly R&S service performed, suggesting the important confluence of service and academics on cognitive competencies.

Emergent response domain	Content from several qualitative data sources	Themes derived from content
Self-efficacy	Sociability/extroversion Capable Self-esteem Improved/changed life outlook Self-awareness Belief I can make a difference Become a better listener, leader, and teacher How to take action/initiative Lifestyle change Proud of actions Problem solving Speak out	Youth reported a change in their life outlook as a result of their participation in Roots & Shoots. Youth cited changes in their self-esteem and self-awareness. Several cited improved cognitive and interpersonal skills such as teaching, leading, or listening. Because of participation in Roots & Shoots, youth came to believe that they could make a difference. "I feel, through my R&S experience, that I can make a difference and that it is important for me to do so. I have gained both a sense of optimism and realism by analyzing problems and forming the best solutions."

Table 2. Self efficacy, or the belief in one's ability to achieve goals, emerged as a dominant theme in youth's interviews and journals.

dominant theme (See Table 2).

Our current research incorporates quantitative measures to assess program outcomes. Using the 6 Cs of PYD as a framework, we provide a description of the measures intended to assess ecopsychological correlates of the R&S program's service learning outcomes: Competence (cognitive, such as planning, organizing and critical thinking and social, such as cooperation and negotiation); Confidence (self efficacy and a sense of purpose); Connections (positive feelings towards people and nature), Caring (sense of social responsibility); Character (commitment to humanitarian values) and Civic Engagement (commitment to ongoing social action) along with some illustrative results from participants who completed the compilation of measures in our Global Youth Survey. Youth were recruited from school-based groups, leadership summits, a refugee camp in Western Tanzania, and a link

Philippines.

Competence

The Civic Attitudes and Skills Questionnaire (Moely et al., 2002, pp. 15-26) contains items in six subscales including: Interpersonal and Problem-Solving Skills - abilities to listen, work cooperatively, communicate, take the role of the other, and think logically (e.g., "I can work cooperatively with a group of people"); Leadership Skills- abilities to lead and effectiveness as a leader (e.g., "I am a good leader"); and, Political Awareness - of local and national events and political issues (e.g., "I am knowledgeable of the issues facing the world"). The three samples, Tanzania, U.S., and Multi-national, were similar in that they reported greater interpersonal problem solving skills compared to leadership skills and political awareness. Although political awareness was the lowest of the subscales in all three groups, com-

Confidence

The Hope Scale reflects: 1) a person's sense of agency, or belief in one's self and one's abilities to sustain goal-oriented action; and 2) pathways, or one's competency in solving problems and facing challenges en route to these goals (Snyder, 1995, pp. 355-360). It includes items such as, "I energetically pursue my goals" and "There are lots of ways around any problem." In the Tanzanian sample, members whose groups were based in the Lugufu refugee camp, scored higher on both subscales compared to members from groups in urban and other rural locations in Tanzania. This finding could be attributed to refugee members' resiliency in surviving conflict and displacement coupled with perceptions of their accomplishments in serving the refugee community.

The General Self-Efficacy Scale (Schwarzer & Jerusalem, 1995, pp. 35-37) assesses the degree to which participants feel they can set and attain goals. It includes items such as "It is easy for me to stick to my aims and accomplish my goals." Similar to The Hope Scale, Tanzanian refugees scored higher than all other members. Generally, youth residing in rural areas scored lower in self efficacy than those from urban areas; this result could be attributed to frustration experienced by youth in rural locations when projects had to be discontinued due to lack of resources or when their sponsoring teachers were relocated to distant schools, a common governmental practice in many developing countries.

Connections

The Connectedness to Nature Scale (Mayer & Frantz, 2004, pp. 503-515) is a measure of emotional connectedness with the natural world, with items such as, "I often feel a part of the web of life" or reverse coded items such as, "My personal welfare is independent of the welfare of the natural world." The youth we surveyed did not differ in their overall feelings of connectivity to the natural world; however, there were some differences in some of the scale's items. Members from the Multi-national sample reported a deeper understanding of how their actions affected the natural world compared to U.S. groups. This might be because members' agrarian livelihoods are noticeably dependent on the land; while U.S. members, especially those from urban areas, are insulated from the negative effects humans have caused to the environment. The U.S. sample reported that they recognized and appreciated the intelligence of other living organisms more than the Multi-national sample, but also they considered themselves to be at the top of the nature hierarchy. Overall, females reported being more connected to nature than males. Females rated a sense of kinship with other animals and plants highly; whereas, males indicated that the natural world was a larger community to which they belonged.

Caring

The Interpersonal Motivation Scale (Jimenez & Park, 2006) measures compassion, defined as affective, cognitive and behavioral response motivated by connection to others and awareness of another's suffering. The scale measures a person's orientation towards others, including altruism (helping), empathy (ability to take another's perspective), and ethic of care and concern. It includes items such as, "I am likely to extend understanding and sensitivity toward someone in pain" and "I am usually the first to notice when someone is in physical or emotional pain." Similar to the connections measures, females were more compassion oriented compared to males.

Character

Two additional subscales on the Civic Attitudes and Skills Questionnaire concern an individual's character: Social Justice Attitudes concerns causes of

Figure 2. Italian Roots & Shoots members fly a peace dove in the village piazza. These youth participate in service projects that benefit an orphanage in Tanzania, East Africa. Photo: Julie S. Johnson-Pynn.

poverty and misfortune and how social problems can be solved (e.g. a reverse coded item, "People are poor because they choose to be poor") and Diversity Attitudes, which concerns relating to culturally different people (e.g. "I enjoy meeting people who come from backgrounds very different from my own"). Tanzanian youth valued diverse cultures and work for social justice more so than youth from the U.S.; and, amongst the Tanzanian sample, youth residing in urban locals reported higher scores on these subscales compared to youth residing in rural locations and the refugee camp. Perhaps this is because youth from the urban locals are in schools on the Swahili coast, which has a long history of settlement and trade from peoples of African, Arabic, and European cultures. Lower scores from the refugee sample could be due to social tensions that arise between locals and refugees, such as competition for resources and differing cultural traditions. Higher scores on these subscales were positively related to age, number of years of school, and

tenure in their R&S group, which suggests that the R&S program, coupled with academic activities, does influence the development of character that appreciates diverse viewpoints and recognizes their importance to civic life.

Civic Engagement

The final scale on the Civic Attitude and Skills Questionnaire measures civic engagement, Civic Action - intentions to become involved in community service or action (e.g. "I plan to become involved in my community"). Civic action was the second highest rated subscale for youth, after interpersonal problem solving skills, underscoring a chief benefit of R&S-- that all youth feel like they have important responsibilities, supporting the notion that R&S's service learning model is powerful to individuals no matter where their groups are based.

The Eco-logical Self

The intertwined concerns of moral and spiritual growth, service behavior, and connection with the natural world reported by youth in R&S programs, show the extent to which ecologically structured environmental education programs encourage and develop living bonds with others. Caring for others, both human and non-human, in service-based learning projects demonstrate that an ecological approach connects strands of cultural and natural life-worlds. Our research suggests that as relatedness and responsiveness to human and non-human, or the eco-logical self, grows in importance, the alienated ego-logical self dissipates. Examining identity developmental constructs, like the eco-logical self, is necessary to understand how youth develop an ethic of care towards the environment, motivation for pro-environmental behaviors, and conviction for environmental activism. In our future research, we hope to explore the relationships between developmental constructs, such as ethnicity, environmental identity, and collective efficacy. Nonetheless, our findings demonstrate that positive developmental programs, like R&S, enhance youth's connectedness to nature and optimize their capacity to create effective and sustainable solutions to the social and environmental challenges they face now, and will face in the future.

References

Belar, C. (2007). Sustained efforts for sustainability. *Monitor 38*, no. 2 (March), http://www.apa.org/monitor/mar07/soe.html (accessed March 7, 2007).

Bowdon, M., Billig, S. H., & Holland, B. A. (2008). *Scholarship for sustaining service learning and civic engagement*. Charlotte, NC: Information Age Publishing.

Bronfenbrenner, U. (2004). *Making human beings human: Bioecological perspectives on human development*. Thousand Oaks, CA: Sage Publications.

Catalano, R. F., Berglund, L. M., Ryan, J. A. M., Lonczak, H. S., & Hawkins, D. J. (2002). Positive youth development in the United States: Research findings on evaluations of positive youth development programs. *Prevention & Treatment 5*(15), http://a:/pre0050015a.htm (accessed September 12, 2005).

Chalwa, L. (2008). Growing up green: Developing agency to care for the natural world. Paper presented at the annual convention of the American Psychological Association, August 2008 in Boston, MA.

Christiansen, C., Matas U., & Vigh, H. (2006). *Navigating youth generating adulthood: Social becoming in an African context*. Uppsala: Nordiska Afrikainstitutet.

Eyler, J. (2000). Studying the impact of service-learning on students. *Michigan Journal of Community Service Learning, Special Issue*, 11-18.

Eyler, J., & Giles, D. E. (1999). *Where's the learning in service learning?* San Francisco, CA.: Jossey-Bass, Inc.†

Flanagan, C. A., & Faison, N. (2001). Youth civic development: Implications of research for social policy and programs. *Social Policy Report, 15*, 3-15.

Flanagan, C., & Van Horn, B. (2001). Youth civic engagement: Membership and mattering in local communities. *Focus, 1*, 1-11.

Giles Jr., D. E., & Eyler, J. (1994). The theoretical roots of service-learning in John Dewey: Toward a theory of service-learning. *Michigan Journal of Community Service Learning, 1*, 77-85.

Goodall, J. (1999). *Reason for hope: A spiritual journey*. New York: Soko Publications.

Guessous, O., & Watts, R. J. (2005). A model of youth sociopolitical development: Empowerment, ethno racial identity, and opportunity structures. Paper presented at the Society for Research in Child Development Conference, April 2005, in Atlanta, GA.

Jimenez, S. & Park, C. L. (2006). Interpersonal motivation scale: Validation of a compassion measure. Paper presented at the American Psychological Association Convention, August 2006, in New Orleans, LA.

Johnson, L. R., Johnson-Pynn, J. S., & Thomas Pynn, T. (2007). Youth civic engagement in China: Results from a program promoting environmental activism. *Journal of Adolescent Research, 22*, 355-386.

Johnson, L. R., & Johnson-Pynn, J. S. (2007). Cultivating compassion and youth action around the globe: a preliminary report on Jane Goodall's Roots and Shoots program for youth. *Journal of Youth Development: Bridging Research and Action, 5*, 1-14.

Johnson-Pynn, J. S., & Johnson, L. R. (2005a). Successes and challenges in East African conservation education. *The Journal of Environmental Education, 36*, 25-40.

Johnson-Pynn, J. S., & Johnson, L. R. (2005b). The Jane Goodall Institute's Roots & Shoots program: Bettering the lives of East African youth and their ecology. *Journal of Ethics in Leadership, 1*, 17-31.

Johnson-Pynn, J. S., & Pynn, T. (2003). Jane Goodall. In L. Baines & D. McBrayer (Eds.), *How to get a life: Empowering wisdom for the heart and soul* (Vol. 1, pp. 136-149). Atlanta, GA: Humanics.

Kahn, Jr., P. H. (1997). Developmental psychology and the biophilia hypothesis: Children's affiliation with nature. *Developmental Review, 17*, 1-61.

Kahn, Jr., P. H. & Kellert, S. R. (Eds.). (2002). *Children and nature: Psychological, sociocultural, and evolutionary investigations*. Cambridge, MA: MIT Press.

Kahn, Jr., P. H. (2001). *The human relationship with nature*. MA: MIT Press.

Kaufman, Natalie. H., & Rizzini, I. (Eds.). (2002). *Globalization and children: Exploring potentials for enhancing opportunities in the lives of children and youth*. NY: Kluwer Academic/ Plenum Publishers.

Kellert, S. R. (2002). Experiencing nature: Affective, cognitive, and evaluative development in children. In P. H. Khan & S. R. Kellert (Eds.), *Children and nature: Psychological, sociocultural, and evolutionary investigations* (pp. 117-152). Cambridge, MA: MIT Press.

Lerner, R. M., Almerigi, J. B., Theokas, C., & Lerner, J. V. (2005). Positive youth development: A view of the issues. *Journal of Early Adolescence, 25*, 10-16.

Lerner, R. M., Brentano, C., Dowling, E. M., & Anderson, P. M. (2002). Positive youth development: Thriving as the basis of pesonhood and civil society. In R. M. Lerner, C. S. Taylore, & A. von Eye (Eds.), *New directions for youth development: Pathways to positive development among diverse youth* (pp. 11-34). San Francisco, CA: Jossey-Bass.

Lerner, Richard M., Celia B. Fisher, and Richard A. Weinberg. (2000a). Toward a science for and of the people: Promoting civil society through the application of developmental science. *Child Development, 71*, 11-20.

Lerner, R. M., Fisher, C. B., & Weinberg, R. A. (2000b). Applying developmental science in the 21st century: International scholarship for our times. *International Journal of Behavioral Development, 24*, 24-29.

Louv, R. (2008.) *Last Child in the Woods: Saving Our Children from Nature Deficit Disorder*. Chapel Hill, NC: Algonquin Books.

Mayer, F. S., & Frantz, C. M. (2004). The connectedness to nature scale: A measure of individuals' feeling in community with nature. *Journal of Environmental Psychology 24*, 503-515.

Moely, B. E., Mercer, S. H., Illustre, V., Miron, D., & McFarland, M. (2002). Psychometric properties and correlates of the civic attitude and skills questionnaire (CASQ): A measure of students' attitudes related to service-learning. *Michigan Journal of Community Service Learning, 8*, 15-26.

Myers, Jr., O. E., & Saunders, C. D. (2002). Animals as links toward developing caring relationships with the natural world. In P. Kahn & S. R. Kellert (Eds.), *Children and nature: Psychological, sociocultural, and evolutionary investigations* (pp. 117-152). Cambridge, MA: MIT Press.

National Clearing House on Families and Youth for the Family Services. (2007). *Putting positive youth development into practice*. National Clearing House on Families and Youth for the Family Services Bureau, Silverspring, MD.

Pelletier, L. G. (2002). A motivational analysis of self-determination for pro-environmental behaviors. In E. L. Deci & R. M. Ryan (Eds.), *Handbook of self-determination research* (pp. 205-232). Rochester, NY: University of Rochester Press.

Population Resource Center. (2005). *Providing the demographic dimension of public policy, 2005 Annual report*. http://www.prcd.org/html/annual-reports.html.

Schwarzer, R., & Jerusalem, M.. (1995). Generalized Self-Efficacy Scale. In J. Weinman, S. Wright, & M. Johnston (Eds.), *Measures in health psychology: A user's portfolio. Causal and control beliefs* (pp. 35-37). Windsor, UK: Nfer-Nelson.

Snyder, C. R., (1995). Hope: Theory, measurement, and interventions. *Journal of Counseling and Development, 73*, 355-360.

Ecocognition

Decision and Understanding in Environmental Context

Matthew J. Sharps & Adam B. Hess

C onsiderations of environmental issues, in general, focus on group behavior. This is logical and unsurprising; it is in groups that people have the greatest influence on their environment. Yet groups are composed of individuals. Even though individuals are socially influenced to a massive degree, they make decisions in their individual human minds. This consideration is important, as it leads directly to a new and productive way of framing environmental considerations. This is environmental cognitive psychology, ecocognition for short: the study of the intellectual processes by which people arrive at their environmental decisions, attitudes, and ideas.

Matthew J. Sharps (PhD, University of Colorado) teaches cognitive psychology, cognitive neuroscience, and the history of psychology at California State University, Fresno. He served as an NIH research associate at the University of Colorado. His teaching credits include Alliant International University, the University of Wyoming, Fresno Pacific University, and invited lectures at Stanford and Stockholm Universities. He is the author of numerous publications and presentations, as well as the book *Aging, Representation, and Thought: Gestalt and Feature-Intensive Processing* (Transaction Publishers, 2003) and the book *Processing under Pressure: Stress, Memory, and Decision Making in Law Enforcement* (Looseleaf Law Publications, 2010). Correspondence concerning this article should be addressed to M. J. Sharps.

Research in environmental psychology, even on environmental education, has to date had little ecocognitive focus. Such a focus is needed.

Consider the realm of environmental education. Education about environmental issues is crucially important, and should hold a high priority in the formulation of national and international environmental policy (e.g., Salmon 2000; Lawton, 1997). Yet environmental education per se has generally, with few exceptions, yielded relatively modest or even minimal effects on actual human behavior (e.g., Dwyer, Leeming, Cobern, Porter, & Jackson, 1993). Why have

Adam B. Hess earned a PhD in Forensic Psychology from Alliant International University in Fresno, California. He works at Sierra Education & Research Institute (SERI) to provide mental health services to at risk populations. Adam is the Coordinator of Behavioral Health at the Fresno County Juvenile Justice Campus (JJC). At the JJC, Adam has developed a treatment program for the high security units dealing with youth that display a pattern of marked behavioral disruptions. In addition, Adam is an adjunct lecturer in the department of Criminology at California State University, Fresno where he teaches undergraduate courses such as The Psychology of Crime and Juvenile Delinquency. His research interests include forensic cognition, eyewitness identification, and ecological and environmental cognitive psychology. Contact Matthew Sharps: Dept. of Psychology, California State University, Fresno, MS- ST- 11, 2576 E. San Ramon, Fresno, CA 93740-8039, matthew_sharps@csufresno.edu, (559) 278-2347.

well-designed educational programs not met with more success?

"Saving the Earth"

In real-world human cognition, there is a tendency to consider any given phenomenon in gestalt rather than feature-intensive terms (Sharps, 2003; Sharps & Nunes, 2002); in other words, we tend to focus on the general gist of an idea, neglecting more detailed, feature-by-feature analysis which might yield a clearer picture (e.g., Sharps & Martin, 2002; see also Dörner, 1996). For example, in the consideration of environmental issues, it is often said that "the Earth" is "in trouble" (e.g., Gillespie, 2007), due to human agency in such unquestionable areas as air and water pollution, and in well-documented realms such as global warming and the looming extinction of food fish stocks (e.g., Burkholder et al., 2007; Elgin, 2007; Gentile, 2007; Kohn, 2007; Perkins, 2007; Dean, 2006; Stokstad, 2006; Baum et al., 2003). This idea of "the Earth in trouble" is a gestalt consideration; the broad semantic system characterized as "the Earth" conceals a plethora of detail which is not explicitly in evidence in the thought of this gestalt system's being "in trouble." A more detailed, "feature-intensive" consideration (Sharps, 2003) reveals that this gestalt platitude is not only oversimplified, but may in fact be misleading for the cognitive processing which ultimately leads to environmental policy. Considered from a more "feature-intensive" perspective, the Earth per se, as a planet and as the vessel for a continually shifting, dynamic and interlocking set of ecosystems, is hardly likely to be destroyed as the result of human depredations. Nor are we likely to be able to exterminate life on this planet. Life in many forms, the majority of which are no longer extant, predated us; nothing in paleohistory suggests that life would not continue after us, in admittedly unpredictable ways. This planet, together with its cargo of mutable life, weathered the Permian extinction, the Cretaceous/Tertiary event, and the climactic see-saw of the Pleistocene ice ages and interstadials. Such global catastrophes, so to speak, outweigh us, outweigh our human influence; yet the Earth, as a constantly changing planetary system, has repeatedly survived them.

In short, the Earth as a planet is not in trouble; we are. More specifically, our activities as a species may place in

We tend to focus on the general gist of an idea, neglecting more detailed, feature-by-feature analysis which might yield a clearer picture.

jeopardy the current state and conditions of the planet, and of the planet's living cargo, *as we prefer or require that state and those conditions to remain* in order to sustain our lives and our lifestyles. Subjectively, one might sense equal measures of despair and perverse pride in our perceived ability to "save the Earth" or to destroy it, but, as the novelist Michael Crichton wrote, "Let's be clear. The planet is not in jeopardy. We are in jeopardy. We haven't got the power to destroy the planet — or to save it. But we might have the power to save ourselves" (1990, p. 369).

Thus, we tend to think about environmental issues in gestalts, rather than in more careful, feature-intensive terms. We may therefore arrive at oversimplified or even erroneous conclusions. A gestalt focus on "saving the Earth" is unlikely to generate useful solutions to specific environmental problems. However, a more feature-intensive focus on specific aspects of our living conditions, or on our relationships to desirable or undesirable species in our environments, is much more likely to yield what Wertheimer (1982) termed "productive thinking," cognition likely to generate useful and creative results.

But how is this to be done? In brief, how can we make ourselves smarter in our environmental deliberations?

Chunking and Gestalts in Environmental Cognition

When we use a term such as "the Earth" as a gestalt, in broad reference to the cognitive construct of ourselves, our lifestyles, and those extant species which we find desirable, we are engaging in "chunking," or inclusion by *category* (see Miller, 1956). This process, known since antiquity and considered by scholars from Aristotle to Wittgenstein (e.g., Lakoff, 1987), is crucially important to virtually all forms of human cognition (e.g., Miller, 1956; Rosch, 1973; Lakoff, 1987). Chunking allows us to function, efficiently and in many important everyday domains. We are able to say "Would you like a drink?" to a guest without having to list the contents of the refrigerator or the cellar; the guest can recognize that "drink" refers to a category of things which are reasonably drinkable, as opposed to, say, pieces of furniture or glasses of antifreeze.

Yet the salutary processes of chunking and categorization have a negative side, discussed in detail by Lakoff (e.g., 1987). Chunking makes it possible to ignore vital subsidiary information and crucial details; in short, it allows us to obviate feature-intensive processing. For example, a person might believe in the

A gestalt focus on "saving the Earth" is unlikely to generate useful solutions to specific environmental problems.

gestalt category of constructs labeled under the rubric "overpopulation is bad for the Earth" without reference to the numbers of his or her own progeny, or to their probable quality of life in an overpopulated future.

In many environmental areas, of course, the average person is unlikely even to be aware of the problems involved, to possess the knowledge which would form the relevant chunks; he or she would have to have training and reasonable access to the scientific literature to have the relevant information available in mind, and consequently to consider it and act on it, chunked or not. Therefore, for situations in which the average person is simply unaware of relevant facts, the solution seems clear: education. People must be informed about environmental issues, as efficaciously as possible. This is, of course, the intent and thrust of environmental education programs.

Yet, as discussed above, such programs have typically influenced human behaviors to a relatively modest degree. We are still faced with the question of why this has been the case for the many sophisticated and salutary efforts at environmental education that have been developed (e.g., Dwyer, Leeming, Cobern, Porter, & Jackson, 1993; Kempton, Harris, Keith, & Weil, 1985; Syme, Seligman, Kantola, & MacPherson, 1987).

To begin to answer this question, let us consider situations in which the availability of technical knowledge is not a problem at all. The issue of overpopulation mentioned above provides a good example. In this situation, *the availability of information for the given individual is very unlikely to be the problem.* Granted, overpopulation is seldom discussed in the majority of public venues, including those directly concerned with environmental issues (e.g., MacLeish,

1994). This is oddly true even though the vast majority of environmental ills could be reduced or eliminated through a conscientious world-wide drive toward a gradual, sustainable, rational reduction of population (see McDougall (2006) regarding world population).

However, regardless of the perplexing human or societal tendency not to discuss the importance of overpopulation (e.g., MacLeish, 1994; McDougall, 2006) in most public venues, it is certainly the case that the existence of overpopulation is known to most literate adults in the Western world. Furthermore, it is vanishingly unlikely that anybody is unaware of the existence or numbers of the children they have knowingly produced. Now, it is obvious how information we do not possess can fail to influence our behavior; but how can information of which we are fully and knowingly in possession fail to do so, as in the case of overpopulation?

Relevant Context

The context of a given decision includes the pertinent knowledge that is directly or indirectly present in the mind, and the ways in which that knowledge is arranged. These factors have long been known to be important for successful reasoning. The Gestalt psychologists (e.g., Wertheimer, 1982; Kohler, 1947; also see Sharps & Wertheimer, 2000) showed that if the context of a cognitive task is understood, "productive," meaningful solutions will be forthcoming; if not, solutions are likely to be "mindless," wrong or too narrow to be useful (Wertheimer, 1982). In other words, information relevant to a given cognitive task must be immediately available in the task context to be useful.

The salutary effects of immediately-available information have been repeatedly demonstrated, given proper arrangement of the information in question. Bransford and Johnson (1973) rendered virtually incomprehensible passages of text comprehensible, and memorable, by means of guiding or organizing pictures or relevant simple phrases made available just prior to passage presentation. Such simple contextual information is most effective when it can be related to

Information must be present in the proximate context of the decision, immediately available in working memory, in order to be effective.

previous ideas (Kieras, 1978); to ideas still available in short term memory (Lesgold, Roth, & Curtis, 1979) at the time of decision (note, here, the importance of immediacy again); and when the relevant ideas have direct, noninferential, explicit linkage to the concepts needed for an effective decision (Haviland & Clark, 1974). These factors, if present, prevent the need for time-consuming searches for pertinent information and organizing frameworks in long term memory (Glenberg, Meyer, & Lindem, 1987; Kintsch, 1979, 1994; Lesgold, Roth, & Curtis, 1979).

Taken together, these studies indicate that *information must be present in the proximate context of the decision, immediately available in working memory*, in order to be effective (Sharps & Martin, 2002). As will be seen, these facts may be critically important for the success of environmental education programs.

But what sort of information must be proximately available for successful reasoning? It might initially appear that if people were constantly reminded to "save the Earth," the mere proximate presence of this information would have salutary effects on their environmentally-related behavior. Yet as we have already seen, this type of "chunked" gestalt concept may be too broad to be of value, and may be actively misleading, in any given consideration of environmental issues. Such broad gestalt concepts must be unpacked into their constituent features, and those features themselves analyzed, if they are to be useful for environmental reasoning and decision (Sharps 2003).

These considerations informed the development of a recent theoretical formulation, Gestalt/Feature-Intensive Processing theory (G/FI; Sharps and Nunes 2002; Sharps 2003) which has been instrumental in conceptualizing the cognitive dynamics discussed here. The utility of the G/FI perspective has been demonstrated in a variety of areas of human cognition (see Sharps, 2003, for review). The considerations involved have been validated in studies across the human lifespan and in over two decades of research (Sharps, 2003).

In brief, G/FI theory holds that cognitive processing lies along a continuum from a feature-intensive consideration of any given phenomenon, in which details are processed relatively slowly and in relative depth, to a more gestalt consideration which deals in chunks and overarching categories. Gestalt processing therefore arrives more swiftly at the general gist of a given sequence of cognitive processing, but does not arrive at in-depth understanding. The reason for this is that when cognitive processing leans toward a more gestalt character, the feature-intensive processing of the given concept is diminished, yielding a general representation of an event or class of event which is relatively barren of details. Since details are reduced in number and significance in gestalt processing, the resulting, relatively barren gestalt representation is more amenable to error (Sharps & Nunes, 2002; Sharps, 2003; Sharps, Hess & Ranes, 2007). Furthermore, in gestalt processing, error is less likely to be detected (see Sharps, 2003).

In contrast, feature-intensive (FI) processing, while slower, is typically anchored in a relatively veridical representation of the actual details of a given situation, especially in such complex areas as environmental reasoning. This has been empirically demonstrated, as will be discussed below (Sharps & Martin, 2002; Sharps, Hess, & Ranes, 2007). In the ecocognitive realm, in which extreme speed of decision making is not typically at a premium, it is important to use educational techniques which maximize feature-intensive processing.

The G/FI continuum provides an explanatory framework within which to conceptualize the important elements of cognitive processing generally and environmental cognition, or ecocognition, specifically. The current state of cognitive knowledge within the G/FI framework (Sharps 2003; Sharps and Nunes 2002) suggests methods by which to optimize environmental education:

1. When possible, necessary information should be provided prior to consideration of the issues at hand (Bransford & Johnson, 1973).

2. This information should be feature-intensive (FI) in nature, and should promote FI processing during the consideration of the issue at hand (Sharps & Nunes, 2002; Sharps, 2003).

3. The information should be available in working memory (Lesgold, Roth, & Curtis, 1979), and explicitly and directly related to the issue at hand (Haviland & Clark, 1974; Kieras, 1978), during active consideration.

4. All of these conditions should be fulfilled for information already known and available in long-term memory, as well as for any new information which may be imparted through, for example, environmental education.

Empirical Tests

We tested these concepts experimentally, with reference to reasoning and to decisions across a variety of everyday and executive contexts (Sharps & Martin, 2002). Respondents were exposed to twelve real-world decision scenarios which had led to negative or disastrous consequences. These respondents read the circumstances leading up to the given decision, and the decision itself, *but were not informed of the outcomes*. Then they were asked, quite simply, whether the given decision was a good one. Interestingly, most of the respondents held positive views of most of these ill-fated decisions.

Other respondents, however, received additional "contextual information," in the form of short passages of explicitly-relevant information. These were provided in the *immediate context of the decision*, and were intended to foster feature-intensive consideration of the primary passages. The crucial point here, however, was that the contextual information provided *was already available in respondents' long-term memory*; in other words, it required no training, as was demonstrated in an additional pilot study (Sharps & Martin, 2002). .

The results of this research were entirely consistent with the G/FI-based hypotheses governing the research. The presentation of contextual information significantly improved participants' abilities to understand the negative consequences of decisions, and to reduce the aforementioned types of "mindlessness" in decision processes (Sharps & Nunes, 2002; Sharps, 2003). Effect sizes were large. The provision of contextual information instantiated a more feature-intensive style of cognition, which was more likely to aid in the detection of logical errors and of failures to consider relevant evidence.

In summary, it is entirely possible to improve reasoning processes in critical decision situations. The obvious next step, for present purposes, was to conduct the same type of experiment in the purely ecocognitive realm. This made it possible to ascertain whether environmental reasoning, specifically, could be enhanced through the provision of relevant contextual information.

Accordingly, we conducted the relevant study, using the same experimental format (Sharps & Martin, 2002). In this new study (Sharps, Hess, & Ranes, 2007), respondents were exposed to twelve real-world decision scenarios concerning a variety of important environmental issues. All had resulted in long-term negative outcomes, in some cases with catastrophic consequences for human welfare. Half of the respondents in this study received these decision scenarios alone, and the others were provided with contextual information in the immediate context of the decision.

The scenarios employed included overexploitation of food resources, the use of pesticides which are also highly toxic to humans, and several instances of avoidable habitat damage. All scenarios were real, drawn from news accounts and professional journals. A pilot study showed that the contextual information provided to respondents in each appropriate condition was already well-known to them, as in the Sharps & Martin (2002) work. Additionally, all respondents filled out an exploratory questionnaire rating their self-reported religiosity, political liberality or conservatism, and self-perceived status as environmentalists or outdoor enthusiasts.

The results of the study were consistent with those of Sharps & Martin (2002), and were exactly as anticipated. Specifically, the contextual information group showed a statistically superior ability to evaluate environmental decision, compared to the control group which did not have this information immediately available in working memory,.

Surprisingly, no significant relationships were observed between the ability to use contextual information in environmental reasoning and self-reported levels of religiosity, political ideation, outdoor interests or environmental orientation. However, from the standpoint of environmental education, this may be seen as encouraging: at least within the framework of this research, neither religious, political, nor specific environmental attitudes diminished the prospect of enhancing environmental reasoning through the systematic use of contextual information. These results demonstrated that it is possible, through relatively simple procedures based in current cognitive science, to enhance the human capacity to reason intelligently about critical environmental issues and policies.

Using What we Know

Gestalt/feature-intensive processing theory (G/FI; Sharps & Nunes, 2002; Sharps, 2003) suggests that the inclusion of relevant information *in the immediate context* of a given decision will tend to result in better cognitive processing than would otherwise be the case, yielding a stronger consideration of logic and evidence. The studies outlined here demonstrated that this is true for ecognition as well as for other areas of cognitive study. Respondents didn't need to be taught anything new; they simply needed to have the information they already possessed arranged properly.

Additional research is needed in this area. The precise cognitive mechanisms underlying these effects should be further investigated. Also, more work should be conducted on issues of self-interest, personal identification with religious, political, or environmental orientations, and similar factors as these interact with more basic ecocognitive dynamics. However, for the present, the findings and considerations presented here may provide a preliminary roadmap for enhanced success in environmental education and environmental thought.

More specifically, this research provides evidence that successful environmental education programs, as well as successful consideration of environmental issues by scholars, policy-makers, and the general public, all require the same basic cognitive dynamics: explicit, relevant information, provided within prior frameworks for understanding when possible, presented in the immediate context of the concepts or decisions to be considered. In the studies described above, these factors resulted in the feature-intensive processing needed for success in the ecocognitive realm, as in other areas of cognition.

The use of these cognitive principles is likely to foster the successful development and implementation of strong, responsible, science-based environmental policies. Otherwise, successful environmental outcomes are improbable, simply because the necessary intellectual resources to develop such outcomes are inefficiently employed. In view of current levels of global environmental deterioration (e.g., Gore, 2006; Gregory, 2000; Harder, 2003; Reid, 2001; Townsend, 2003), and especially in view of our rising global population, it is increasingly important to formulate and implement well-reasoned environmental policies (Gregory, 2000; United Nations Environment Program, 2004). An empirically-based approach to ecocognition is needed to understand the psychological bases of such policies if they are to be successful.

References

Baum, J., Myers, R. A., Kehler, D. G., Worm, B., Harley, S. J., & Doherty, P. A. (2003). Collapse and conservation of shark population in the Northwest Atlantic. *Science, 299,* 389.

Bransford, J. D., & Johnson, M. K. (1973). Considerations of some problems of comprehension. In W. G. Chase (Ed.), *Visual Information Processing* (pp. 383-438). Orlando, FL: Academic Press.

Burkholder, J. Libra, B., Weyer, P., Heathcote, S., Kolpin, D., Thorne, P. S., & Wichman, M. (2007). Impacts of waste from concentrated animal feeding operations on water quality. *Environmental Health Perspectives, 115,* 308-312.

Crichton, M. (1990). *Jurassic Park.* New York: Ballantine.

Dean, C. (2006, November 3). Study Sees Global Collapse of Fish Species. *The New York Times,* p. A21.

Dorner, D. (1996). *The logic of failure: Why things go wrong and what we can do to make them right.* New York: Metropolitan Books.

Dwyer, W. O., Leeming, F. C., Cobern, M. K., Porter, B. E., & Jackson, J. M. (1993). Critical review of behavioral interventions to preserve the environment: Research since 1980. *Environment and Behavior, 25,* 275-321.

Elgin, B. (2007). How 'green' is that water? *Business Week, 4046,* 18.

Gentile, A. (2007). Cleaning the dust from the air by 2010. *American City and County, 122,* 20-22.

Glenberg, A. M., Meyer, M., & Lindem, K. (1987). Mental models contribute to foregrounding during text comprehension. *Journal of Memory and Language, 26,* 69-83.

Gore, A. (2006). *An inconvenient truth.* Emmaus, PA: Rodale.

Gregory, R. (2000). Using stakeholder values to make smarter environmental decisions. *Environment, 42,* 34-44.

Harder, B. (2003). Catch zero: What can be done as marine ecosystems face a deepening drisis? *Science News, 164,* 59-61.

Haviland, S. E., & Clark, H. H. (1974). What's new? Acquiring new information as a process of comprehension. *Journal of Verbal Learning and Verbal Behavior, 13,* 512-521.

Kempton, W., Harris, C. K., Keith, J. G., & Weil, J. S. (1985). Do consumers know what works in energy conservation? *Marriage and Family Review, 9,* 115-133.

Kieras, D. E. (1978). Good and bad structure in simple paragraphs: Effects on apparent theme, reading time, and recall. *Journal of Verbal Learning and Verbal Behavior, 17,* 13-28.

Kintsch, W. (1979). On modeling comprehension. *Educational Psychologist, 14,* 3-14.

Kintsch, W. (1994). Text Comprehension, memory, and learning. *American Psychologist, 49,* 294-303.

Kohler, W. (1947). *Gestalt psychology.* New York: Mentor.

Kohn, M. (2007). The Arctic killers. *New Statesman, 137,* 24-26.

Lakoff, G. (1987). *Women, fire, and dangerous things: What categories reveal about the mind.* Chicago: University of Chicago Press.

Lawton, M. (1997). Quality of environmental texts found uneven. *Education Week, 16,* 1.

Lesgold, A. M., Roth, S. F., & Curtis, M. E. (1979). Foregrounding effects in discourse comprehension. *Journal of Verbal Learning and Verbal Behavior, 18,* 291-308.

MacLeish, W. H. (1994). *The day before America: Changing the nature of a continent.* New York: Houghton-Mifflin.

McDougall, R. (2006). Overpopulation denial is a fatal game. *Biologist, 53,* 115-116.

Miller, G. A. (1956). The magical number seven, plus or minus two: some limits on our capacity for processing information. *Psychological Review, 63,* 81-97.

Perkins, S. (2007). Asian forecast: Hazy, warmer. *Science News, 172,* 68.

Reid, W. V. (2001). Biodiversity, ecosystem change, and international development: Issues for the new U.S. administration. *Environment, 43,* 20-26.

Rosch, E. H. (1973). Natural categories. *Cognitive Psychology, 4,* 328-350.

Salmon, J. (2000). Are we building environmental literacy? The Journal of *Environmental Education, 31*(4) 4-10.

Sharps, M. J (2003). *Aging, representation, and thought: Gestalt and feature-intensive processing.* New Brunswick, NJ: Transaction.

Sharps, M. J., Hess, A. B., & Ranes, B. (2007). Mindless decision making and environmental issues: Gestalt/feature-intensive processing and contextual reasoning in environmental decisions. *Journal of Psychology, 141,* 525-537.

Sharps, M. J., & Martin, S. S. (2002). "Mindless" decision making as a failure of contextual reasoning. *Journal of Psychology, 136,* 272-282.

Sharps, M. J., & Nunes, M. A. (2002). Gestalt and feature-intensive processing: Toward a unified model of human information processing. *Current Psychology, 21,* 68-84.

Sharps, M. J., & Wertheimer, M. (2000). Gestalt perspectives on cognitive science and on experimental psychology. *Review of General Psychology, 4,* 315-336.

Stokstad, E. (2006). Global loss of biodiversity harming ocean bounty. *Science, 314,* 745.

Syme, G. L., Seligman, C., Kantola, S. J., & MacPherson, D. K. (1987). Evaluating a television campaign to promote petrol conservation. *Environment and Behavior, 19,* 444-461.

Townsend, J. W. (2003). Reproductive behavior in the context of global population. *American Psychologist, 58,* 197-204.

United Nations Environment Program (2004). *Global environment outlook year book.* New York: United Nations.

Wertheimer, M. (1982). *Productive thinking.* Chicago: University of Chicago Press.

Imagination

Showing the Sense of Environmental Ethics

Sam Mickey

A s awareness of the global ecological crisis has become increasingly common in recent decades, ecologically oriented investigations in psychology and philosophy have articulated theoretical and practical issues regarding the attitudes, images, beliefs, values, practices, and habits with which humans relate to the natural world. In addressing the ethical implications of such issues, these investigations often raise questions about what humans hold to be of central importance or central value. More specifically, it is common to distinguish between anthropocentrism and non-anthropocentrism, the former designating orientations wherein value and meaning are centered primarily on the human (*anthropos*), and the latter des-

Sam Mickey is the web content manager and newsletter editor for the *Forum on Religion and Ecology* (http://yale.edu/religionandecology). He is an adjunct professor in the Engaged Humanities program at Pacifica Graduate Institute, and an adjunct professor in the Theology and Religious Studies department at the University of San Francisco. Aiming to integrate multiple theories and practices for engaging in the complex entanglements of human-Earth relations, Sam's research focuses on the philosophical and religious implications of postmodernism. Sam is working toward his PhD in the Philosophy, Cosmology, and Consciousness program at the California Institute of Integral Studies. Contact: sam_mickey@yahoo.com, 1608 Delaware St. Apt. B, Berkeley, CA 94703, 510-981-0296

ignating orientations wherein value and meaning center more primarily on life (biocentrism) or on ecosystems and the environment as a whole (ecocentrism) (Nash, 1989, pp. 153-160).

By some accounts, a sustainable world requires that humans participate in the value of the environment from biocentric, ecocentric, or other non-anthropocentric orientations. These accounts often claim that anthropocentrism, by reducing the value of the natural environment to a peripheral status relative to the human being, supports actions that abuse and destroy the environment. However, non-anthropocentric orientations are likewise untenable insofar as they reduce humans to a peripheral or marginal status. While anthropocentric orientations tend to support manipulative and exploitative relations between humans and the environment, non-anthropocentric orientations such as eco- and bio-centrism tend to foster misanthropy and social irresponsibility insofar as they marginalize the struggles of humans who face problems such as poverty, racism, sexism, disenfranchisement, etc.

Although arguments for anthropocentrism, biocentrism, and ecocentrism are often articulated in response to environmental problems and unsustainable practices that are associated with a dichotomy or disassociation separating the human from the natural world,

these varieties of "centrism" all tend to presuppose and perpetuate the very dichotomy that they purport to transform: value is centered *either* on the human *or* on the non-human. In contrast to the either/or dichotomy manifest in these centrisms, I articulate a phenomenological description of the relationship between humans and the natural world in terms of the elemental force of imagination, which discloses the human and the cosmos not as mutually exclusive opposites but as mutually constitutive vectors of sense. Irreducible to the dichotomy between anthropocentric and non-anthropocentric, participation in the force of imagination can be described better with the term "anthropocosmic"—an adjective indicating that the human and the cosmos are intimately intertwined and interconnected. Participation in the force of imagination would thus facilitate a turn away from the dichotomy between anthropocentric and non-anthropocentric environmental ethics and a turn toward anthropocosmic environmental ethics.

Before explicating the sense of environmental ethics that shows itself through participation in the force of imagination, I first describe the role of dream and imagination in relations between humans and the natural environment, I propose a monstrous phenomenology of the force of imagination, and then I consider the anthropocosmic relationships facilitated by imagination.

Earth Dreams and the Elemental Turn

Dream of Earth. As the "geologian" Thomas Berry expresses in *The Dream of the Earth*, participation in such a dream can open up the human species to an ecologically viable future (Berry, 1988, p. 194). Transforming the relation of the human being to itself, to the planet, and to the elements of the cosmos, dreaming can facilitate a reinvention of human nature: dreaming of Earth "to reinvent the human—at the species level" (Berry, 1999, p. 159). This reinvention would re-place the human in such a way as to "place the human within the dynamics of the planet" and the evolving cosmos (p. 160). Moreover, to reinvent the human is neither a merely cognitive endeavor nor a merely personal mission. It is "the historical mission of our times," a mission that calls for the emergence of a human species that can enact socially just and ecologically sustainable ways of dwelling in the world (p. 159).

Shared dream experience makes possible a reinvention that would reorient the human to its place within the natural world. Not merely a human faculty, dreaming can reorient the human to the natural world because it is part of the natural world, part of the same elemental creativity manifest as the evolutionary processes of the cosmos. Berry observes that, in human and cosmic manifestations of this creativity, something is given "in a dim and uncertain manner, something radiant with meaning that draws us on to a further clarification of our understanding and our activity" (p. 164). Such creativity "can be described in many ways, as a groping or as a feeling or imaginative process" (pp. 164-5). The imaginative process enacted in a dream of the marriage of earth and sky is the same process enacted in the groping or feeling whereby a predator seeks its prey or whereby an atom bonds or refuses to bond with another atom.

Imagine. Dream of Earth. Participation in this imaginative process requires that one attend to the dual sense of the genitive: dream of Earth, both in the sense of dreaming about Earth and in the sense of dreaming that comes from Earth. The imaginative process is thus at work not only in human beings, but also in the elemental forces of nature, which are "forces of primitive imagination" (Berry 1988, pp. 201-2). Human imagination and the elemental forces of primitive imagination are aspects of the co-constitutive imagination enacted in dreaming of Earth. The "social construction of nature" is thus balanced with a "natural construction of the social," such that social or psychological imagination is complemented with what the liberation ecologists Michael Watts and Richard Peet call an "environmental imaginary"—"a way of imagining nature" that includes images of "those forms of social and individual practice which are ethically proper and morally right with regard to nature" (Watts & Peet, 1996, p. 263). Through the notion of environmental imaginary, one experiences "nature, environment, and place as sources of thinking, reasoning, and tional stage in the development of cognitive functions, a stage of "egocentric representational activity" (Casey 2004, p. 31). This dismissal of imagination also pervades the history of philosophy, with imagination often being ignored or reduced to a subordinate or degenerate type of perceiving or thinking (pp. 32-34).

The general trend in Western thinking has been to reduce imagination to a faculty or power of the human, whether as an unrestrained or immature function of the ego or as a degenerate power of perception or thought. However, if imagination shows the mutual constitution of the natural and the social, then imagination is not merely a *faculty* of the human subject or soul. It is more fundamentally an *elemental force* at work in humans and in nature. Accordingly, John Sallis describes how the word "force" conveys "the deconstruction of the most global philosophical determinations of imagi-

Irreducible to the dichotomy between anthropocentric and non-anthropocentric, participation in the force of imagination can be described better with the term "anthropocosmic"—an adjective indicating that the human and the cosmos are intimately intertwined and interconnected.

imagining" (p. 263).

The co-constitutive sense of imagination is considerably different from the understanding of imagination that has dominated the history of Western science and philosophy. The phenomenologist Ed Casey mentions that, throughout the history of psychology, imagination has often been disparaged or dismissed: Freud reduced imagination to mere daydreaming, which he considered to be the result of a temporary loss of control by the ego; Jung emphasized the therapeutic potential of "active imagination," but never developed a thorough elucidation of imagination itself; and Piaget saw the imagination of the child as a transi- nation," which is to say, force marks the deconstruction of determinations that reduce imagination to a mere faculty or power of the human (Sallis, 2000, p. 129). For Sallis, this deconstruction accompanies a turn to the elemental, a turn that "would reinstall the human in wild nature and in its bearing on the earth and beneath the sky, returning human nature to nature" (p. 25).

If this operation of deconstruction is to be sustained, it must include new rigorous determinations that do not efface the force of imagination. For Sallis (2000), this demand "makes phenomenology indispensable" to an understanding of imagination, because phenomenology provides rigorous determinations of things as they show themselves, and it holds in abeyance any determinations that efface manifestation or fail to adhere to the self-showing of things (p. 8).[1] The importance of phenomenology for a rigorous account of imagination is similarly observed by Andy Fisher, whose radical approach to ecopsychology overcomes the dualisms for which imagination is a subjective faculty, egocentric activity, or anthropomorphic representation of an objective world.

Invoking Maurice Merleau-Ponty's phenomenology of the "flesh," Fisher articulates "a nondualistic and naturalistic psychology" that describes imagination not as mere anthropomorphism, but as a way of contacting the flesh of the world and participating in the intertwining of oneself with all other beings (Fisher, 2002, pp. 133-136). For Merleau-Ponty, phenomenological reflection attends to the things of "wild" Being to express the contact we have with these things "when they are not yet things said" (Merleau-Ponty, 1968, p. 38, p. 168). Before humans and nature are expressed in terms of opposition, they intertwine with one another in the crucial criss-crossing of the elemental flesh of wild Being, or in other words, they intertwine in "the chiasm" whereby sensing (subject) and sensed (object) participate in an interconnected unity (pp. 139, 147, 215). In the flesh, humans and nonhumans emerge from the same sensing/sensed Being, wherein consciousness and wild nature overlap and interlace, exceeding the limits of any oppositional schema.

Monstrous Phenomenology

Phenomenology mutates with this turn to the elemental and to the deconstruction of traditional philosophical determinations of imagination. Such a muta-

tion requires that phenomenology adhere more rigorously to the complexity of what shows itself, and thus rather than confining itself to the phenomena that are present to consciousness as objects to a subject, phenomenology becomes what the French phenomenologist Gaston Bachelard calls "a phenomenology without phenomena" (Bachelard, 1994, p. 184). This mutant phenomenology takes into account the overlap, interplay, difference, absence, and excess that are at work (but not simply present to consciousness) in the constitution of things as they show themselves. By articulating what shows itself as it exceeds the limits of presence, phenomenology attends

Photo: Glenn McCrea, www.dewdropworld.com

to an exorbitant sense of "showing" (from Latin, monstrare) and mutates into "monstrology" (Sallis, 2000, p. 42).

Monstrology is exposed to what shows itself in its irreducible excess, anomaly, and exorbitance, which is to say, its "monstrosity" (from Latin, monstrum, "monster," "portentous sign"). Monstrology does not assimilate the self-showing of things into traditional philosophical determinations that reduce phenomena to binary oppositions (e.g., subject/object, nature/culture, appearance/reality, matter/form, and sensible/intelligible). Whereas such determinations subordinate the world of sense to an intelligible world of truth, monstrous phenomenology interprets the world of

sense without recourse to any schema that dichotomizes the sense of things in their self-showing. If one adheres to the exorbitant and ineffable sense of things in their self-showing, then the sense of the world is not a meaning or truth behind, beyond, or otherwise opposed to the world. Rather, the sense of the world is the world of sense. As the contemporary French philosopher Jean-Luc Nancy observes, the phrase "'the sense of the world' is a tautological expression," which is to say, the world does not have a sense, "but it is sense" (Nancy, 1997, p. 8).

The sense of imagination shows complex criss-crossings between opposites like subjective/ objective and intelligible/sensible. This is evident in the ambivalent sense of the word "sense," which can refer to subjectivity (sensing; apprehension) and to objectivity (sensed; apprehended), and also to an intelligible sense (meaning) and an aesthetic sense (perception) (Sallis, 2000, p. 32). According to this monstrous phenomenology, the force of imagination is not merely a subjective faculty or a perceptual or mental power of the soul, but is always a movement of intimately intertwined vectors of sense, always effecting combinations and separations that gather things into the horizons where they show themselves (pp. 129-133). To impel things to show themselves, the force of imagination gathers together the monstrous ambivalence of sense, the ambivalence that marks the indeterminacy of the multiple senses of sense. Following the German idealist philosopher Johann Gottlieb Fichte, one can describe this imaginal gathering as a "hovering" (Schweben) that brings together determinate phenomena while also wavering between these phenomena and the radical indeterminacy pervading the ambivalence of sense (p. 127).

In gathering together the horizons in which things show themselves, imagination can be described as simultaneously originary and memorial: "originary" because imagination is a creative force that draws things into presence, and "memorial" because that which imagination draws into presence is already there (at least potentially or implicitly) before it is gathered into presence (p. 138). Imagination lets that which is already

---

[1] The word "phenomenology" is derived from the Greek words phainomenon and logos, with the former deriving from phainesthai ("to show itself"). Phenomenology is thus a discourse (logos) on that which shows itself. According to Martin Heidegger's etymological interpretation of the word, phenomenology is a way of letting phenomena shows themselves in their self-showing: "phenomenology" means "to let that which shows itself be seen from itself in the very way in which it shows itself from itself" (1962, 58).

there show itself (again) for the first time. Hovering between the determinations and indeterminacy of the originary/memorial, the intelligible/perceptual, and the subjective/objective, the force of imagination draws things into the horizons where they show themselves: "imagination composes monstrosity" (p. 139).

Imagination is not a reproduction or degeneration of the true world, for truth only shows itself as such insofar as imagination draws things into their self-showing (p. 144). Nor is imagination a faculty of the human subject, for a subject only shows itself as such through the force of imagination (p. 145). Imagination does not belong to the human. The human belongs to imagination. The force of imagination gathers the vectors of sense whereby the human and the world show themselves. With imagination, the human shows itself not as isolated or alienated but as situated within the sense of the world, and the natural world shows itself not as a homogeneous groups of objects but as "a kind of hypernature within nature," that is, an elemental nature that encompasses and exceeds the limits of things (p. 158).

The monstrous force of imagination operates as an "elemental imagination" through which "humans draw around themselves the elementals that will always have encompassed them" (p. 172). Imagination opens possibilities for re-placing and reinventing the human by reorienting the species to its place in the elemental flesh of the world. The human and the natural world thus show themselves not as mutually exclusive opposites but as mutually constitutive sites of elemental imagination. The elemental force of imagination returns the human to its place within the sense of the world, reorienting the human to its abode within the encompassing horizon opened by earth and sky and the other elemental forces of wild Being.

Anthropocosmic Relations

Through participation in the elemental force of imagination, the relationship between the human and the natural world exceeds the limits of binary oppositions like subject/object and anthropocentrism/non-anthropocentrism. With imagination disclosing the intertwining of

the human and the world, their relationship can be described as anthropocosmic. Along these lines, the French phenomenologist Gabriel Marcel notes that "an anthropocosmic relation can only be established beyond the opposition of subject and object," and this anthropocosmic criss-crossing of subject/object is evident insofar as the human is always already "in a situation," which is to say, anthropology is always already "oriented in a cosmological direction" (Marcel, 2002, p. 83). Marcel's phenomenology of anthropocosmic relations resonates with the accounts of anthropocosmic relations articulated by other French phenomenologists, including Bachelard and Paul Ricoeur.

Bachelard describes anthropocosmic relations in his phenomenological ontology of poetic images, wherein he explores the "onset of the image" as it shows itself prior to any assimilation of the image into a dualistic opposition between the human and the world (Bachelard, 1994, p. xix). According to Bachelard, the onset of the image is particularly evident in reverie (Bachelard, 1971, pp. 11, 19, 57). Characterized by the intervention of waking consciousness in the dream, reverie is not mere daydreaming, but "puts us in the state of a soul being born," that is, "a soul which is discovering its world"(p. 15). With the onset of images in "cosmic reverie," the cosmos and the dreamer emerge together (Bachelard, 1994, p. xxiv). To attend to the onset of the image is to attend to the elemental flesh, "the anthropo-cosmic tissue" intertwining the human and the cosmos (p. 22). In working toward the articulation of images that show the intertwining of the human and the cosmos, the phenomenology of imagination becomes "anthropo-cosmology" (p. 47).

Bachelard draws on diverse selections of poetry to explore the images disclosed in reverie, as in The Poetics of Space, throughout which he reflects on poetic images of intimate spaces (e.g., houses, cradles, corners, nests, shells, etc.). From the miniature to the vast, poetic imagination discloses the "intimate immensity" of space, according to which the intima-

An ethical response to the environmental crisis does not require universal ethical theories or moral prescriptions but a new sense of the place of human nature in elemental nature.

cy of human spaces is intertwined with the immensity of the cosmos (pp. 183-185). Whether through poetry or reverie, phenomenological explorations of the "anthropocosmic complexes" that condition relations between the human and the world open possibilities for reorienting the human to its cosmic situation and tightening anthropocosmic ties that have become slack (Bachelard, 1971, p. 123). Moreover, Paul Ricoeur points out that "the sectors of anthropocosmic experience" include not only poetic and oneiric experience but also hierophantic experience, as anthropocosmic experience weaves poetry and dream together with sacred phenomena (i.e., hierophanies) (Ricoeur, 1967, pp. 11-14).

As with other sectors of anthropocosmic experience, the sacred is not a matter of intelligibility opposed to sensibility, transcendence opposed to immanence, or ideal truth opposed to illusory appearance. The sacred appears with the sense of the world. The human "first reads the sacred on the world, on some elements or aspects of the world" (p. 10). The anthropocosmic ties between the human and the world gather together vectors of sense that can show themselves as manifestation of the sacred, as oneiric events of the psyche, or as poetic expressions of language. In referring to the place of the sacred in anthropocosmic experience, Ricoeur cites the use of the term "anthropocosmic" by Mircea Eliade.

For Eliade, "anthropocosmic experiences" occur when the human recognizes itself as a porous microcosm, "a living cosmos open to all the other living cosmoses" in which the human is embedded (Eliade, 1970, p. 455). The history of religions can help the human being recover the symbols and images of its body, "which is an anthropocosmos," and it does this by providing determinations of "the archetypal positions" of the body (Eliade, 1991, p. 36). These archetypal positions manifest "anthropo-cosmic homologies" that appear throughout the history of religions as "a whole system of micro-macrocosmic correspondences," including the correspondence "of the belly or womb to a cave, of the intestines to a labyrinth, of breathing to weaving, of the veins and arteries to the sun and moon, of the backbone to the axis mundi" (Eliade, 1987, p. 169). In rediscovering the archetypal positions and micro-macrocosmic correspondences of the anthropocosmic body, the human and the world show themselves not as mutually exclusive opposites but as mutually constitutive partners in the manifestation of the sacred.

Furthermore, Eliade's discussion of anthropocosmic relations in the history of religions has been taken up by contemporary scholars who draw attention to the environmental implications of anthropocosmic images in Confucianism, Daoism, Islam, and other religious traditions (Mickey, 2007).

Whether enacted through religion, poetry, dream, reverie, or otherwise, participation in the force of imagination makes it possible for the human and the world to show themselves as vectors of the same elemental sense. Hovering between the determinations and the indeterminacy of sense, imagination composes the anthropocosmic tissue of the human and the world. To participate in the force of imagination is thus to reinvent the human and rediscover its anthropocosmic ties to elemental nature.

The Place of Ethics

By disclosing the intimate intertwining of the human and the world, the force of imagination makes possible a reinvention that rediscovers the anthropocosmic element of the flesh and places the human and its cultural traditions back into their cosmic context. This cosmic context, this place in which imagination places the human can also be called the ethos of the human, in the original meaning of ethos as "abode" or "dwelling place." Such an ethos resonates with what Sallis calls "exorbitant ethics," which names an approach to environmental ethics that would accompany the return of the human to the wildly exorbitant sense of the world, that is, an ethical

Photo: Glenn McCrea, www.dewdropworld.com

approach that emerges with "the turn to the sensible and to elemental nature" (Sallis, 2000, p. 206).

The reinvention of the human through poetic, oneiric, or religious engagements in the force of imagination constitutes an ethical injunction. Indeed, this is Berry's claim: the reinvention of the human is "the ethical imperative of our times" (Berry, 1999, p. 164). It is the imperative to turn away from the currently dominant ethic of anthropocentrism, which dichotomizes the human and the natural world, and turn toward the elemental exorbitance of anthropocosmic ethics, according to which the human and the world show themselves in their intertwining, gathered together by the force of imagination. Moreover, the anthropocosmic turn in environmental ethics replaces anthropocentrism, but not with non-anthropocentric approaches like biocentrism and ecocentrism.

Anthropocosmic relations exceed any dichotomy between human/nonhuman or between anthropocentrism/nonanthropocentrism. This means that a turn toward anthropocosmic environmental ethics calls for neither another, perhaps more encompassing, non-human center nor a modified version of a centralized human. Rather than placing value exclusively on the human (anthropocentric), on life or living organisms (biocentric), on ecosystems or the planet as a whole (ecocentric), or on any determinate center which would exclude or marginalize some periphery, an anthropocosmic approach to environmental ethics overcomes the center/periphery dualism and facilitates the mutual interpenetration of values, such that the values of humanity and the values of the natural world are interconnected vectors of sense drawn together by the same elemental force of imagination.

An anthropocosmic approach to environmental ethics does not tend to any one determinate center but to the imaginative force that gathers the human and the world into their elemental relationship, according to which central and peripheral values show themselves not

Imagination fundamentally is an elemental force at work in humans and in nature.

as fixed determinations but as oscillating waves of sense. As the force of imagination gathers together the sense of the world, it impels the human and the world to show themselves in their monstrosity. The human being is thus reoriented to its ethos not through a determinate center, but through participation in the imaginal hovering that intertwines the anthropocosmic ties of the human and the world.

The hovering of imagination makes it possible for the human to engage in ethical deliberation. The force of imagination draws together various possible directions for the sense of the world, and it frees these possibilities by suspending them between determinate and indeterminate vectors of sense. With a possibility in suspense, one can begin to deliberate, "weighing out" (from Latin, de-liberare) the pros and cons of a possibility. As Sallis observes, one can thus "remain suspended between alternatives, hovering between various possibilities in such a way as to weigh them against one another, that is, to deliberate about them, between them" (Sallis, 2000, p. 204). Deliberation opens possibilities for deliberative action, which is not a practice that emerges from a prior ethical theory or system, but a practice that emerges with the self-showing of things.

If anthropocosmic environmental ethics includes a theory, it is a theatrical theory. Whereas "theory" (theoria) derives from Greek words for "viewing" (thea) and "seeing" (oros), a theatrical theory conveys a viewing that takes place, a theatron (the suffix tron connotes "place"). As imagination frees possibilities for deliberation, it opens the horizon wherein deliberative action takes place, it opens "the theatre of action" (Sallis, 2000, p. 205). Deliberative action is determined through participation in the shows that take place on the anthropocosmic stage.

This sense of deliberative action works against hegemonic systems of environmental ethics and politics (Sallis, 2000, p. 25). Anthropocosmic deliberation would contest the hegemony of ethics and politics that assimilate the exorbitant sense of what shows itself and reduce it to systems, pre-programmed responses, overgeneralizations, and conceptual schema. Replacing hegemonic systems, the reinvention of the human reorients ethics and politics to the place of the human in the elemental sense of the world. With the turn to the elemental that takes place in anthropocosmic environmental ethics, there is no fixed determination of what is good, right, or valuable, no rigid system that determines once and for all the proper conduct of the human in its engagements with the world.

Hovering between determinations and indeterminacy, the human deliberates and acts according to what shows itself through the force of imagination. Imagination does not center exclusively on the human, on living organisms, or on the environment as a whole. It provides no final determination that answers in advance any ethical questions raised by issues of climate change, pollution, human overpopulation, food production, water scarcity, species extinction, or any other impasses of the current global ecological crisis. An ethical response to the environmental crisis does not require universal ethical theories or moral prescriptions but a new sense of the place of human nature in elemental nature.

With an anthropocosmic sense of environmental ethics, the only imperative is to reinvent the human, to let the human and the world show themselves as they intimately intertwine with one another through the force of imagination. Deliberately, reinvent the human: let the force of imagination open up places on the anthropocosmic stage where actors can show themselves and sustain their action in the show.

References

Bachelard, G. (1971). *The poetics of reverie: Childhood, language, and the cosmos* (Trans. D. Russell). Boston: Beacon Press.

Bachelard, G. (1994). *The poetics of space* (Trans. M. Jolas). Boston: Beacon Press.

Berry, T. (1988). *The dream of the earth*. San Francisco: Sierra Club Books.

Berry, T. (1999). *The great work: Our way into the future*. New York: Bell Tower.

Casey, E. S. (2004). *Spirit and soul: Essays in philosophical psychology* (2nd ed.) Putnam: Spring Publications.

Eliade, M. (1970). *Patterns in comparative religion* (Trans. R. Sheed). Cleveland: World Publishing Company.

Eliade, M. 1987. *The sacred and the profane: The nature of religion* (Trans. W. Trask). San Diego: Harcourt Brace Jovanovich.

Eliade, M. 1991. *Images and symbols: Studies in religious symbolism* (Trans. P. Mairet). Princeton: Princeton University Press.

Fisher, A. (2002). *Radical ecopsychology: Psychology in the service of life*. Albany, NY: SUNY Press.

Heidegger, M. (1962). *Being and time* (Trans. J. Macquarrie & E. Robinson. New York: Harper and Row.

Marcel, G. (2002). Phenomenological notes about being in a situation. In *Creative fidelity* (pp. 82-103, Trans. R. Rosthal). New York: Fordham University Press.

Merleau-Ponty, M. (1968). *The visible and the invisible* (Trans. A. Lingis). Evanston: Northwestern University Press.

Mickey, S. (2007). Contributions to anthropocosmic environmental ethics. *Worldviews: Environment, Culture, Religion, 11*(2), 226-247.

Nancy, J.-L. (1997). *The sense of the world* (Trans. J. Librett). Minneapolis: University of Minnesota Press.

Nash, R. (1989). *The rights of nature: A history of environmental ethics*. Madison: University of Wisconsin Press.

Ricoeur, P. (1967). *The symbolism of evil* (Trans. E. Buchanan). New York: Harper and Row.

Sallis, J. (2000). *Force of imagination: The sense of the elemental*. Indianapolis: Indiana University Press.

Watts, M., & R. Peet. (1996). Towards a theory of liberation ecology. In R. Peet & M. Watts (Eds.), *Liberation ecologies: Environment, development, social movements* (pp. 260-269). London and New York: Routledge.

Digitizing the Psyche

Human/Nature in the Age of Intelligent Machines

Fernando Castrillon

T his article systematically explicates and examines a deep psychological and cultural process I have termed the *digitization of the psyche*, also referred to as *the production of digitized subjectivities*. The digitization of the psyche refers to an internal and relational mirroring of our larger discursive interaction with progressively digitized culture. Under this process, the dynamic construction of our psyches begins to take on an increasingly digitized, binary, and standardized feel. How we experience and articulate emotion and cognition, and

Fernando Castrillon, Psy.D., is an assistant professor in the Community Mental Health Department at the California Institute of Integral Studies (CIIS) in San Francisco. Dr. Castrillon is the director of CIIS' "Clinic without Walls", Senior Mental Health Specialist with Instituto Familiar de la Raza, Candidate Analyst at the Lacanian School of Psychoanalysis in Berkeley, California, and is on the editorial board of the journal Ecopsychology. His clinical, teaching, and research interests include the production of subjectivity (both human and more-than-human), psychoanalysis, community mental health, ecopsychology, and post-structuralist social/cultural theory. Currently he is working on a book based on his dissertation research, in which he examines the psychological and inter-subjective consequences of the hyperdigitization of contemporary Western culture. Contact information: fcastrillon@ciis.edu. Mailing address: CIIS, 1453 Mission St., San Francisco, CA. 94103, Phone: (415) 575-3487.

how we relate to others begins to mimic (and acts to support) the functioning of the digital machines we engage with in our everyday practice. As we become progressively enveloped in electronically mediated bubbles, traversed with

"I've gotten so much into code that I expect everything in my life to be as efficient as my software," he says. "I get into arguments with my wife because I'll present situations to her and expect her to produce the results like a program. She'll get very angry and yell, "I'm not a computer program, damn it! I'm a human being." But soon, will there be less of a difference? (Dawkins, 2005, 81)

flows and processes that are digitally encoded and articulated, our lives start to resemble a vast landscape of biomechanical interaction wherein the currency of communication is not the smooth ebb and flow of the natural world, but the neatly packaged, black and white,

on/off cyber-utterance of the bit and the byte. Our movements become more mechanical, more ordered; our range of motion more restricted, more controlled; our muscles and sinews becoming constellated in a digital synchronicity; the

parceling out of energy throughout our bodies takes on the character of a robot, a cyborg, an android, a human increasingly devoid of wild, undomesticated nature.[1]

I regard the digitization of the psyche as a subset of a larger cultural process of digitization that is currently in ascendancy within Western culture and in many respects globally. I define this larger process of digitization as the privileging of instrumental rationality, computational logic and symbolic manipulation over intuition, emotion, nonlinear logic and the ebb and flow of the natural, undomesticated world.

Gilles Deleuze and Felix Guattari (1987) and Manual De Landa (1991) refer to the overall set of self-organizing processes in the universe, including the self-organizing processes of the natural world, as the machinic phylum. "These include all processes in which a group of previously disconnected elements suddenly reaches a critical point at which they begin to 'cooperate' to form a higher level entity" (De Landa, 1991, pp. 6-7). I am arguing that digitization is one such self-organizing process. It is a coming together, an arranging that brings various and often disparate elements, humans and machines, into a particular constellated synchronicity or ecology that I will refer to as a machinic assemblage. The digitization of the psyche occurs within these super-networked and hyperlinked machinic assemblages, particularly at the level of the human-machine discursive interface.

The focus of this article, then, is an examination of how our psyches and our ways of relating are being discursively digitized within the ecologies of these super-networked and hyperlinked machinic assemblages that we are increasingly a part of. These machinic assemblages can be seen as ecologies that produce digitized subjectivities, and the more digitized the psyches and relations operating therein, the greater and more intense the digital nature of the machinic assemblages themselves. Many of us experience the above, in one form or another, and we see the myriad ways

Photo: Glenn McCrea, www.dewdropworld.com

to the way we interact with the different parts of ourselves, the deep psychological and cultural process of digitization marks many aspects of our contemporary existence. The point of this article is to provide a theoretical framework or language that allows us to think critically about the contours of the digitized psyche and its implications for our personal lives and the cultures we discursively construct. As well, the article examines various contemporary cultural responses to this process of digitization, including that emanating from the field of ecopsychology.

Digitization: Psychological and Cultural

My work on the digitization of the psyche, while original, is an outgrowth and meld of several theoretical orientations; among others, the work of Gilles Deleuze and Felix Guattari (1987), Manuel De Landa (1991), Lewis Mumford (1963), Max

Our lives start to resemble a vast landscape of biomechanical interaction wherein the currency of communication is not the smooth ebb and flow of the natural world, but the neatly packaged, black and white, on/off cyber-utterance of the bit and the byte.

in which the process impacts our lives. From the way we interact with others

Acknowledgments: As with all human productions, this work is the result of many conversations, both real and imagined. I cannot possibly name all the different people that have influenced me and my thinking on the myriad themes addressed in this work, but I will attempt to name a few. In particular I would like to thank Kaisa Puhakka, Raul Moncayo, Christian Erickson, Doug Vakoch, Erik Davis, my colleagues and students at the California Institute of Integral Studies, my fellow travelers at the Lacanian School of Psychoanalysis in Berkeley, and my wife Holly S. Castrillon for their support. This work is dedicated to my newly-born son David Paolo Castrillon. May you choose wisely the relationships you enter into in this world.

Weber (1921-1922/1978) and the field of ecopsychology more generally. A definition of a few key concepts derived from the work of these authors will help to lay out the theoretical foundations of this article.

Machinic Phylum

As noted above, Gilles Deleuze, Felix Guattari, and Manual De Landa refer to the overall set of self-organizing processes in the universe as the machinic phylum. "These include all processes in which a group of previously disconnected elements suddenly reaches a critical point at which they begin to 'cooperate'

[1] Domestication refers to the fundamental changes that have occurred to human subjectivity as the inverse result of the human domestication of plants and humans. Hence, the standardizing, controlling, and instrumental denaturing of animals and plants by humans also worked to domesticate humans themselves. Domestication is understood to be diametrically opposed to "wild," feral, or undomesticated nature, in which there is a relative lack of standardization and control.

to form a higher level entity" (De Landa, 1991, pp. 6-7). Understood more deeply, the term "machinic" refers to the existence of processes that act upon an initial set of merely coexisting, heterogeneous elements, and induce them to assemble together and constellate into a new and original synthesis (Deleuze & Guattari, 1987, p. 330). Machinic, then, is synony-

I am arguing that we are fast approaching the terminal point of this teleology; as rationalization drove and fulfilled modernity, so digitization as the progeny of rationalization is driving and fulfilling hyper-modernity.

mous with Ilya Prigogine's and Isabelle Stenger's (1984) principle of self-organization, or autopoiesis as described by Francisco Varela, Humberto Maturana and Ricardo Uribe (1974).

The term "phylum" is derived from biology and refers both to the evolutionary category and the idea of a common, universal "body-plan" that gives rise to many different organic designs depending on the operations that are undertaken. Put together, machinic phylum refers not only to all the self-organizing processes in the cosmos, both living and non-living, but to the fact that all these machinic processes find their common origin in a basic design. Machinic phylum also refers to the fact that the machinic process, or self organization, is a key aspect of existence itself (De Landa, 1997).

Abstract Machines

Within this larger, all encompassing machinic phylum we encounter *abstract machines* and *machinic assemblages*. For the purposes of this work, abstract machines can be understood as supra-high level self-organizing processes. Not to be confused with technical machines, such as cars or computers, abstract machines impart or disassemble form to the variable flows we find in nature

(Deleuze & Guattari, 1987). The process of digitization is one such abstract machine.

The work of Max Weber (1921-1922/1978), particularly his examination of an antecedent abstract machine, namely rationalization, can help us to understand the abstract machine process of digitization. Weber, a German sociologist, focused much of his work on the process of *rationalization*. Rationalization, as defined by Weber, and later by the Frankfurt School theorists Max Horkheimer and Theodor Adorno (1973), as the hyper-privileging of *instrumental reason*, is a key component of the process of digitization.

For Weber, the process of rationalization involves six cultural sub-processes:

1. The disenchantment and intellectualization of the world, and the resultant tendency to view the world as a causal mechanism subject, in principle, to rational control;

2. the emergence of an ethos of impersonal worldly accomplishment, historically grounded in the Puritan ethic of vocation;

3. the growing importance of specialized technical knowledge in economy, administration, and education;

4. the objectification and depersonalization of law, economy and polity, and the consequent increase in the regularity and calculability of action in these domains;

5. the progressive development of the technically rational means of control over man and nature; and

6. the tendential displacement of traditional and value-rational (wertrational) by purely instrumental (zweckrational) action orientations. (Brubaker, 1994, pp. 546-547)

This extension of the logos of science and technology into every conceivable sphere of human activity and being (including the psyche) is considered the work of modernity for Weber (1921-1922/1978). As such, it is a revolutionary teleology that "might engender a world without caritas, without freedom, dominated by powerful bureaucracies and by the 'iron cage' of the capitalist economy" (Brubaker, 1994, p. 547). To a large extent, I am arguing that we are fast approaching the terminal point of this teleology; as rationalization drove and fulfilled modernity, so digitization as the progeny of rationalization is driving and fulfilling hyper-modernity.[2]

The abstract machine of digitization, while encompassing and extending all the above six cultural sub-processes of rationalization, goes beyond it in two key respects. First, digitization at its core aims at extreme levels of manipulation. We now often hear of efforts to "digitize" libraries or picture galleries or even whole fields of study. What is meant by this is that the field in question has its myriad components reduced to a binary code or information. Once reduced to "pure information" the possibilities for manipulation are seemingly limitless. Witness for example, music

Digitization, as an abstract machine, seeks to deterritorialize life and reality themselves.

production which has become almost entirely digitized. Recombinant articulations of previously independent musical

---

[2] I purposely do not use the term "postmodern," as it suggests that modernity is over, and that we have somehow left it behind. Like Paul Virilio (1997), I believe that the contemporary situation is instead an intensification and deepening of modernity, hence the term "hypermodernity." For more on this see Virilio's *Open Sky* (1997), and John Armitage's *Beyond Postmodernism?: Paul Virilio's Hypermodern Cultural Theory* (2004).

[3] It is interesting to note potential connections between this alluring power of digitization and its seemingly limitless potential for manipulation, and Lacanian psychoanalytic thinking around the issue of castration. It would seem that this "drive" towards limitless manipulation might serve as a way of circumventing the whole issue of castration or boundaries or even the "law" of nature. This is not new of course. Fantasies of unlimited power are a deep trope of civilization itself.

forms is now the mainstay, and this is due to digitization which allows for limitless manipulation.[3]

Digitization also goes beyond rationalization in that it is hyper-deterritorializing. As Deleuze and Guattari (1987) use the term, it refers to a process in which a thing or the content of something is ripped off its moorings, or the site in which it was engendered. All abstract machines do this type of "decoding" (pp. 142-145). Within the larger sphere of capitalism and modernity that rationalization was a part of, the cash-nexus, or the reduction of everything to a cash equivalency, accomplished this deterritorialization to a vast degree. Hence, human labor came to equal apples which equaled childcare which equaled nuclear submarines; and the intervening currency of equivalency was cash.

Digitization, however, goes beyond this already far-reaching cash equivalency of commodities. Digitization, as an abstract machine, seeks to deterritorialize life and reality themselves. The Human Genome project is one clear example. By reducing it to a binary code, in other words deterritorializing it, the very blueprint of the human organism is made equivalent to everything else that has also been reduced to a binary code. So the human genome now equals the U.S. Library of Congress, which equals the latest Hubble Telescope pictures which equals GPS data for Yellowstone National Park; and the intervening currency of equivalency is digitization. It is like something out of the film The Matrix (L. Wachowski & A. Wachowski, 1999), where reality and all its different components and processes are reduced to digital code or information. So while the engine of deterritorialization under modernity was the cash-nexus, it is the the digital-nexus that drives deterritorialization under hypermodernity. All aspects of reality

are made equivalent and could potentially be stored side by side, if we were only able to build a large enough memory storage device.[4]

Machinic Assemblages

Abstract machines in turn give rise to machinic assemblages, wherein previously independent and heterogeneous elements, both discrete entities and dynamics, enter into a cooperative arrangement with each other (De Landa, 1991). In the case of the abstract machine I have termed digitization, the machinic assemblage engendered is specifically digital. In these digital machinic assemblages, humans and technical machines, such as computers, are brought together by the abstract machine process of digi-

Photo: Glenn McCrea, www.dewdropworld.com

tization into a cooperative set of relationships.

Digital Machinic Assemblages and the Production of Subjectivity

Digital machinic assemblages are different from other types of machinic assemblages, such as a 1920s automobile assembly line, in that they operate on a digital code. As such, the humans involved in these assemblages are also entrained to operate on a digital code. It is posited that this discursive interaction between humans and machines that occurs in digital machinic assemblages results in the production of digitized subjectivities.

So what does it mean to "produce" a certain type of subjectivity? The work of Felix Guattari (1996) proves instructive in this regard.

To consider subjectivity from the perspective of its production in no way implies, I suggest, a return to traditional systems of determination involving a material infrastructure and an ideological superstructure. The different semiotic registers that contribute to the engendering of subjectivity do not maintain obligatory, hierarchical relations that are fixed once and for all. It could happen, for example, that economic semiotization becomes dependent on collective psychological factors, as one sees with the sensitivity of the stock market indexes to fluctuations of opinion. In fact, subjectivity is plural — polyphonic, to borrow a term preferred by Mikhail Bakhtin. It is not constituted by a dominant, determining factor that directs other factors according to a univocal causality. (p. 192)

Therefore, subjectivity is derived from many different sources, not just the material substratum as many Marxists would argue. Subjectivity, understood here as one's particular and individual sense of self-hood, is a production of a discursive interaction with ideas, things, beings and processes in one's environment (Guattari, 1995, p. 7). If this is the case, then our discursive interaction with machines must also be implicated in the production of our human subjectivity.

Must we keep the semiotic productions of the mass media, of computers, of telecommunications, robotics, etc., outside of psychological subjectivity? I don't think so. … technological machines for information and communication operate at the heart of human subjectivity — not only within its memories and intelligence, but also within its sensibilities, affects, and unconscious fantasies. (Guattari, 1996, p. 194)

And the greater and more intense our interaction with these technological machines, the more digitized the subjectivities that are produced.

The Production of Digitized Subjectivities

We now turn to the particulars of how this discursive digital interaction between humans and machines produces digitized psyches. In order to do that, however, it is useful to look at how previous mechanical machinic assemblages

---

[4] The radical deterritorializing nature of digitization seems to have spurred a kind of thinking which posits that absolutely everything is information and that the universe is simply a giant information-processing computer. For more on this, see Seth Lloyd's Programming the Universe: A Quantum Computer Scientist Takes on the Cosmos (2007).

produced certain machinified human subjectivities.

Lewis Mumford's Technics and Civilization (1963), is a history of the machine and a critical study of its effects on civilization and psychology over the

The various practices of rewilding can be seen as a set of subversive methodologies whose aim is that of disrupting the production of digitized subjectivities through the deployment of counter-digital epistemologies and ways of being.

last one thousand years. Originally published in 1932, Mumford's *Technics and Civilization*, was far ahead of his time, as exemplified by the following quote.

If we wish to have any clear notion about the machine, we must think about its psychological as well as its practical origins; and similarly, we must appraise its esthetic and ethical results. ... We find that there are human values in machinery we did not suspect; we also find that there are wastes, losses, perversions of energy which the ordinary economist blandly concealed. The vast material displacements the machine has made in our physical environment are perhaps in the long run less important than its spiritual contributions to our culture. (Mumford, 1963, p. i)

Mumford is the first scholar to have systematically examined the impact of machines on society and the psyche, and how our society and psyches gave birth to machines. In this regard, his work is highly original and critical.

Mumford's work on the antecedents to the machinification of labor demonstrates how the production of machinified human subjectivity is accomplished. He argues that the breakdown of complex craftsmanship down to simple routine tasks during the long nightmare of the Industrial Revolution, preceded machinification. "Once human motions had become simplified, however, they were

ripe for imitation by machines" (1963, pp. 180-181, illustration #4). And once these simple human motions were enacted on a consistent basis by machines, they were then privileged as the kind of motions appropriate to humans. It was at this point that humans increasingly took these motions and ways of being on, resulting in a machinified human subjectivity. As Mumford put it, there arose a

contempt for any other mode of life or form of expression except that associated with the machine. ... For a new type of personality had emerged, a walking abstraction: the Economic Man. Living men imitated this penny-in-the-slot automaton, this creature of bare rationalism. (pp. 176-177)

This new type of human personality or subjectivity was a production of this new arrangement between machines and humans that made up what we could refer to as mechanical machinic assemblages. As human interaction with the novel machines of the 19th century intensified, so did this discursive migration of privileged motions. From humans to machines, and from machines to humans, a privileging occurred that served to create a new type of human being. One in line with the particular exigencies of these early machines. It is important to note that while this new subjectivity was machinified, it was not digital. These early machines worked on a different basis. The production of digitized subjectivities and psyches would have to await the invention of the microchip.

As many a scholar has argued, the microchip signals a giant and fundamental sea change in human history. This is due not only to its enormous computational power but its central place within the culture at large. As Kirkpatrick Sale (1996) notes,

I think it can be truly said that nothing has had as reticulate and reverberating an effect on industrial society as the electronic digital computer, the "master technology" that stands behind so many other inventions and processes of our lives, which has many antecedents but is appropriately dated from the perfection of the microchip and microprocessor in 1971 ... in the last two decades, a powerful and sweeping alternation of the industrial world has taken place as a result of technological changes that go to the very core of our lives, creating a revolution in work and thought, politics and markets, culture and leisure, at least as profound as that of the first Industrial Revolution ... with effects that many have seen as sweeping: computers and electronics have wrought a "Digital Revolution" is the way a magazine called Wired put it in 1993, with "social changes so profound their only parallel is probably the discovery of fire" (p. 206).

For the purposes of this article, the most salient aspect of the microchip is that it operates on a digital code. This digital mode of operation, fundamentally distinguishes most contemporary

Photo: Glenn McCrea, www.dewdropworld.com

technology that relies on the microchip (i.e., computers, stereos, communication systems, etc.) from previous analog technology. What I am arguing is that this digital basis for operation and interaction has profound effects on the humans that are brought into its discursive sphere of influence.

Perhaps the best way of understanding the particulars of how the digital basis of contemporary human interaction with machines impacts both human subjectivity and relationality is to see it as a reinforcing series of three movements. The first movement is partially based on De Landa's work (1991), but the second and third movements are original and work off the widely held cultural belief that machines are inherently more efficient than humans.

1. Certain aspects of human psychological and cognitive functioning (particularly instrumental rationality, computational logic and symbolic manipulation) "migrate" to digital machines in the form of encoded heuristics and algorithms (De Landa, 1991, pp. 4 & 146).

2. We then privilege these machine-embodied processes because they maintain our phantasies of omniscience and allow and instrumentalize our mapping and conquest of nature.

3. As our interaction with these digital machines increases both in frequency and intensity, these privileged heuristics and algorithms "migrate" back to humans displacing those human psychological characteristics (i.e., intuition, non-linear logics, emotions) that were not part of the original migration to the machines.

This migration to and from machines constitutes the particulars of contemporary human interaction with digital machines. Remarkably similar to how the machinified human subjectivity of the 19th century was achieved, this is "how" the digitization of the psyche occurs. I have termed this three-fold movement, *the ascending integrative discursive dialectic of the digitizing process*. It is ascending and integrative in that it reaches towards a certain terminal point, namely a totalizing integration of humans and machines on a common digital basis. And it is discursive in that the movements are part of a discourse between and within machines and

humans in which meanings and values are assigned and shared.

Responses to Digitization

In this section, I examine various cultural responses to the process of digitization outlined above. This list is by no means exhaustive and only covers a few of the many articulations of resistance to be found on the contemporary scene.

Ecopsychological Weapons of Mass Disruption

Rewilding is one of many reactions to digitization. Coming from the Green

> By calling on humans to base their relationships and internal dynamics on undomesticated, natural bases, ecotherapy serves as a practice of resistance for those who find the digitizing process antithetical to their values or to their conception of what it means to be truly human.

Anarchy and ecopsychology[5] movements, it is an attempt to reconnect with wildness at the everyday level of practice and to approximate some sort of feral state of being. The various practices of rewilding can be seen as a set of subversive methodologies whose aim is that of disrupting the production of digitized subjectivities through the deployment of counter-digital epistemologies and ways of being.

> Rewilding is a process that is going on all around us, all the time. It's going on in our

---

[5] Ecopsychology, a meld of psychological and ecological sensibilities, includes practices such as ecotherapy (discussed below) nature-oriented awareness practices, earth sustaining work, and art and ritual. For a fuller description of ecopsychology and its subcomponents refer to Roszak, Gomes, & Kanner (1995).

heads, our bodies, our communities, and any forest or river that is recovering from damage. It's the most irrefutable physical fact that we are capable of observing: the reversion to wild form, uncontrolled by the domesticating grip of one species.... Rewilding is as much affirmation as reaction. It's the unmediated adventure we dream about and talk of romantically, the original source from which all adventure springs forth. The trust and receptiveness to let what happens, combined with a hyper-awareness of and synchronicity with physical surroundings, and a lifetime of learning while watching and doing, is the daily attitude of the forager ... On a practical level, rewilding involves both accessing our present situations, and looking back to what has been done before by people. By developing blends of old traditions and new adaptations that are suited to our habitats and all the complexities of modern life, we can reclaim our wildness little by little. (Green Anarchy & the Wildroots Collective, 2004, p. 1)

Rewilding includes the learning of "primitive skills" such as the building of earthlodges for shelter, predicting the weather, tracking wild animals, and tanning hides and furs for clothing. Other rewilding practices include bioregionalism, which is a way of identifying and interacting with our physical surroundings that is rooted in a sense of belonging to a particular ecological place, and permaculture, a holistic approach to food cultivation that emphasizes working with the patterns and resources in nature rather than controlling them with external energy and inputs (Green Anarchy & the Wildroots Collective, 2004, pp. 7-10).

While all these practices may seem like the simple learning of skills, the underlying and explicit emphasis throughout these skill-learning exercises is to "change our psychological conditioning" by undoing our learned domestication (Green Anarchy & the Wildroots Collective, 2004, p. 2). This kind of thinking is in line with Felix Guattari's (1995) theorizing, discussed above, wherein subjectivity is understood as being the on-going production of a discursive interaction with ideas, things, beings and processes in one's environment (p. 7). Hence, if humans change the content and character of their discursive interaction with the world, their subjectivity also changes. It would go from being progressively digitized to less domesticated.

Ecotherapy

Ecotherapy, a set of nature-based psychotherapeutic practices, is another of the cultural forms that has arisen partly as a reaction against the process of digitization. Ecotherapy healing modalities include Sarah Conn's (1995) self-world model of psychotherapy, wherein the client's individually experienced suffering is connected to the ecological crisis of the planet (pp. 156-171), Leslie Gray's (1995) shamanic counseling (pp. 172-182), and extended wilderness treks like those practiced by Stephen Foster, Meredith Little, Robert Greenway, Rick Medrick, Dolores LaChapelle, and Steven Harper (Harper, 1995, p. 200).

Joanna Macy's (1995) despair and empowerment workshops can also be considered a type of ecotherapy. These workshops encompass a set of "introspective techniques that help people find a sense of empowerment through an honest confrontation with such paralyzing negative emotions as rage, guilt, and despair" (p. 240). Her more recent work is the much-heralded "Council of All Beings, a collective mourning ritual that allows participants to work through their deeply repressed emotional responses to ecological disaster" (p. 240).

Ecotherapy's focus and emphasis on a return to our primal matrix, defined by Chellis Glendinning (1994) as "the state of a healthy, wholly functioning psyche in full-bodied participation with a healthy, wholly functioning Earth," (p. 5) could be interpreted as a powerful counterpoint to the digitizing process. By calling on humans to base their relationships and internal dynamics on undomesticated, natural bases, not digital ones, ecotherapy serves as a genus or practice of resistance for those who find the digitizing process antithetical to their values or to their conception of what it means to be truly human.

Cyber and Viral Warfare

Other possible reactions against the process of digitization include the incapacitation of digital machinic assemblages through cyber and viral warfare. Cyberwar, or the use of computers and the internet to wage war, could incapacitate intelligence and military machinic assemblages through concerted efforts to disable centralized and decentralized command and control structures. This objective can be accomplished through denial of service attacks on critical node servers, contamination of intelligence data, equipment disruption and attacks on power and communication infrastructures that support digital machinic assemblages (McWilliams, 2003, p. 1). Viral warfare could affect the same sort of results through the dispersal of computer viruses that bring down both specific machinic assemblages and their surrounding computer environments.

References

Armitage, J. (2004). "Beyond Postmodernism?: Paul Virilio's Hypermodern cultural theory" In A. & M. Kroker (Eds.), *Life in the wires: The ctheory reader* (pp. 354-368). Victoria, Canada: New World Perspectives/CTheory Books.

Brubaker, R. (1994). "Rationalization". In W. Outhwaite & T. Bottomore (Eds.), *The Blackwell dictionary of twentieth century social thought* (pp. 546-547). Oxford, England: Blackwell Publishers.

Conn, S. A. (1995). "When the Earth hurts, who responds?" In T. Roszak, M. E. Gomes, & A. D. Kanner (Eds.), *Ecopsychology: Restoring the Earth, healing the mind* (pp. 156-171). San Francisco: Sierra Club Books.

Dawkins, N. (2005). "Interview with Joshua Davis." *ZINK*, March.

De Landa, M. (1991). *War in the age of intelligent machines.* New York: Zone Books.

De Landa, M. (1997). "The machinic phylum." V2. http://framework.v2.nl/archive/archive/node/text/.xslt/nodenr-70071 (accessed May 14, 2007)

Deleuze, G., & Guattari, F. (1987). *A thousand plateaus.* Minneapolis: University of Minnesota Press.

Glendinning, C. (1994). *My name is Chellis and I'm in recovery from western civilization.* Boston: Shambala.

Gray, L. 1995. "Shamanic counseling and ecopsychology." In T. Roszak, M. E. Gomes, & A. D. Kanner (Eds.), *Ecopsychology: Restoring the Earth, healing the mind* (pp. 172-182). San Francisco: Sierra Club Books.

Green Anarchy and The Wildroots Collective. (2004). "Rewilding: A primer for a balanced existence amid the ruins of civilization." *Green Anarchy: An Anti-Civilization Journal of Theory and Action, 16*(Winter), 1-16. http://zinelibrary.info/files/ga16.pdf

Guattari, F. (1995). *Chaosmosis An ethico-aesthetic paradigm.* Bloomington: Indiana University Press.

Guattari, F. 1996. "Subjectivities: For better and for worse." In G. Genosko (Ed.), The Guattari Reader (pp. 193-203). Oxford, England: Blackwell Publishing.

Harper, S. (1995). "The way of wilderness." In T. Roszak, M. E. Gomes, & A. D. Kanner (Eds.), *Ecopsychology: Restoring the Earth, healing the mind* (pp. 183-200). San Francisco: Sierra Club Books.

Horkheimer, M., & Adorno, T. (1973). *Dialectic of enlightenment.* New York: Continuum International.

Lloyd, S. (2007). *Programming the universe: A quantum computer scientist takes on the cosmos.* New York: Vintage.

Macy, J. (1995). "Working through environmental despair." In T. Roszak, M. E. Gomes, & A. D. Kanner (Eds.), *Ecopsychology: Restoring the Earth, healing the mind* (pp. 240-259). San Francisco: Sierra Club Books.

McWilliams, B. (2003, May 22) "Iraq's crash course in cyberwar." Wired. http://www.wired.com/politics/law/news/2003/05/58901?currentPage=all (accessed May 14, 2007

Mumford, L. (1963). *Technics and civilization.* New York: Harcourt BraceJavanovich.

Prigogine, I., & Stengers, I. (1984). *Order out of chaos: Man's new dialogue with nature.* New York: Bantam.

Roszak, T., Gomes, M. E., & Kanner, A. D. (Eds.). (1995). *Ecopsychology: Restoring the Earth, healing the mind.* San Francisco: Sierra Club Books.

Sale, K. (1996). *Rebels against the future, the Luddites and their war on the industrial revolution: Lessons for the computer age.* New York: Addison Wesley.

Wachowski, L. & Wachowski, A. (Producers & Directors). (1999). *The matrix.* USA: Warner Bros.

Varela, F., Maturana, H. R., & Uribe, R. (1974). Autopoiesis: The organization of living systems, its characterization and a model. *Biosystems, 5,* 187-196.

Virilio, P. (1997). *Open sky.* (J. Rose, Trans.). London: Verso.

Weber, M. (1978). *Economy and society: An outline of interpretive sociology* (Eds. G. Roth & C. Wittich). Berkeley: University of California Press. (Original work published 1921-1922)

The Western Mind, Terror of Death, & Environmental Degradation

Mark McKinley

L ife is a precarious enterprise with death being its ever present and complementary aspect. Beyond the typical hazards of survival, however, today we face an increasingly dangerous world in which the ability of the planet to support its myriad forms of life is threatened. The environmental crisis is in full force. Species extinctions are occurring at alarming rates, while fragile eco-systems are being destroyed. There are drastic reductions in wilderness areas, increased desertification, reductions in potable water, and an inordinate amount of toxic material emitted into the atmosphere, dumped into the water supply, or buried in once fertile ground. These atrocities, among many others, bring into stark relief the perilous nature of life in catastrophic proportions.

Ecopsychology is a burgeoning field that studies the complex interconnection of the environment on the human

Mark McKinley is a doctoral candidate in clinical psychology at the California Institute of Integral Studies. He has presented at two ecopsychology colloquiums on topics related to ecopsychology and transpersonal psychology. Mark is exploring various applications of ecopsychology, both in his clinical work and as a broader critique on American culture. Contact: Access Institute, 110 Gough Street, Suite 301, San Francisco, CA 94102, 415-861-5449 x338, Bradshaw219@yahoo.com

psyche and humankind's relationship with nature. A central focus in ecopsychology is the relative ineffectiveness the environmental movement has had on promoting large scale change in social attitudes or behaviors related to environmental concerns (Brown, 1995). The earth continues to deteriorate and yet there are only incremental or "shallow" solutions offered to address the magnitude of the ecological crisis. With more than 50 years of campaigning, why has the environmental movement failed to galvanize mainstream America to respond to the enormity of the environmental crisis? A partial answer can be found, I will argue, by examining the psychological underpinnings that prevent a cultural paradigm shift that would organize society and the individual to support a sustainable worldview perspective.

To guide my inquiry, I will draw on the theoretical framework of terror management theory (TMT). TMT is predicated on the work of cultural anthropologist Ernest Becker (1973) who argued that the fundamental anxiety that shapes individual psychologies and subsequently cultures is a terror of death. With the capacity for self-awareness, humans can remember the past, perceive the present, and anticipate future events, including the inevitability of one's death. This foreboding knowledge of one's own

mortality results in a pervasive and crippling anxiety, in which one can only seek refuge by using culture to provide psychological value and security. TMT empirically extended Becker's theory by revealing that when one is saliently reminded of one's mortality, one engages in culturally sanctioned behaviors that support one's self-esteem and reinforce faith in one's cultural worldview in order to restore and maintain psychological equanimity (Arndt, Solomon, Kasser, & Sheldon, 2004).

Using the theoretical formulations of TMT provides a lens to examine the psychological underpinnings that support the current values and behaviors associated with the dominant Western worldview. These salient values and behaviors include maintaining an anthropocentric view that seeks domination and control over the environment, and confers self-esteem through the acquisition of material wealth and possessions. TMT thus offers crucial insights to understanding the insecurities of the human psyche and how specifically Western values and beliefs contribute to the environmental crisis.

But why has the Western worldview developed to alienate humankind from nature and lead to values and beliefs that threaten to eradicate life on earth? To answer this question and to understand what has prevented large scale social changes regarding environmental issues, we will explore the psychological foundation of the Western mind through understanding the human predicament and tracing the historical development of the dominant Western worldview. From this vantage point, we can see how TMT elucidates the psychological mechanisms behind the environmental degradation and offers insights into the challenges in developing an alternative worldview that values ecological sustainability.

The Human Predicament

Erich Fromm (1964, p. 116) spoke of the human predicament as a "contradiction inherent in human existence" by virtue of humans being both animals and self-aware, symbolic creatures. This situates humankind in a dialectical conflict between being physically constrained by

is threatened." Unlike fear, in which one can respond decisively to a specific object, anxiety can only be managed, since it is integrally related to one's subjective understanding of self and world. Consequently, anxiety permeates all facets of human life.

This understanding of the nature of anxiety helps elucidate the motivation behind human behavior. Becker (1962, p. 39) noted that, "Anxiety is the prime mover of human behavior, and man will do anything to avoid it." In fact, an individual's maturation may be seen as an increased sophistication of psychological mechanisms to manage anxiety and the development of strategies to avoid physical and symbolic dangers. This comes at a price, however, in that one is restricting experience in service of maintaining perceived security. But

and through the course of history has widened the gap between the two. This exacerbation of the human predicament has had the unfortunate consequence of inflaming humankind's experience of anxiety. Fromm (1956, pp. 8-9) noted, "the experience of separateness is the source of all anxiety [and] the deepest need of man is to overcome his separateness." The solution to this existential anxiety, according to Becker (1973), is for people to act heroically within culturally meaningful ways to attain self-worth that may symbolically transcend their animal nature and defy the inevitable fate of death, the final separation. This is primarily achieved through the psychological mechanisms of denial and repression, which collectively help inform the cultural worldview.

Fromm (1964) observed that this heroic attempt to transcend nature to maximize the full potential of symbolic humanness is one means to overcome the separation of the human predicament. This effort, however, lacks a realistic appraisal and is doomed to fall short of being an adequate solution. Not only does this solution further estrange humankind in a perverted sense of reality, but as Becker (1973, p. 66) poignantly articulated, the irony of the human condition is that humankind's "deepest need is to be free of the anxiety of death and annihilation; but it is life itself which awakens it, and so we must shrink from being fully alive." This insight renders impossible the desire to cleave our animalistic nature in pursuit of human potential. Therefore the only possible way to maintain psychological equanimity is for people to remain in denial and repression, enacting what Becker (1973) called the vital lie.

All actions endeavored upon in the human symbolic world, Becker (1973) argued, are an effort to overcome the inevitable fate of death. Principal in this pursuit, denial and repression represent the foundation of cognitive distortions in which humans are able to deceive themselves of the terrifying realities of their world. Becker (1973) called this the vital lie, in that it is a necessary deception in order to preserve the functioning capabilities of humans. He argued that if one truly appreciated the fragility of life, the awesome power of nature,

Why has the environmental movement failed to galvanize mainstream America to respond to the enormity of the environmental crisis?

nature and simultaneously being free to experience the infinite expression of human intellect, including such notions as immortality. This conflict alienates humankind, positioning them in a unique bind in which humans are neither fully a part of nature, nor emancipated from it. As such, this conflict yields a humankind that is separate, isolated, and ultimately frightened in the world (Fromm, 1964).

The felt experience of the human predicament is one of anxiety. Rollo May (1977) acknowledged anxiety as a purely human phenomenon by distinguishing anxiety from fear. According to May, fear represents an emotional and physiological response to a specific threat, whereas anxiety represents a capacity to be aware of potential threats that may or may not manifest. As such anxiety is primal, while fear derives from one's capacity to be aware of danger. May (1977, p. 181) further articulated this distinction when he asserted, "An individual experiences various fears on the basis of a security pattern he has developed; but in anxiety it is this security pattern itself which

no matter how securely an individual may construct his or her life, the inevitable reality of death pierces through all constructions and will ultimately destroy the individual. Thus death serves as the fundamental anxiety, the final separation that spurs all human behavior (Becker, 1973; May, 1977).

The greatest manifestation of human behavior is the development of culture. Cultures were carved out of the chaos and danger of the natural world to bring a shared symbolic system to organize, protect, and provide stability to the human experience. Becker (1973, p. 5) argued that each culture was designed as a hero-system "in which people serve in order to earn a feeling of primary value, of cosmic specialness, of ultimate usefulness to creation, of unshakable meaning." Thus culture represents a haven that insulates humans from the realities of a dangerous environment and provides a consensually agreed upon worldview that brings forth meaning and purpose. Culture has mediated the relationship between humankind and nature

and the unpredictability of death, one would be rendered paralyzed in terror. Such a state threatens the survival of the human species, and as a result, humans developed a symbolically meaningful worldview to buffer such anxiety. This worldview prescribes the socialization of particular psychological defenses and behaviors that bring a sense of predictability, security, and agency to the human experience. The vital lie enables humans to exercise their heroism, achieving self-worth, purpose, and meaning in an otherwise nihilistic world red in tooth and claw.

Development of the Western Cultural Worldview

The aforementioned analysis of the human predicament is situated in a Western psychological perspective, which assumes the construction of the self to be bounded, and therefore existing as a separate entity, and is volitionally oriented towards developing mastery and control (Taylor, 1989). It also assumes a relationship in which the human species is pitted against the whole of nature in a zero-sum game for survival. To understand potential new ways to construct a worldview that is more ecologically sustainable it is important to examine the history of the dominant Western worldview to elucidate the development of certain values and beliefs that guide our contemporary paradigm.

Throughout the ancient world, nature was perceived as enchanted and sacred (Tarnas, 1991). The awesome powers of nature were attributed to Gods and Goddesses and "The earth was sacred

the Abrahamic religions and the dictate expressed in Genesis 1:28: "God blessed them (humankind) and said to them, "Be fruitful and increase, fill the earth and subdue it, have dominion over the fish in the sea, the birds in the air, and every living thing that moves on the earth" (The

Photo: Glenn McCrea, www.dewdropworld.com

Oxford Study Bible 1992, p. 12). Within the Judeo-Christian canon, this is God's first command to humankind and establishes a hierarchical relationship between humankind and the rest of nature. It categorically places humankind above the rest of nature and implies that nature

relationship with nature in that prior to the expulsion it appears that nature is abundant and accessible to humankind. Following the banishment from Eden, however, God claims the earth is cursed and humankind will have to labor and toil to acquire food that was once bountiful. Through this act, earth, the sacred source of life has been disenchanted and reduced to mere objective materiality. This further reinforced the attitude that inhabiting this world is a form of divine punishment and represented the scourge of human folly. Philosopher Richard Tarnas (1991, p. 137) succinctly described this situation when he noted, "But with man's sin and fall, both man and nature lost their divine inheritance, and thus began the Judeo-Christian drama of man's vicissitudes in relation to God, amidst a backdrop of a spiritually destitute and alienated world." Collectively, the sentiments of Genesis have opened the door for a gradual but pervading desacralization of nature. As such, the contemporary theologian Larry Rasmussen (1994, p. 174) noted, "Christianity bears a huge burden of guilt for the ecocrisis" in that elements of the Judeo-Christian ethic validate an anthropocentric worldview.

As Christianity spread out from Galilee through the pagan Greco-Roman civilization it encountered many local earth-based religions. Many of these religions had seasonal ceremonies and rituals which that were absorbed in Christianized form; moreover, these religions sanctioned pilgrimages to sacred places, such as mountains, rivers, and tree groves (Sheldrake, 1991). Through this process Christianity retained some connection to nature despite its dualistic theology. However, with the advent of the Protestant Reformation many of these adulterated practices were purified. The Protestant Reformation valued "Personal faith and repentance [and] ritual observances, seasonal festivals, pilgrimages, devotion to the Holy Mother, and cults of saints and angels were

Humans are neither fully a part of nature, nor emancipated from it.

both as the source of life and as the receiver of the dead" (Sheldrake, 1991, p. 13). Though nature inspired reverence, it also inspired fear and a desire to control nature. This visceral experience of nature can be seen as the antecedent to the anthropocentrism that has been present through most of Western history.

Historically, the centrality of an anthropocentric ethic can be traced to

exists for the sole benefit and pleasure of humankind. This categorical differentiation also suggests that humankind is ontologically privileged and therefore entitled to plunder, exploit, and destroy the inferior resources of nature.

Additionally, roots of anthropocentrism can be traced to the story of Adam and Eve's expulsion from the Garden of Eden. This story shifts humankind's

all denounced as pagan superstitions" (Sheldrake, 1991, p. 28). The result of this purification was the disenchantment of the world. Spirit was conceived as residing only in the confines of humanity and in humankind's personal relationship with God. The rest of the world was considered inanimate matter. As a result of expunging any connection to nature and only valuing spirit within humankind, Rasmussen (1994, p. 174) concluded that our current "spiritual crisis rest in the alienated way in which we conceive ourselves apart from nature." According to Fromm (1956), this has exacerbated humankind's existential anxiety and promulgated a further isolation of human culture in an ill-conceived solution to overcome humankind's separation.

The perpetuation of human isolation from nature was solidified in the Protes-

This new empiricism sought knowledge through a systematic reduction of nature into its smallest parts in order to understand, control, and manipulate it for the purposes of humankind. Through this endeavor, control and predictability supplanted nature as the divinely inspired laws of the Newtonian universe operated like clockwork. This cultural shift and rise of intellectualism reoriented the prevailing anthropocentric worldview by predicating it on materialism and the myth of progress (Swimme & Berry, 1992).

Cosmologist Brian Swimme and philosopher Thomas Berry (1992) assert humankind is currently under the siren's song of progress. The myth of progress is the anthropocentric view that due to humankind's unique cognitive abilities and its derivatives of knowledge, tech-

lack of awareness of the interrelatedness of one's self and nature has led humankind into a perilous environmental crisis.

Terror Management Theory

From this vantage point, we can appreciate the psychological as well as the cultural composition of the Western mind. To see how this psychological mechanism works in relation to environmental degradation, it is helpful to understand the basic tenets of terror management theory (TMT). TMT is predicated on the assumption that humans are predisposed towards self-preservation and reproduction, and that humans are unique in that they are self-aware creatures. As noted earlier, the awareness of death induces a debilitating terror, which needs to be mitigated to preserve human life. This is accomplished through behaviors that reinforce a cultural worldview and bolster one's self-esteem within that cultural worldview (Arndt et al., 2004).

The protection from mortality is the driving force (often unconsciously) behind human motivation and behavior (Ardnt et al., 2004). As a child develops, TMT purports, that the child begins to learn the cultural worldview, which imbues life with meaning "through accounts of the origin of the universe, prescriptions for behavior, and explanations of what happens after death" (Solomon, Greenberg, & Pyszczynski, 2000, p. 201). Through socialization, the child learns a security pattern by behaving in culturally sanctioned ways. These prescribed behaviors bring a sense of control and predictability to the world, which allows the child to feel safe. Additionally, the child learns to feel good about himself or herself (self-esteem) through personal achievement of culturally valued possessions, roles, and contributions. Self-esteem is important for providing value and agency within the symbolic world of human culture. Through cultural domestication the child learns appropriate behaviors that reinforce a sense of security and value.

Unfortunately, within the dominant Western worldview, this has had deleterious effects on the environment. The formulaic mechanism behind TMT suggests that humans within Western cultures have sought to maintain a sense of meaning and "cosmic specialness"

Terror Management Theory elucidates the psychological mechanisms behind the environmental degradation and offers insights into the challenges in developing an alternative worldview that values ecological sustainability.

tant Reformation and the burgeoning scientific revolution. The Reformation laid the foundation for a scientific revolution which would create a new mechanistic cosmology, which completely divorced the subjective human from the objective universe (Sheldrake, 1991). Integral to this intellectual and eventually cultural transition was the French philosopher, Rene Descartes. In his methodical search for epistemological certitude, Descartes found "human reason established first its own existence, out of experiential necessity, then God's existence, out of logical necessity, and thence the God-guaranteed reality of the objective world and its rational order" (Tarnas, 1991, p. 279). Thus Cartesian dualism emancipated the world from any sacred or human qualities and opened it up for scientific exploration and ultimately exploitation.

nology, and skills, humankind is able to progress. Swimme and Berry (1992, p. 241) noted that "Progress has been measured by the extent of human control over the nonhuman world and the apparent benefits that emerged for humans." The consequence of this progress is the exploitation of nature, the depletion of resources, and a toxication of the environment that is destroying the sustainability of earth. This progress is a myth insofar as humankind's achieved comforts and conveniences are endangering the survivability of the human and nonhuman world. From this anthropocentric perspective of separation and individualism, humans are collectively too blind to their technological addiction to realize "that what humans do to the outer world they do to their own inner world" (Swimme & Berry 1992, p. 242). This

through the control and domination of nature, and achieving a sense of esteem by amassing wealth, power, and possessions (Kasser & Sheldon, 2000; Koole and Van den Berg, 2005). Rollo May (1977, p. 206) noted that social prestige within American culture is defined primarily in economic terms and that "the acquisition of wealth is accepted as proof and symbol of individual power." This meaning system, which emphasizes individual accumulation of material goods have wrought havoc on the environment.

Disrupting this defensive posturing as articulated by TMT is particularly difficult in light of environmentalists' attempts to alter social attitudes and behaviors related to the environmental crisis. It is a challenging proposition insofar as raising awareness of the environmental crisis induces, at least to some degree, a mortality salient experience that triggers individuals to exhibit behaviors that reinforce their cultural worldview and bolster their self-esteem. Employing rhetoric that uses fear tactics to convey the urgency of the crisis or doomsday-like predictions about the earth's demise produces a response of denial and reliance on culturally ingrained values and behaviors to recover a sense of psychological security. Consequently, the environmental movement is faced with a paradoxical situation in which the more ardent or radical arguments to engender social change may impel a stronger psychological resistance. It may even encourage greater environmental degradation as the populace struggles to retain a sense of security through the purchasing and disposing of material goods. This represents an insidious cycle that thwarts significant cultural changes, which appear necessary to resuscitate earth's beleaguered biosphere. It appears this psychological quagmire is in part responsible for the resistance and apathy associated with mainstream responses to the environmental crisis and is rarely addressed.

The basic dilemma of the human predicament cannot be changed, but the cultural meanings promulgated by the West-

Culture represents a haven that insulates humans from the realities of a dangerous environment and provides a consensually agreed upon worldview that brings forth meaning and purpose.

ern worldview can be altered to support a more ecologically friendly displacement of humankind's terror of death. Theoretically, the way out of this vicious cycle is to change certain values within the Western worldview to reflect modes of gaining self-esteem and security within an ecologically friendly paradigm. There is evidence that such changes in

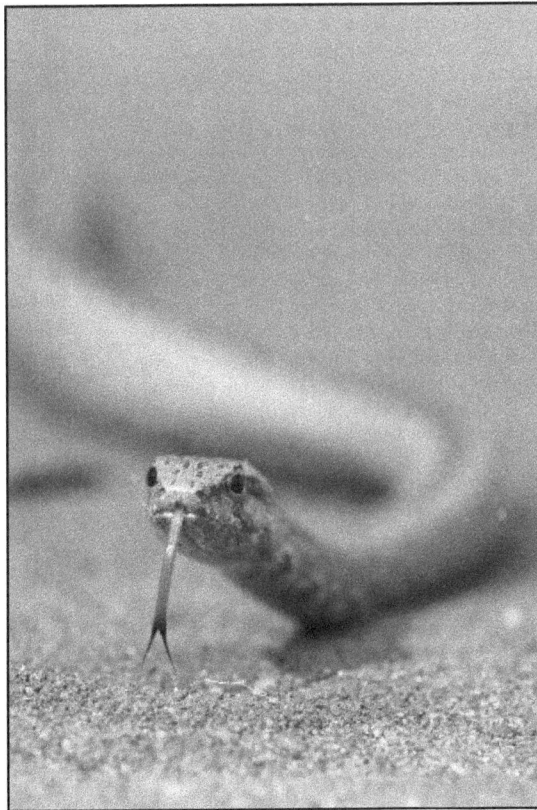

Photo: Glenn McCrea, www.dewdropworld.com

worldview do in fact result in more proenvironmental behaviors when people are exposed to mortality salient experiences (Vess & Arndt, 2008). This further supports the notion that environmental discourse needs to focus on discussing and altering values embedded within the dominant Western worldview in order to lay the foundation for changes in economic, political, and social structures.

Challenges to Shaping a New Worldview

There are many challenges to making sweeping cultural changes. As TMT suggests, people are interested in maintaining a sense of psychological security and value in the how they symbolically perceive and interact in the world. The dominant Western values of anthropocentrism, individualism, and materialism have guided how Westerners relate to the environment for thousands of years. Changing this relationship dynamic, in which humans have been the sole beneficiary, has psychological consequences. It is important to understand what is psychologically at stake in shifting this worldview perspective.

I believe there are two fundamentally perceived losses (from an anthropocentric view) which inhibit Westerners from fully participating in behaviors to significantly mitigate the environmental crisis. These perceived losses include a loss in ontological stature and a loss of selfhood as traditionally defined in Western values. These perceived losses are especially vulnerable in a cultural transformation from an anthropocentric ethic to an ecocentric ethic. Members of the deep ecology movement have argued that the only sustainable change that ensures the viability of the biosphere is to acknowledge the intrinsic value of all life forms, not just what is useful to humankind (Sessions, 1995). Deep ecologists are often misrepresented as being misanthropic, and I believe this charge is a reaction to the loss of ontological privilege suggested in an ecocentric perspective. The result of disabusing humanity from its ontological superiority to the nonhuman world is a deep narcissistic blow to humanity's sense of "cosmic specialness." It fractures an integral construction in the Western worldview, dismantling the symbolic foundation that grants transcendence. The relinquishing of ontological privilege also results in a tangible redistribution of power, which may engender feelings of deflation and impotence. This is especially true if there is not a substituted worldview to furnish a sense of meaning or value to one's recent loss of ontological stature.

Additionally, the ecocentric ethic also challenges Western conceptions of selfhood. An ecocentric perspective refutes the notion that the self is a discretely bounded, self-sufficient, separate entity. It suggests that the self exists in an interconnected and interdependent matrix composed of the cosmos, the biosphere, and humanity (Roszak, 1995). This ecological self may be viewed as an expansion and perceived by some as beneficial. However, from an anthropocentric view, it represents a loss in the treasured ideal of a self-reliant and independent self that is integral in the Western worldview. To successfully advance the environmental movement's agenda to a more sustainable worldview perspective, there needs to be greater discussion, mourning, and reworking of humankind's ontology and requisite conception of selfhood.

The shift from an anthropocentric to an ecocentric ethic has immense implications and seems to require a transitional worldview to bridge from an old meaning system to a new, ecologically sustainable worldview. An essential component to this transition is identifying the psychological hurdles that resist change and begin crafting a new values system that can absorb the emergent anxieties while paving the way for a more ecologically sustainable worldview. The specific steps needed to transform the economic, political, and social structures of society to accord with an ecocentric ethic is beyond the scope of this article, but such steps would require highlighting the psychological dimension by appreciating the necessity and utility cultural worldviews provide for human beings.

References

Arndt, J., Solomon, S., Kasser, T., & Sheldon, K.M. (2004) The urge to splurge: A terror management account of materialism and consumer behavior. *Journal of Consumer Psychology 14*(3), 198-212.

Arndt, J., Greenberg, J., Solomon, S., Pyszczynski, T., & Simon, L. (1997) Suppression, accessibility of death-related thoughts, and cultural worldview defense: Exploring the psychodynamics of terror management. *Journal of Personality and Social Psychology 3*, 5-18.

Becker, E. (1962). *The birth and death of meaning.* New York: The Free Press of Glencoe.

Becker, E. (1973). *The denial of death.* New York: The Free Press.

Brown, L. R. (1995). Ecopsychology and the environmental revolution: An environmental foreword. In T. Roszak, M. E. Gomes, & A. D. Kanner (Eds.), *Ecopsychology: Restoring the Earth, healing the mind* (pp. xiii-xvi). San Francisco: Sierra Club Books.

Fromm, E. (1956). *The art of loving.* New York: Harper Perennial Modern Classics.

Fromm, E. (1964). *The heart of man: Its genius for good and evil.* New York: Harper and Row.

Kasser, T., & Sheldon, M. (2000). Of wealth and death: Materialism, mortality salience, and consumption behavior. *Psychological Service, 11*(4), 348-351.

Koole, S.L., & Van den Berg, A.E. (2005). Lost in the wilderness: Terror management, action-orientation, and nature evaluation. *Journal of Personality and Social Psychology, 88*(6), 1014-1028.

May, R. (1977). *The meaning of anxiety.* New York: Pocket Books.

Rasmussen, L. (1994). Cosmology and ethics. In M. E. Tucker & J. A. Grim (Eds.), *Worldviews and Ecology: Religion, Philosophy, and the Environment* (pp. 173-180). New York: Orbis Books.

Roszak, T. (1995). Where psyche meets Gaia. In T. Roszak, M. E. Gomes, & A. D. Kanner (Eds.), *Ecopsychology: Restoring the Earth, healing the mind* (pp. 1-17). San Francisco: Sierra Club Books.

Sessions, G. (1995). Preface. In G. Sessions (Ed.), *Deep ecology for the 21st century: Readings on the philosophy and practice of the new environmentalism* (pp. ix-xxviii). Boston: Shambhala Publications, Inc.

Sheldrake, R. (1991). *The rebirth of nature: The greening of science and god.* New York: Bantam Books.

Solomon, S., Greenberg, J., & Pysszczynski, T. (2000). Pride and Prejudice: Fear of death and social behavior. *Current Directions in Psychological Sciences, 9*(6), 200-204.

Swimme, B., & Berry, T. (1992). *The universe story: From the primordial flaring forth to the ecozoic era-a celebration of the unfolding of the cosmos.* San Francisco: HarpersSanFrancisco.

Tarnas, R. (1991). *The passion of the Western mind: Understanding the ideas that have shaped our world view.* New York: Ballantine Books.

Taylor, C. (1989). *Sources of the self: The making of modernity identity.* Cambridge: Cambridge University Press.

The Oxford Study Bible: Revised English Bible with the Apocrypha. (1992). Eds. M. J. Suggs, K. D. Sakenfeld, & J. R. Mueller. New York: Oxford University Press.

Vess, M. & Arndt, J. (2008). The nature of death and the death of nature: The impact of mortality salience on environmental concern. *Journal of Research in Personality, 42*, 1376-1380.

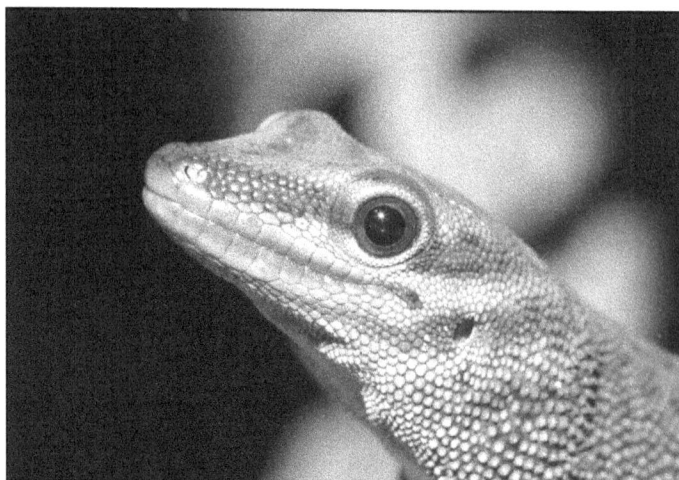

Photo: Glenn McCrea, www.dewdropworld.com

Global Warming, Ecological Psychology, & the Call to Higher Maturity

Jeff Beyer

Our solutions for the fundamental problems of living with nature have not often been very wise or mature solutions. Although our cleverness did thankfully get us through many predicaments, it usually did so only temporarily, and the real consequences of these clever solutions were delayed for another time, mostly kept hidden from view. We might now come to realize that we are not doing well. We humans collectively are not unlike the very bright but struggling college freshman, that guy who was able to breeze through elementary and high school and who is dismayed to discover that he never really developed the study skills and personal maturity he now desperately needs to make it in college. To now get himself to do what it takes to survive, he must first face the agonizingly real possibility that he may not. The story of the human-nature relationship is one littered with such examples of "just getting by." The

air outside is becoming too polluted? If you can't move away then just keep the windows closed--hide inside. But because of all the toxic substances we use to make the things in our homes, the air we breathe inside may be even more toxic than the air outside--do you keep the windows opened or closed? You can't get away from it anymore. Our clever but not particularly mature solution: get away from it, try to wall yourself off from it. And, for thousands of years at least some people must have known what utter folly it is to cut down all of the trees of the land; but deforest the land we did anyway, and then we moved on to cut elsewhere. Our solu-

I am convinced that climate change, and what we do about it, will define us, our era, and ultimately the global legacy we leave for future generations.... We hold the future in our hands.... Together, we must ensure that our grandchildren will not have to ask why we failed to do the right thing and let them suffer the consequences. Ban Ki-moon[1]

tion: just move on. But now, not surprisingly, we discover that there is nowhere left to move on to. Again, throughout all of history, the problem of what to do with massive quantities of daily waste was solved by bundling it up and throwing it away someplace; out of sight, out of mind. Our solution: just throw it away. But now it is becoming so apparent to us that my "away" is actually someone else's "here." In truth, there has never been any real throwing "away," not really--it's really always been just throwing "over there." The list goes on and on. These less than wise, tragically short sighted solutions gave us easy access to the handy and comforting illusion that everything was going ok (well, kind of ok, as long as you didn't look too closely). And we can appreciate that life for most people seemed plenty difficult as it was; we're just trying to get by. So it was apparently deemed "good enough for now" to employ these patchwork solutions to keep the ship on course for the time being, even if, in truth, that course insidiously (or otherwise) engen-

Jeff Beyer Please see first article in this issue for bio.

[1] UN Secretary-General Ban Ki-moon to the UN General Assembly, 9/24/07 (LA Times, 9/25/07)

dered its own problems--psychological, social, environmental--and was, or will be, in the end, catastrophic and maybe even suicidal for our species. Clever, effective, efficient--well, maybe; but so clearly not wise. We'll worry about the bigger problems when the time comes, we must have thought.

are those who would bet everything that we will some day, somehow, come up with yet another clever technological solution to our problems, one which will simply erase our past indiscretions and clear the environmental slate--a kind of glorious high tech absolution. For these

of relating with nature. This threat of global destruction comes from all of us just doing what we are doing now. Our way of life is being called into question in a most dramatic way: if we continue along our present, alienated-from-nature course, we may not even survive as a species, at least not at all in the way that we hope to. The peril arises from the way we live, and it is my contention that the way we live thrives on a posture of experienced alienation from the rest of nature.

Will it be in this, our own generation that the cumulative debt of the human species will finally come due?

Well, has the time come? Could it be that now, after so many generations of human existence, we are finally being forced to realize that there is no place left to hide, that there is no more running away, that if we keep this up, we'll soon be standing knee deep in our own pile of toxic waste? Inevitably, as we could have known we would if we kept multiplying, we have encircled the earth with our numbers and we are bumping into each other on all sides. And thousands of years of an ever exacerbating posture of alienation from and careless exploitation of nature is taking its toll. Will it be in this, our own generation that the cumulative debt of the human species will finally come due? Is there no more room for denial and deferment? Will the bright but failing college student be able to let go of problematic and habitual youthful ways and start growing toward greater maturity and wisdom? Will he do it in time? Can he? Will we humans flunk out of the evolutionary story for lack of sufficient wisdom and maturity?

Throughout most of history the relatively small number of human beings compared to the apparent vastness of the earth must have made it easier, I suppose, to remain in denial about what we were really doing, doing both to ourselves and to the rest of the natural world. While there must have been those whose eyes remained open to the psychological and environmental folly--those who could see the illusion for what it was and who knew well that the path was unsustainable in the long run, these people were apparently too few or too powerless or too otherwise occupied to significantly change our trajectory. And then there

optimistic and flatteringly self confident people the battle cry is "More of the same and full speed ahead!" It is for them a high stakes, "all in" wager that our growing technological cleverness will outpace our ongoing destruction of natural systems. And, lastly, there will always be those who are willing to avert their gaze altogether, who would refuse even to see, much less fully appreciate, the reality of what we were doing to ourselves and to the rest of nature. "Refusal to see" is not often hailed as an indicator of psychological health or maturity in a relationship of any kind, and it can only impede the development of good judgment and wisdom. Because of our failure to act, our reluctance to change, or our refusal see, we have effectively bequeathed to other people at other times the compounding fundamental problems of our way of relating with nature; our children's inheritance includes the consequences, whatever they may be, of our denial and our refusal to address the quality of this relationship.

This is not the first time in history in which we have been invited to face the possibility of global destruction--the jolting threat of nuclear weapons and global war, for example. But these predicaments, at best, have only called us to question our ways of relating with each other, human to human. The new and interesting thing about the global climate chaos predicament is that it is primarily a call to question our basic ways

We should be clear that the problem of global warming is not really just a CO_2 problem, one that simply needs an urgent, narrowly focused, high tech solution; true, the current and projected CO_2 levels are the legitimate focus of our concerns today, and we must do something about it now. But, like toxicity, deforestation, waste disposal, and all the rest of the serious and compounding problems, the real issue is whether or not we begin to act more wisely, with a significantly increased measure of maturity, with much greater sensitivity and concern for the genuine well being

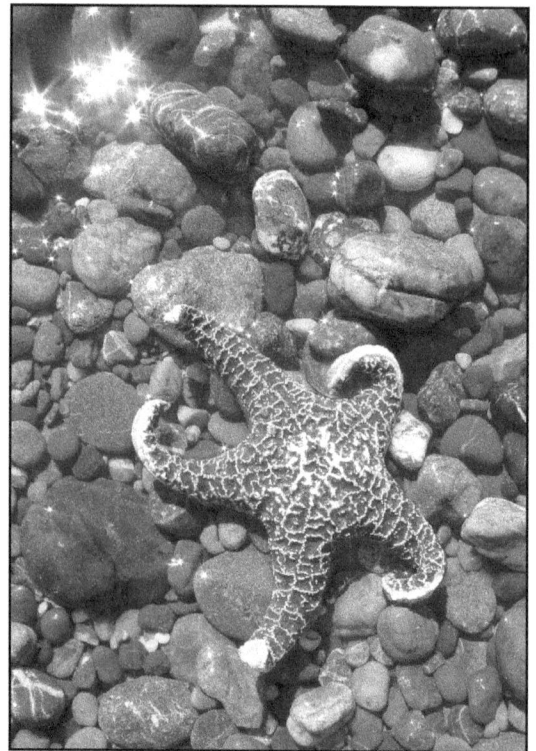

Photo: Glenn McCrea, www.dewdropworld.com

of all of nature, including all of each other. By and large, maybe even from the beginning of agriculture some 10 or 12 thousand years ago through modern times, these necessary levels of sensitivity and concern have apparently not been found in our pervasive alienated posture toward nature (White, 1967, p. 1203). Real solutions require a more mature psychological openness to the reality of our interconnectedness with nature and the wisdom borne of that intimate involvement. The current CO_2 level problem is just another symptom beckoning our greater wisdom. It is the first weakest link in a long chain that was going to break anyway unless something basic changed in our relating with the rest of nature. If it wasn't CO_2 levels it would have eventually been something else.

The good news is that this may be the first time in human history in which this call to question the human-nature relationship has been so poignant and so global. Recent surveys have shown that the issue is now among the central concerns of people in virtually every country on earth, and many consider their very existence to be at stake (BBC World Service Poll, 2007). Just within the past year or so the daily media in this country have become saturated with stories of serious concern about the natural world and about changes in policy and business practices already underway in response to global warming. For so long a taken for granted non-issue, assumed by most to be a given and a done deal, our relationship with the rest of nature is now being called into question urgently, ominously, in virtually every place on earth. It has never before happened quite like this.

But we should pause here and ask: Why not? Why are we apparently so willing to push it to the very edge of catastrophe? What is it about our relationship with nature that makes it so difficult for us to question it? And why is it so difficult to make changes to what is so obviously a problematic course? What "in" the world are we in denial of? Well, perhaps that's exactly it: we are in denial about being "in" the world. The central and most pathogenic problem in our relating with nature is that we like to think of ourselves as being "apart from it" rather than as being "a part of it" (Leff, 1978, p. 285). We like to think of ourselves as being somehow higher up in the order of things, as a special case

in the universe. We like to tell ourselves that though the world is a dangerous and scary place, luckily we humans are in some way separate from it and above it all. We have been granted dominion over nature, our task: to dominate and control it, to subordinate it, and to otherwise feel free to use it for our own purposes. The habitual way we think and the social institutions we inhabit are replete with these kinds of sentiments (Shepard, 1995, pp. 131-140). We fall into believing that the whole point of the earth and nature is to be merely the stage on which the human drama is played. Nature is an

object, the background, just a place for us to stand as we deliver our soliloquies. This assumed and not-to-be-questioned posture of separateness, the scaffolding with which we make meaning of our experience, makes it difficult for many to accept or even to be aware that the way we choose to live our relationship with nature could be problematic--problematic for our own psychological health as well as for the health of rest of nature (Cushman, 1990, p. 599). After all, nature is and has always been simply there for us, we believe, and we hear no complaints if we choose to not listen. So on we go, supposedly separate and surely alienated, as always, and heavily invested in the denial of any indications to the contrary for as long as we can. And if nature "out there" is adversely or even fatally affected, our anthropocentric creed assures us that it has nothing to do with us or the posture we adopt in

relating with it. Nothing fundamentally wrong here, of course, just a new problem in need of an old solution. After all, who's more important, a human being or a spotted owl? We believe that we just need to repeatedly reassert and redouble our dominance and control to further reign in this wild and unruly rascal of an earth so that we can continue on our way.

Modern cultures are saturated with various kinds of highly valued anthropocentric sentiments, and we have become numbingly habituated to those ways of relating, to those ways of thinking, and to those ways of experiencing (Fox, 1995,

Because of our failure to act, our reluctance to change, or our refusal see, we have effectively bequeathed to other people at other times the compounding fundamental problems of our way of relating with nature; our children's inheritance includes the consequences, whatever they may be, of our denial and our refusal to address the quality of this relationship.

p. 18). We should appreciate that it is quite understandable that, in the interest of insulating ourselves from the danger and pain of more reciprocal and intimate involvement with the natural world, we have also endeavored to psychologically protect ourselves by pretending to be somehow essentially outside of nature. Psychological distance, the denial of connectedness, seems to offer us a quick and easy sense of safety and security. So we construct and then inhabit and submit to a cultural ethos which inclines us to wall ourselves off from nature, from each other, and even ultimately from the experience of the whole of our selves. We build psychological barriers to defend ourselves against the presumed threats of intimacy, and then, borrowing a phrase from Maslow (1971, p. 336), we commit ourselves to "taking up residence" within these impermeable and constricted boundaries of our now supposedly free standing, and safe, ego. We do this with the best of intentions, for our own well being, in anticipation of pain or danger, even if none exists or presents itself.

It all makes some sense, of course--but it may not be very wise, and it may be stunting our psychological growth a bit. When you live behind psychological walls and invest heavily in them, it can get pretty lonely, and the flow of emotional nourishment is by design likewise restricted and meager. There is

The well being of nature and the well being of humans are thus inextricably intertwined; it seems we will have them both, or we will have neither.

a high price to pay for denial and presumed separateness (Glendinning, 1995, pp. 41-54). The deal is this: we trade the psychologically healthy capacity for intimate relating and connectedness for a supposed inoculation from pain and danger. Safe and sound. And alienated. And empty. We are left to live our lives so many steps removed from the full richness of genuine presence and nourishing intimate relating, and we are too alone, and there seems to be something missing. It is for want of greater intimacy that we are left immature and empty and our earth overheats. So we try blindly and in vain to fill this culturally promoted and sanctioned emptiness--fill it with work, maybe, or consuming, or entertainment, or drugs, or texting, or some other modern way of distracting ourselves from the discomforting effects of this prophylactic psychological disconnection.

So while the prospect of global climate chaos certainly reveals an inherent vulnerability of nature, it also reveals a corresponding, longstanding vulnerability for humans: that our predominant, anthropocentric way of relating with nature incurs seriously problematic psychological consequences. It is thus critically important for us to realize, at long last, that this most challenging and

important of contemporary issues is not just an environmental issue--not in the traditional, anthropocentric sense. It's not just a problem "out there." And it is not only a psychological issue in the traditional sense, either. It's fundamentally a relational issue. It has to do with the quality of the experience of the relating between humans and the rest of the natural world (both built and wild), the quality of the experience of the "intertwining," as Merleau-Ponty puts it: "... and between them there is a relation that is one of embrace. And between these two vertical beings, there is not a frontier, but a contact surface" (1968, p. 271). At issue is the experience of the ongoing level of intimate and open presence, on the one hand, vs. the experience of disconnected and objectifying alienation, on the other, in any and all instances of our relating. The well being of nature and the well being of humans are thus inextricably intertwined; it seems we will have them both, or we will have neither.

If we do in fact look closely at the structure of the experience of this relating,

This threat of global destruction comes from all of us just doing what we are doing now.

we find in the experience of alienation from nature the incubator for paranoid-like fearfulness, careless exploitation, and destruction (Beyer, 1999, pp. 133-143). When it comes to relating with other people, we have long known about the dangers inherent in disconnection and objectification. We can be careless, we can hurt, we can destroy others so readily when we experience ourselves as different from them, separate from them, superior to them. (We are reminded here of Buber's I-Thou/I-It distinction, Heidegger's Meditative Awareness, May's Genuine Encounter, Maslow's

Self Actualization.) The argument presented here is that this alienated posture is equally problematic with respect to relating with nonhuman nature. From an alienated posture we objectify and commodify, effectively insulating ourselves psychologically from experiencing the full richness and significance of how we are being and what we are doing: food becomes just something we buy at a store, animals become just so many head of cattle, a forest becomes just a stand of timber, and the land becomes just undeveloped real estate. Denial of the experience of one's self as being a part of nature provides the only ground for such careless exploitation and ruination. From this alienated posture responsible environmental action becomes a huge and hopeless impediment to progress, a hassle, a sacrifice. It seems all we can do is turn our gaze away from this discomforting realization. Just as it is in human to human relating, this habitual turning away from an impasse to greater levels of intimacy is at the same time a turning away from psychological growth toward full maturity, and it perilously inclines one toward unwise actions.

In the direct experience of intimate relating, on the other hand, one always finds a profound sense of care and compassion toward one's self AND the other, and one finds a univocal inclination to act in accordance with the wellbeing of the self AND the other. The care and compassion expands with the experienced sense of self to include the other, as if the other were now being realized as a part of ones self. One's sense of well being and that of the other are experienced as distinguishable but not at all separate (Adams, 1996, p. 28). Intimacy is not experienced as me against the other, me vs. nature, jobs vs. the spotted owl—these hostile, adversarial sentiments only arise as such and only make sense from an anthropocentric, alienated posture. Again, this is the case whether the intimate relating is with other people or with the rest of nature.

It is important to note that this powerful and significant inclination to act in accordance with the well being of all of nature comes to us as an event, it comes in a moment of direct experience of open and intimate relating. It is in principle available to each and every one of us through our direct experience at every moment. If these events are rare, if they are neglected instead of being adequately validated and nurtured, or if they are deemed taboo and quickly extinguished under the weight of anthropocentric investments, then they will not be adequately integrated into the whole of the self, and all of the potentially valuable and even critical sentiments and inclinations otherwise gained will be mostly lost on ourselves and on the rest of nature. If, on the other hand, this powerful experience of care and concern and identification is allowed into our reflective awareness, and if it is nurtured and supported by others around us, and--just imagine--even by the culture at large, then it starts to become integrated into the whole of the self, and one is naturally inclined to live one's life accordingly. Mature, wise, and responsible social and environmental practices would be inclined to follow with relative ease.

And herein we find reason for hope and optimism. If because of the problem of global climate chaos the political and social realities of the day require us to make significant changes relatively quickly in our daily lives, it's easy to see that this is more likely to be accomplished in an atmosphere of supportive political will. But from within the anthropocentric posture so prevalent today a significant change in lifestyle can only mean giving something up. What, no SUV? Only one Large Screen Plasma TV? For those so afflicted, it can only seem that nothing is gained by a change in how we relate with nature-- it's only a major setback, a real blow to whatever comforts and enjoyment there was to be had. From that posture one

is not likely to be able to see clearly enough that there has always been something missing, something problematic

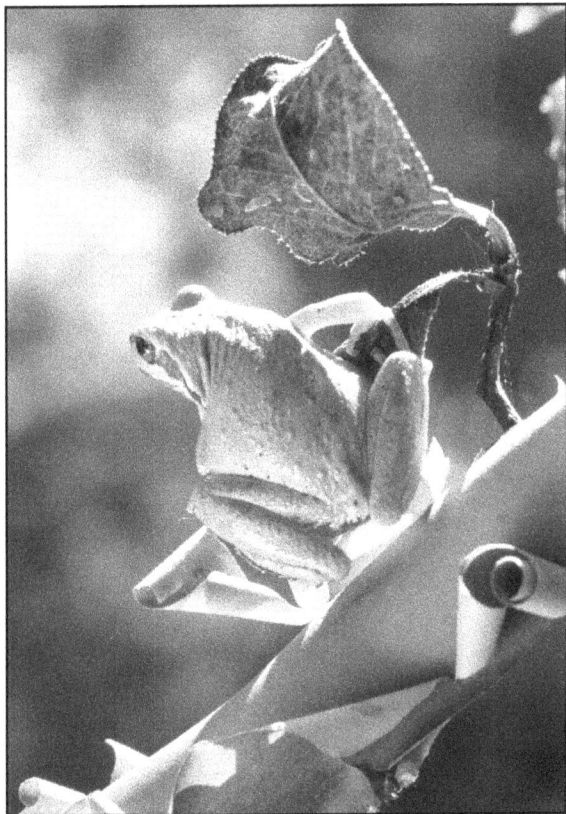

Photo: Glenn McCrea, www.dewdropworld.com

psychologically, and that more consuming, etc, is not going to remedy it. So, in classic neurotic form, we are inclined to do more of that which we already do too much. We will dig in and hold on, as we always have, resisting the psychological growth and maturity which would have come from a genuine openness to exploring the relationship. And the global climate chaos problem is likely to be worse than it would otherwise be--it's bad news for the earth and it's bad news for us. But if we can come to realize that there is actually something very significant to be gained from more intimate relating with each other and with the rest of nature, then being open to a change can suddenly become an intriguingly attractive possibility. It then becomes not so much a setback as a movement forward, a letting go, a letting go of the endless pursuit of modern society's holy grails, a letting go of the surplus impediments to intimacy, a letting go in order to embark on a more healthy and rewarding path of intimate relating. Through a renewed commitment to direct experience of intimate relating with nature we may come to realize a way of experiencing our lives which we may have almost forgotten, or only vaguely remember. We may experience life in even greater richness and depth than ever before, with a more frequent and profound sense of contentment, and with a sense of wholeness of self, and at last feeling more thoroughly saturated in the comforting familiarity of at-homeness.

We are being called as never before by our urgent circumstances to address an issue that needed to be addressed anyway. While it may be easy to fall into despair about our future, these may in fact be just the kind of circumstances we needed to finally call into question and weaken the grip of anthropocentric relating, to usher us into a new era of environmental sustainability, and to move us forward toward higher levels of psychological maturity. One of the most hopeful truths is that our habitual anthropocentric ways may be less the intractable juggernaut than they seem, and that this rigid monolith may actually prove as fragile as a house of cards, vulnerable by just being called into question by direct experience; "Look! The king has no clothes!" As unlikely as it may at first sound, part of the solution to global

We fall into believing that the whole point of the earth and nature is to be merely the stage on which the human drama is played. Nature is an object, the background, just a place for us to stand as we deliver our soliloquies.

climate chaos is, I suggest, that we allow ourselves to be open to our direct experience in relating with nature. There is no need for advanced specialized knowledge or training to do so, no need for indoctrination of any sort into a new way of thinking about nature, no need for preaching to the masses the axioms of some environmental creed. For each and every one of us the posture of open and intimate relating provides the basis for coming to know how to be with the rest of nature, and, moreover, provides the basis for being inclined to actually be that way. So, among the first and most important things that need to be done to affect a foundation of change and action is to go outside and see what happens to you; give yourself enough time to allow yourself to be open to your experience in the relating, and then just notice it and nurture the experience along in your own way. You may find that the denial of your sense of being a part of nature may burn off like the morning fog, and you may find that a renewed sense of interconnection with nature will incline you to act in the best interest of all of nature, including humans.

Our impending environmental crisis is thus a call, a call to revisit our direct experience of relating with nature, a call to finally set aside the anthropocentric assumptions which have left us so alienated and brought us to this precipice. We are being called again to greater levels of human maturity and to a more sane and sustainable relationship with the rest of nature. This may be our last good opportunity to heed the call.

References

Adams, W. (1996). Discovering the sacred in everyday life: an empirical phenomenological study. *The Humanistic Psychologist, 24*, 28-54.

BBC World Service Poll. (2007). Man causing climate change—poll. BBC News [updated: Tuesday, 25 September 2007, 00:13 GMT 01:13 UK]. http://news.bbc.co.uk/2/hi/7010522.stm.

Beyer, J. (1999). *Experiencing the self as being part of nature: A phenomenological-hermeneutical investigation into the discovery of the self in and as the flesh of the earth* (Unpublished doctoral dissertation). Pittsburgh, PA: Duquesne University.

Cushman, P. (1990). Why the self is empty: Toward a historically situated psychology. *American Psychologist, 45*, 599-611.

Fox, W. (1995). *Toward a transpersonal ecology: Developing new foundations for environmentalism.* Albany, NY: State University of New York Press.

Glendinning, C. (1995). Technology, trauma, and the wild. In T. Roszak, M. E. Gomes, & A. D. Kanner (Eds.), *Ecopsychology: Restoring the Earth, healing the mind* (pp. 41-54). San Francisco: Sierra Club Books.

Leff, H. L. (1978). *Experience, environment, and human potentials.* New York: Oxford University Press.

Maslow, A. (1971). *The farther reaches of human nature.* New York: The Viking Press.

Merleau-Ponty, M. (1968). *The visible and the invisible* (Trans A. Lingis). Evanston, Il: Northwestern University Press. (Original work published in 1964).

Shepard, P. (1995). Ecology and man—a viewpoint. In G. Sessions (Ed.), *Deep ecology for the 21st Century: Readings on the philosophy and practice of the new environmentalism* (pp. 131 - 140). Boston, MA: Shambhala Publications.

White, L. 1967. The historical roots of our ecological crisis. *Science, 155*, 1203-1207.

Photo: Glenn McCrea, www.dewdropworld.com

www.ingramcontent.com/pod-product-compliance
Lightning Source LLC
Chambersburg PA
CBHW081157270326
41930CB00014B/3184